To Tabor College
Library for the
many hours
spent there

N Alete

John 150

A THEORY OF PERSONALITY DEVELOPMENT

Recent titles in the

Wiley Series on Personality Processes

Irving B. Weiner, *Editor*

University of South Florida

A Theory of Personality Development

Luciano L'Abate
with the assistance of
Charles H. Bryson

A WILEY-INTERSCIENCE PUBLICATION

JOHN WILEY & SONS, INC.

New York • Chichester • Brisbane • Toronto • Singapore

In recognition of the importance of preserving what has been
written, it is a policy of John Wiley & Sons, Inc., to have
books of enduring value published in the United States
printed on acid-free paper, and we exert our best efforts
to that end.

Library of Congress Cataloging-in-Publication Data

L'Abate, Luciano, 1928–
    A theory of personality development / Luciano L'Abate with
the assistance of Charles H. Bryson.
        p.   cm. — (Wiley series on personality processes)
    Includes bibliographical references and index.
    ISBN 0-471-30303-8 (cloth)
    1. Personality development.   I. Bryson, Charles H.   II. Title.
    III. Series.
BF723.P4L27   1993
155.2'5—dc20   93-12795

Printed in the United States of America

10 9 8 7 6 5 4 3 2 1

To the memory of

Uriel Foà

Fellow expatriate, world citizen

Series Preface

This series of books is addressed to behavioral scientists interested in the nature of human personality. Its scope should prove pertinent to personality theorists and researchers as well as to clinicians concerned with applying an understanding of personality processes to the amelioration of emotional difficulties in living. To this end, the series provides a scholarly integration of theoretical formulations, empirical data, and practical recommendations.

Six major aspects of studying and learning about human personality can be designated: personality theory, personality structure and dynamics, personality development, personality assessment, personality change, and personality adjustment. In exploring these aspects of personality, the books in the series discuss a number of distinct but related subject areas: the nature and implications of various theories of personality; personality characteristics that account for consistencies and variations in human behavior; the emergence of personality processes in children and adolescents; the use of interviewing and testing procedures to evaluate individual differences in personality; efforts to modify personality styles through psychotherapy, counseling, behavior therapy, and other methods of influence; and patterns of abnormal personality functioning that impair individual competence.

IRVING B. WEINER

University of South Florida
Tampa, Florida

Preface

To write a book about a theory of personality development in this day and age takes considerable gall and a great deal of ambition, if not grandiosity. The field of personality theory has not progressed as much as it could because most authors, especially researchers, seem to shy away from "grand" theorizing and what they perceive as a too-demanding (actually impossible) task. Furthermore, most psychologists with empirical interests are trained, hired, and rewarded for their analytical rather than their global skills. Theorizing becomes a dangerous territory when your colleagues may snipe at you for being too theoretical and not supporting your ideas with evidence. Theory building and testing may become an even more solitary pursuit within the family psychology paradigm, about which most academic psychologists are ignorant or disinterested. Personality, for all practical purposes, is still viewed as developing in a vacuum, away from relationships and especially (God forbid!) from intimate relationships. Until recently, most psychologists have shied away from this area. Fortunately, love and intimacy are no longer strange or weird concepts. They are becoming more and more a legitimate field of study.

Social psychological concepts have been my avocation as a practicing clinician since I became involved in family psychology. I will readily admit to being a rank amateur as a social psychologist. I have not been specifically trained in this field, nor have I performed any specific research in it. I have been interested, however, in seeing how developmental and social psychological concepts can be applied to a description and understanding of personality development as a relational, interpersonal process, especially in intimate relationships, such as the family.

In this book, I have attempted to integrate what I have experienced and seen as a practicing family clinical psychologist and as an academician with more than 30 years of clinical practice, teaching, and research. Can there be isomorphism between the problems we see in our offices and what we can test out in the laboratory? I do believe that it is possible to conceptualize personality development in ways that are isomorphic in both settings. Furthermore, how can we separate issues of normative personality development from issues of deviant and psychopathological development? I do not think we can. On practically every page, I try to show how normative and deviant personality developments are extensions and amplifications of each other.

In Part One (Chapters 1 through 3), I define and expand upon each term: theory, personality, and development. Part Two (Chapters 4 and 5), focuses on the two assumptions of the theory (space and time). In Part Three, the substance of the theory is considered in Being (Chapter 6), Doing (Chapter 7), and Having (Chapter 8). Part Four examines the settings where personality development takes place—home (Chapter 9), work (Chapter 10), and leisure (Chapter 11)—together with priorities (Chapter 12), a concept that would relate to the two previous parts and all the preceding chapters. Part Five considers the assessment and verification of the theory through evaluation (Chapter 13) and interventions (Chapter 14). Finally, Part Six (Chapter 1) looks at the validity of the theory and its expansion to include sexuality and addictions.

This book is, primarily, an outline of a theory of personality development. A full-fledged theory of personality development would take much more room than can be allotted to any author by any publisher. Hence, I slighted many topics that deserved much fuller treatment than they received here, particularly in Chapters 7, 8, 9, 10, and 11. On the other hand, so much has been written about the topics covered in these chapters that the major function of the theory consists of relating them together. Thus, it is possible to criticize this book on grounds of being superficial, on one hand, as well as of trying to cover too much ground, on the other. I spent a large amount of space on topics that had not been adequately covered in the literature. An author has to decide from the very outset of writing a book whether to stress intensity or extensity. In this case, my choice was to favor extensity in the chapters that received short shift, mentioned earlier, and intensity for the remaining chapters, which received relatively more space. I take responsibility for the present outcome.

As a student of personality for 64 years, I hope that this book will be useful to other students who are interested in the same exciting topic. They may range in age from undergraduates to their teachers and to the teachers of teachers of courses on personality theory. A book dedicated to personality development and psychopathology naturally will be of interest to most therapists, who need to make sense of their clients' behaviors as persons, as partners, and as parents.

Charles H. Bryson, a former student, assisted in the typing of this book. Because he is familiar with my thinking, he was able to clarify my grammar and syntax. He is not responsible for the substantive aspects of the theory.

I am grateful to Professor Stanley Krippner, of the Saybrook Institute, for thoroughly reviewing the manuscript and pointing out various conceptual errors. If any mistakes remain in this manuscript, I am solely responsible for them.

LUCIANO L'ABATE

Atlanta, Georgia
September 1993

Contents

PART ONE
Definition of Terms

CHAPTER 1

What Is a Theory?

The individual remains the principal unit of analysis for most social science research.
(WHITE, 1991, p. 118)

Individuals are the fundamental units of society.
(GERGEN, 1991, p. 156)

This chapter delineates some of the epistemological hurdles that a theory must face to go forward and progress beyond current thinking about personality development. Among the many possible issues, the following ones need elaboration: (a) distinction between a paradigm, a theory, and a model, with the definition of an appropriate theory for *a relational and contextual theory of personality development* (personality does not develop in a vacuum—as suggested by most traditional textbooks on personality—personality develops in relationship to intimate others in specific settings, especially the home); (b) points of emphasis in the theory that would justify its use and applications; (c) criteria to evaluate the theory, some of these criteria being more rigid than others; and (d) relationships between theory (or epistemology) and practice or applications. These points of emphasis should attempt to answer the question: "What is the good of a theory if it cannot be verified in the laboratory as well as in the clinic?" Although many solutions could be proposed for each of these issues, additional topics deemed just as important by other investigators would warrant different answers from the ones proposed here.

DEFINITIONS OF A THEORY

Before defining a theory, we need to distinguish between a paradigm, a theory, and a model. Although the three often have been confused and equated with one another, a theory is different from a paradigm or a model. Such an equation is epistemologically inaccurate, unnecessary, and unwarranted. A paradigm encompasses a view of reality that supersedes and is superordinate to a theory. Dewey and Bentley (1949) summarized the evolution of our views of reality according to three major paradigms: (a) *actional*—behavior without any connection to any other behavior and without any rational connection or explanation or, as by magic; (b) *reactional*—behavior in response to other behavior; and (c) *transactional*—behavior in a bidirectional exchange between two individuals that is observed by another individual looking over the interaction. Interactions between and among human beings are not seen as being separate from the observers who, by the very act of observing, become part of the whole transaction.

When we apply this transactional view to personality development, we readily can see it as the outcome of interactions that we have observed among family members, making it, therefore, an ecological transaction. We, the observers, are looking at it with our own biases, and in doing so, we may wittingly or unwittingly influence it. Personality development and family behavior are interconnected; they are not isolated or independent from the behavior of other family members. In a family, everybody matters. Each person influences and is influenced by everybody else in the family—positively or negatively. Thus, by omission or by commission, we have bi- and multidirectional effects taking us away from the traditional monadic psychology and. traditional personality theories, which view personality development in a vacuum, or as action or reaction (Pervin, 1990; Spiegel, 1971). Thus, the encompassing paradigm that is superordinate to the present theory is *contextual* because the family is the most influential and relevant setting for the origin and development of personality. Among other influential settings, work and leisure are the most important ones, depending on individual proclivities and priorities.

A transactional ecological paradigm, supposedly a new way of thinking about the interconnectedness of individual and family behavior, has been confused as being a theory, mixing levels of abstraction. A paradigm describes how behavior takes place in general and abstract terms. It could be called a metaphor or a metatheory, as represented by systems thinking, for instance, but it is not a theory. Systems thinking, unfortunately, took this paradigm wholesale and tried, unsuccessfully, to make it into what it is not, a theory (L'Abate & Colondier, 1987). A theory is a more specific and concrete view of behavior. A paradigm, because of its abstract and general nature, is untestable, whereas a theory is testable. Even though we can see the interconnectedness of family members as individuals, we need to have more information and make many more assumptions about behavior than a paradigm permits.

Hence, the overarching paradigm that forms the background to the present theory is contextual-relational: Personality development takes place in various contexts according to a normative/hierarchical arrangement—family first, then work, then leisure, transit, and transitory settings (Part Four). A theory makes some informed guesses on how each setting affects personality development. A theory, therefore, is a set of interconnected statements or propositions linked by a communality of purpose or topic ultimately leading to empirical verification. The purpose of the present theory is to understand personality and its development in various contexts or settings.

Personality development is interconnected with the development of other personalities, but how? A paradigm is insufficient to help us understand personality development except in general and vague terms of interconnectedness or interdependence. A paradigm accepts this interconnectedness as a given, but it is up to the theory to explain specifically how this interconnectedness and interdependence take place. A theory can be dialectical—operating within the context of discovery—like many family theories, or demonstrative—operating within the context of demonstrativeness—as in some psychological and sociological theories of behavior in the family (L'Abate, 1986). A theory is an invention for interpreting behavior: (a) *as an umbrella* to cover and encompass certain behaviors, in this case, personality development; (b) *as a map* to show us the territory covered, routes for traversing that territory, and the obstacles and limitations we will encounter in getting there; (c) *as a compass* to point us in the direction we should follow to get where we want to go within the territory covered by the theory; and (d) *as a straitjacket,* narrowing our views and perspectives.

A theory, by definition, is *testable;* a paradigm is not. If a theory representing a particular paradigm is found to be valid, this validity reinforces the significance of the underlying paradigm. For instance, if a theory of personality development, based on the interconnectedness of a family member with other family members, were found to be valid, then it would reinforce the ecological transactional paradigm. Furthermore, a theory becomes testable through models derived from the theory. We bring down the level of abstraction another considerable notch when we go from a theory to models. Both paradigms and theories supposedly explain behavior. Models, however, do not have such an explanatory power, because their function is to test parts of a theory through description. Models are more modest and restricted, usually based on concrete and specific views of behavior that may or may not derive from a theory; therefore, they serve as ways of testing theories, or they may operate by themselves, separate and isolated from any theory. Eventually, even isolated models will need to be reconciled with existing theoretical frameworks. Theories may be formal or informal, reductionistic or nonreductionistic, structured or unstructured.

A theory is an attempt at interpretation and explanation of reality as one sees it. Let us analyze some of the words in this sentence. "Attempt" indicates the tentativeness of a theory: There is nothing sacred or absolute about it. The word in and by itself denotes tentativeness. For "interpretation," we should include the notion of subjectivism versus objectivism, which is discussed later in this chapter. For instance, the theory of personality (Chapter 2) development (Chapter 3) presented here (Figure 1.1)

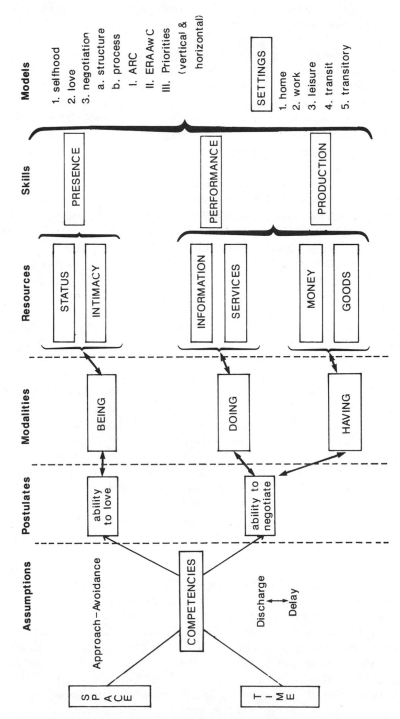

Figure 1.1. A developing theory of interpersonal competence.

consists of two assumptions of space and time, postulates, modalities, competencies, skills, models, and settings.

Space modulates attachments based on emotional and interpersonal distance, underlying the dimensions of internal and external distance respectively, as assessed by extremes of approach–avoidance (Chapter 4). Time modulates control along extremes assessed by discharge delay functions (Chapter 5). These assumptions underlie two postulates about the ability to love (Chapter 6) and the ability to negotiate respectively. Both postulates define personalities as interpersonal competence, defined by how one is, does, and has (Chapter 2). The three modalities of Being, Doing, and Having were derived from Foà and Foà's (1974) resource exchange theory. These authors postulated six resource classes that are continuously exchanged (given and received) between and among us: status, love, information, services, money, and goods (L'Abate, 1986). These postulates link modalities to resources exchanged, which are then linked to competencies and then to verifiable models, according to what resource is exchanged, as summarized in Figure 1.1.

The ability to love is linked to the modality of Being (Chapter 6). Being is made by exchange of resources in status and in love and is expressed personally and interpersonally through presence, being emotionally available to self and to significant others. Presence is evaluated (tested, verified) through two models: one is a model of self-definition through the attribution of importance to self and to others, and the second is a model of love and intimacy. Both models have either been verified through paper-and-pencil self-report tests (L'Abate & Wagner, 1985, 1988; Stevens & L'Abate, 1989) or are in the process of being verified.

The ability to negotiate is linked to the modalities of Doing and Having (Chapters 7 and 8). Doing is made up by exchange of resources in services and in information, and is expressed through performance. Doing is measured by *how well* the person performs on various roles and tasks at home, as a provider, partner, and parent; at work, as an employer or employee; and in leisure-time activities, such as hobbies, avocations, games, and sports. Having is made up by exchange of resources in goods and in money and is expressed through production (Foà & Foà, 1974). Having is measured by how much one produces at home, at work, and in leisure-time activities (Part Four). *Importance* as used here refers to the process of attribution whereby a person perceives a resource and/or setting as being necessary for enjoyment and survival in life. *Resource* refers to any of the six variables considered in Part Three. *Settings* are considered in Part Four.

The two assumptions, therefore, lead respectively to two postulates about the ability to love and to negotiate (Part Two), modalities, competencies, and eventually models derived from the modalities (Part Three). Postulates derive from assumptions, whereas models derive from postulates. These competencies interact with various settings (Part Four). The theory is tested in the laboratory or it can be verified through paper-and-pencil self-report tests or through actual interventions (Part Five). The adequacy of the theory is also evaluated by how it attempts to integrate various developmental and social psychological theories or models and how it expands to cover sex, sexuality, and addictions (Chapter 15).

POINTS OF EMPHASIS IN THE THEORY

This theory of personality development concentrates on five epistemological issues: (a) width and range, (b) depth, (c) units, (d) cause-effect relationships in personality development, and (e) independent variables. A theory may be rather informal and unstructured; many theories in personality development have an inadequate or unclear structure so that we cannot identify a theory's limits or what subordinate part derives from another superordinate part. This theory starts with seemingly abstract assumptions of space and time (Part Two), progresses to less abstract postulates of modalities and competencies (Part Three), and ends with concrete, testable models, going, therefore, from the abstract to the concrete, and from the general to the specific (Figure 1.1).

Width and Range: The Experiencing and Expressing of Behavior

The first point of emphasis for this theory is how behavior takes place spatially (i.e., width and range, within, between, and among individuals). Externally, width and range are shown by the emotional and physical *distance between and among individuals.* The width and range of spatial behavior changes from emotional (receptive-experiencing) to physical (external-expressing) distance. Experiencing is internal, but expressing is external and usually includes interpersonal consequences. We may be spatially distant but very close emotionally to someone we love; and we may be spatially close to someone but at the same time emotionally distant or indifferent. This distance is modulated, modified, and moderated by an internal dimension that covers the range of extremes in experiencing on the receiving, input side to the external, expressing, output side. We need to differentiate strongly between what we experience inside of us and how we express it, otherwise we are in trouble, theoretically and experientially (L'Abate, 1985a). Hence, this theory emphasizes the importance of experiencing—the process of receiving information (input), its processing (throughput), and its expression (output) within a context of relationships.

.

The Importance of Experiencing and Expressing in Intellectual Functioning

This dimension was originally applied to intellectual functioning (L'Abate, 1971; Wildman & L'Abate, 1979) as derived from psycholinguistics, which stressed the importance of distinguishing between comprehension on the incoming side and production on the outgoing side of the experiencing-expressing continuum (Lenneberg, 1967; McNeil, 1968). Developmental psychologists have referred to the same distinction as "recognition–production" (Flavell & Wohlwill, 1969): ". . . any adequate output model must specify both what the child knows and the manner in which the knowledge is represented . . ." (p. 75). Maccoby (1968) referred to the same distinction in the visual-motor modality as the lag between perception and performance. The distinction between fluid and crystallized intelligence (Horn, 1968) essentially refers to the same type of behavior covered by the receptive/experiencing-expressive distinction (Olsen & Pagliuso, 1968) (Table 1.1).

This distinction may place the old heredity-environment controversy in a different light, in which input functions (experiencing) are more closely related to biological factors than are expressive functions. Output functions (expressing) are more related to environmental and cultural factors. This hypothesis was tested with kindergarten and adolescent children using two tests (Peabody Picture Vocabulary Test and Columbia

TABLE 1.1. The Continuum of Experiencing–Expressing, the ERAAwC Model,* Psychological Theories, and Representative Theorists

Experiencing	Reasoning	Activity	Awareness	Context (Settings)
Humanism	Psychodynamics	Behaviorism	Gestalt	Home
Body emphasis	Cognition	Empiricism	Eastern	Work
Phenomenology	Rational–Emotive	Materialism	philosophies	Leisure
				Transitory
				Transit
S. Kierkegaard	S. Freud	J. Watson	F. Perls	A. Adler
L. B. Binswanger	C. G. Jung	B. F. Skinner		H. S. Sullivan
V. E. Frankl	E. H. Erickson	H. Eysenck		K. Lewin
M. Heiddeger	G. A. Kelly	O. H. Mowrer		E. Berne
E. Husserl	A. Ellis	N. E. Miller		R. Barker
A. H. Maslow	A. Bandura	J. B. Rotter		Family
C. R. Rogers	D. Meichelbaum			Therapists
R. D. Laing				
W. Reich				
A. Lowen				
R. May				

* Adapted from Hansen & L'Abate, 1982; L'Abate, 1986.

Mental Maturity Scale) of perceptual functions (receptive) and two tests of expressive functioning (Vocabulary and Draw-A-Person). At both age levels, socioeconomic factors were more influential on the expressive than on the receptive side (L'Abate, 1971). These results were supported by Wildman and L'Abate (1979), who used a specifically constructed test that evaluated in an equivalent manner the auditory, visual, oral, and manual modalities. We usually experience more than we can express. For instance, our receptive vocabulary is greater than our expressive one; we can enjoy a beautiful painting, but we cannot paint it ourselves; we can enjoy music but we cannot compose or perform it.

Although the receptive, experiencing side may have not been considered sufficiently by past researchers interested in intelligence (Baron, 1985; Cancro, 1971; Dockrell, 1970; Eysenck, 1973; Hunt, 1972; Staats, 1971; Vernon, 1969), it seems to enter into more recent views (Sternberg, 1986), but not enough to alter our understanding of behavior and especially of personality development. How is this distinction relevant to personality development?

The Experiencing-Expressing Continuum in Personality Development

The jump from intellectual to personality functioning is not as wide as it would seem at first blush. Gardner (1983) as well as Cantor and Kihlstrom (1987) stresses the importance of a special kind of "social" intelligence. Even though these authors fail to mention that such an intelligence is nurtured in the family, it is the very context where social sensitivity becomes attuned. A great deal of the information we give to and receive from significant others is emotional. Whether it is within the confines of the home or with friends, neighbors, acquaintances, or co-workers, any human encounter encompasses some emotional exchange, ranging from exciting-pleasurable, to neutral, to unpleasant, and even to painful. Hence, experiencing represents the subjective, private side of how we receive information from others and how we perceive it (Singer & Bonanno, 1990).

This personally subjective, phenomenologically private side maintains: "The psychological significance of an event is a critical determinant of how a person responds to the event . . . [which] is the product of both the person and the situation" (Higgins, 1990, p. 302). This experiencing includes feelings and emotions, self-beliefs, self-ideals, discrepancies, fantasies, dreams, and daydreams. These topics form the experiential basis or the private repertoire that makes knowledge accessibility and assimilation the process whereby we receive and process interpersonal information. The process of receiving this information involves the appraisal and interpretation of the received information. On the expressive side, this output has also been called "applicability," how we use the assimilated information once we have processed it (Higgins,

1990). Thus, the experiencing-expressing continuum is equivalent to what Higgins calls the continuum of "accessibility-applicability."

By necessity, the process of receiving emotional information is selective and, therefore, highly individual. What may be a pleasant experience to one, may be painful to another. As a result, we vary on how we perceive, assimilate, process, and store the same type of information. Not only do we vary in receiving and processing similar information, we vary also in expressing it. Being stared at in an apparently menacing manner may cause one individual to turn and walk away, whereas someone else may find the glance a sufficient motive to take out a weapon, ostensibly for defensive purposes, and shoot the person who looks menacing.

Most theories of personality development can be placed along a continuum of how they deal with the reception of experience, on one hand, and the expression of that experience, on the other. The sequence from experiencing (input) to expressing (output) allows us to locate many existing theories according to their specific contribution at any one point on this continuum (Table 1.1). For instance, at the extreme of experiencing, the humanistic school and its various subschools (phenomenology, existentialism, logotherapy, transpersonal, etc.) stress the importance of feelings and emotions in the development of mature behavior and of a functioning personality. The encouragement of free and uncritical expression of these feelings allows change to take place. The subjective perceptions of the individual in the present are valid and often more important than thoughts and actions.

Psychoanalysis, on the other hand, stresses the importance of thinking and logical structures, as they developed from past traumatic and, therefore, affective events. The verbal unraveling of these events, conscious or unconscious, brings about change. Thus, whereas humanism contributed to our valuing feelings and emotions, psychoanalysis and related schools (psychodynamic, reality, rational-emotive, cognitive psychology, etc.) contributed to our understanding and valuing how interpersonal, and therefore emotional, information is processed through rational processes (throughput).

The behavioral school stressed the importance of actions and the immediate consequent contingencies and contingent reinforcements that derive from those actions. In this regard, behaviorism was interested mainly in what we do and in what we say—whatever is visible and verifiable—without the need to study subjective feelings or thoughts. Thus, this school contributed to our valuing the expression of behavior rather than its reception or processing.

Finally, family therapy stressed the importance of the family context for an understanding and treatment of dysfunctional behavior. Whereas previous theories considered the development of personality in a vacuum, family therapy stressed the importance of the family context in this development. Each school or viewpoint contributes to our overall understanding of behavior along a continuum of experiencing-expressing. This integration of past theories finds its practical application in the ER-AAwC (*E*xperiencing, *R*easoning, *A*ctivity, *Aw*areness, *C*ontext) model.

The Experiencing and Expressing Continuum in Personality Theory

Once this spatial continuum of experiencing-expressing is stressed as being basic to personality development and to interpersonal competence, we can make sense of placing previous schools of thinking along a continuum covered by these extremes. The ERAAwC model has been used to integrate past theories of personality development and of family functioning (L'Abate, 1986). Humanism has been useful in stressing the value of experiencing—the subjectively felt perceptions (*E*motionality). Psychodynamic and cognitive schools have underscored the value of processing emotionality through logical schemes and thinking (*R*ationality). Behaviorism has focused on the value of expressing ourselves in observable, and hence measurable, verbal and nonverbal actions (*A*ctivity). Gestalt psychology and Eastern philosophies have stressed the value of *A*wareness as a change mechanism that feeds back to *E*motionality, *R*ationality, or *A*ctivity. The field of family therapy and the ecological, transactional schools have identified the value and role of *C*ontexts in giving meaning to behavior (L'Abate, 1986). We cannot understand personality development in a vacuum. It is a function of the many different contexts in which it takes place, and the context most relevant to personality development is the family setting. This emphasis, however, does not mean that other settings—work, leisure, transit, and transitory environments—are any less meaningful, even though they may be less powerful in their lasting effects. The experiencing-expressing continuum is relevant to how we approach and avoid other people. It is dealt with in greater detail as an assumption of the theory in Chapter 4, for *E*motionality, and Chapter 5, for *R*ationality.

Distortions can take place in any one of these five components along the continuum of experiencing-expressing. Any distortion in a component will affect the other components (Broun, 1986). For instance, if the family setting (C) is abusive physically, sexually, or verbally, or is apathetically neglectful, or alternates inconsistently between these two extremes, it will reduce and limit the *e*motionality and *aw*areness of the child. Emotional growth will then be stunted and distorted. The restriction in the emotional repertoire and awareness could detour the processing of emotions into either exaggerated *r*ationality, which would transform itself into obsessions and, in its extreme form, psychotic behavior; or into the exaggerated *a*ctivity of hyperactivity or impulsivity leading to compulsions, acting out, and in its extreme form, criminality (L'Abate, 1986).

Besides the confluence from various sources cited here and elsewhere (L'Abate, 1986, 1990), including Higgins (1990), to support the epistemological validity of this continuum, it appears to have received support from at least three other sources. Brody (1980) in his review of social motivation distinguished between prophenomenological and antiphenomenological approaches. Among the former, he included Bandura's (1977) self-efficacy theory, self-focused attention (Duval & Wicklund, 1972; Scheier & Carver, 1977), perceived self-motivation (Pittman, Cooper, & Smith, 1977), Klinger's (1977) inner experience, Weiner's (1978) analysis of affect and cognition, and Lazarus's (Lazarus, Kanner, & Folkman, 1980) phenomenological theory of emotions. Among the latter, Brody included Nisbett and Wilson's (1977) arguments about the need to look at people's behavior rather than to their verbal reports, Berkowitz's (1978) findings that people "behave aggressively even though they may not attribute their state of arousal to anger" (p. 146), noncognitive explanations of social phenomena relating to Zajonc's (1965) drive theory of social facilitation, and the motivated unconscious as seen in self-deception (Gur & Sackheim, 1979; Sackheim & Gur, 1978). These two seemingly contrasting viewpoints, when considered on a continuum of experiencing and expressing, would indicate that the phenomenologically oriented psychologists are more interested in the inner experience of individuals, whereas the antiphenomenologically oriented ones are more interested in what people do and say, and the congruence or incongruence between doing, talking, and expressing.

In a second instance, Huston and Rempel (1989) distinguished between two viewpoints:

> Two almost separate literatures have developed about family and other close relationships. One focuses on general interpersonal attitudes and dispositions, such as love, commitment, and trust; the other centers on the analysis of behavioral exchanges, usually concentrating on the detailed examination of behaviors that take place during face-to-face interaction . . . close relationships must consider the links between the behavioral and attitudinal/dispositional levels. (p. 177)

In the third instance, Broun (1988) used what he called the *BASK* model to explain how the process of disassociation in multiple personalities resulting from severe childhood sexual, physical, or emotional trauma, may affect any of these four components. *B* stands for behavior (*A*ctivity), *A* for affect (*E*motionality), *S* for sensation (*Aw*areness), and *K* for knowledge (*R*ationality). The similarities between this model and the ERAAwC are evident. The *C*ontext in Broun's model is specifically an abusive-apathetic household or family. In most instances, therefore, *c*ontext "causes" personality functionalities and dysfunctionalities.

This point of emphasis about an experiencing-expressing continuum is important for two reasons. First of all, the theory presented here (Figure 1.1) starts with the experiential, phenomenological level as shown in the subjective side of personality (assumptions) on the left and ends with the expressing side of visible, observable, and verifiable behaviors (competencies in presence, performance, and production) on the right of the figure. Second, these two aspects of personality development are relevant to the distinction between the two postulates about the ability to love on the subjectively receptive, felt side (Chapter 6), and the ability to negotiate, which is more on the expressive side (Table 1.1) (Chapters 7 and 8). For instance, a person may feel love toward his or her partner, but the way a person shows the love may vary from frequent beatings to the partner in one case to frequent compliments and gifts in another case. If you were to ask the abusive partner how he or she feels about the battered partner, the answer would be an expression of love. Even perpetrators of incest claim undying feelings of love for their victims. In cases of marital murder, the assassin often expresses tremendous guilt for the loss of the loved one. Thus, it is impossible to equate what another person feels with how that person will express those feelings. The number of subjective feelings is pretty well finite. How those feelings are expressed is practically infinite. The implications of this continuum for personality development will be elaborated in Chapter 4.

The Depth Dimension:
Levels of Interpretation

A second point of emphasis for this theory is how personality development takes place at different levels of interpretation. These levels deal with the depth and height of how we look and describe and explain personality development. We use the term interpretation to avoid or try to solve the controversy about whether reality is invented or discovered. Rather than argue whether reality is constructed or invented, the term and process of interpretation attempts to take us away from that controversy because some of our reality, especially the interpersonal, is constructed, whereas our physical reality is discovered.

There is a wide range of possibilities between discovery and invention. Although many theorists assume an absolutistic either-or position—"Reality is *all* invention" versus "Reality is *all* discovery"—I prefer the position that some reality indeed is invented and some is discovered. Galileo Galilei discovered the law of gravity and Einstein discovered the theory of relativity. Christopher Columbus discovered America. He, like Galilei or Einstein, did not invent his find. Edison, however, invented the incandescent bulb. He did not discover it! In borderline cases, such as whether Darwin discovered or invented the theory of evolution, it is necessary to distinguish whether the person created something (like the electric bulb) or found something that already existed. Whatever did not exist before has been invented; whereas gravity and relativity existed long before Galilei and Einstein discovered them.

This distinction begs the question, What is existing? Some theories may find internal states: "Does the 'ego' really exist?" or, "Was it invented or discovered?" Here the distinction becomes more difficult. Some of our behavior is discovered, in the sense that it can be recorded, videotaped, scored, and shown again on film, an approach that reproduces the same behavior. This descriptive level of behavior—its self-presentational and phenotypical aspects—can be recorded, reproduced, and shown almost ad infinitum. From these tapes and scores, we may discover some new patterns. Those patterns, however, were there before we discovered them. On the other hand, we make attributions about descriptive levels, such as the self-presentational and phenotypical levels, on the basis of inferred, hypothetical, and presumptively internal genotypes, or states or traits, including anxiety, self, and other inferred or hypothetical intervening variables.

These internal states are used to explain behavior: "He was jittery because he was anxious." Statements of this kind are inventions and may seem useful devices to understand external, recordable behaviors. We may even develop paper-and-pencil, self-report tests to measure such internal states or traits. But they still remain inventions, no matter how much their creators reify them. Consequently, we can feel more comfortable in interpreting behavior if we are aware that some behavior is discoverable by looking really hard, whereas other behavior, especially if it involves inferences about people in terms of internal states, is most often invented, or constructed, as a useful device (as in the case of the attribution of importance and a continuum of likeness described in Chapter 3).

Constructivism, as represented for instance, by Berger and Luckman (1966), influenced the thinking of Reiss (1981) who provided the first solid indication that, indeed, members of families construct realities of their own. As Scarr (1985) described it (without acknowledging the contribution of Berger and Luckman.):

> . . . a constructionist position on epistemology . . . knowledge of all kinds, including scientific knowledge, is a construction of the human mind . . . We do not discover scientific fact; we invent them (p. 499) . . . science is constructed knowledge (p. 500) . . . The admission that reality is a construction of the human mind does not deny the heuristic value of the construction. Indeed, we get around in the world and invent knowledge that is admirably useful. But the claim that science and reality are human constructions denies that there is any set of facts that is absolute and real. Instead, it asserts that there are many sets of "fact" that arise from different theory-guided perceptions. (p. 501)

Whether we invent on one hand or discover on the other, somewhere in the middle we need to interpret the complexity of personality development according to different levels of description and explanation. For instance, thus far we have had multileveled versus unileveled interpretations of behavior. Psychoanalysis sees behavior as a four-leveled house, with a basement (the id impulses), two floors (the ego and superego), and an attic (the unconscious, where we store all past memories). Humanism and behaviorism, on the other hand, are essentially unileveled in their views of behavior; there is no depth to behavior except what we perceive (humanism) or what we do or say (behaviorism). What we see is what we get. In the view of both schools, we do not need to assume unconscious motivation to make sense of behavior, even though a great deal of what we learn about ourselves and intimate others as we develop takes place outside our conscious awareness (Kihlstrom, 1990).

Hence, levels of interpretation need to be differentiated into descriptive and explanatory (L'Abate, 1964, 1976, 1985a). Each level subsumes two different sublevels. In description, it is necessary to distinguish between presentational and phenotypical sublevels of behavior. Both behaviors can be observed and recorded relatively easily. This is not the case in explanation, where we must distinguish between inferred, attributional, and hypothetical underlying entities such as mastery, self-esteem, and ego (intrapsychically), or dominance, submission, and enmeshment (interpersonally). These factors provide the foundation for ahistorical explanations, whereas historical explanations are based on generational and developmental antecedents. Thus, reality is not only what we make it but also consists of levels or layers of realities, where we must distinguish descriptive realities from explanatory guesses.

Descriptive Levels of Interpretation

Description means that we can observe, record, and even count behavior with mechanical devices such as direct observation or audio- and videotapes. However, we need to distinguish (Table 1.2) between two descriptive sublevels—the sublevel of our public, self-presentational facade and the phenotypical sublevel often hidden from public view.

Self-Presentation.   The self-presentational sublevel tries to answer the question: "How does a person present him- or herself to others in superficial and short-lived relationships?" For instance, how does the person present him- or herself outside the family? This sublevel may include physical appearance (neat–disorderly, clean–dirty), first impressions, impression management (good–bad, remarkable–indifferent). It represents the social facade (nice–nasty, smooth–rough) as well as the self-handicapping or self-enhancing strategies we use to relate to others (Berglas, 1987). Some of us may stress this sublevel of appearance at the

TABLE 1.2.   Levels of Interpretation in Theory Construction*

A. Descriptive Levels: Visible and recordable.

  1. *Self-presentational sublevel:* How does the individual present him/herself to others? How does the individual present him/herself inside and outside the family (e.g., in the workplace)?

    a. Superficial and short-lived.

    b. Physical appearance (neat–disorderly, clean–dirty).

    c. First impression, impression management (good–bad, remarkable–indifferent).

    d. Social facade (nice–nasty, smooth–rough).

    e. Self-handicapping or self-enhancing strategies.

    f. Degree of emphasis on this level at expense of phenotypical level ("Make a good impression at all costs").

  2. *Phenotypical sublevel:* How does the individual behave in close and prolonged relationships or under stress?

    a. How does the individual function affectively, intellectually, and behaviorally in relation to intimate others *over time?*

    b. Consistence–inconsistence, congruence–incongruence with presentational level.

B. Explanatory Levels: Why do individuals behave the way they do? Inferential or hypothetical levels, not available to naked eye or direct observation.

  1. *Genotypical level:* Self-view or concept, underlying structure of self.

    a. Consistence–inconsistence, congruence–incongruence with descriptive levels.

    b. Self-differentiation according to the likeness continuum (Chapter 3).

    c. Attribution of importance to self and intimate others (Chapter 6).

    d. Self-determination.

  2. *Historical or present situation:* How did the individual develop such a genotype?

    a. Transgenerational transmission from family of origin (parental practices and siblings).

    b. Developmental determinants specific to the individual.

    c. Situational determinants at the moment.

    d. Determinants from the family of procreation (marriage and children).

    e. Relationship with other levels.

* Adapted from L'Abate, 1964, 1976.

expense of how we behave in close and prolonged, but not always committed, relationships. Too much emphasis at this sublevel, "making a good impression," may be achieved at the expense of the phenotypical sublevel (i.e., "Make a good impression at all costs, no matter what.").

Self-presentation has also been called "impression-management" by social psychologists. Schlenker (1980) defined impression management as "the conscious-unconscious attempt to control images that are projected in real or imagined social interactions." Schlenker specified further: "When these images are self-relevant, the behavior is termed self-presentation" (p. 6). Thus, the terms *impression management* and *self-presentation* could be differentiated on the dimension of relevance—

inner relevance relates to self-presentation; outer relevance, or relevance to others, relates to impression management. According to Schlenker:

> Impression management is a central part of the very nature of social interaction, it is inconceivable to discuss interpersonal relations without employing the concept. . . . All people control, more or less, through habit or conscious design, the ways they appear to themselves and others. (p. 7)

In reviewing the dramaturgical approach to self-presentation pioneered by Goffman (1956), Schlenker dealt with the issue of self-presentation and self-distortion:

> The boundary between accurate self-presentation and self misrepresentation further blurs when we realize that people are often taken in by their own performances, coming to believe that they really are the idealized or dramatized identities they project. (p. 39)

Even though Schlenker differentiates between impression management (external) and self-presentation (internal), in actual practice he seemed to use both terms interchangeably.

The discrepancy between public and private levels has been evaluated by Snyder and his associates on self-monitoring (Snyder & Swann, 1976; Snyder & Tanke, 1976). They found low self-monitoring individuals exhibit a high correspondence between their private attitudes and their consequent behaviors, whereas high self-monitors exhibit little correspondence. Higgins, Snyder, and Berglas (1990), on the other hand, focused on identifying self-handicappers, who are invested in presenting themselves in a poor or negative light.

Phenotype.   This sublevel tries to answer the following questions: "How does the individual behave in close and prolonged relationships or under the stress of such relationships?" "How does the individual function affectively, intellectually, and behaviorally in relation to intimate others over time?" "How consistent–inconsistent, congruent–incongruent is this sublevel with the preceding presentational sublevel?" Most of us may behave well (according to accepted norms of behavior) in both settings, the one external to the home, requiring some extent of self-presentation, and in the home itself, where most close and prolonged relationships take place. Some of us may behave well ("nice") outside the home but behave horribly ("nasty") in the home. Some of us may behave nastily outside the home and nicely in it. Some of us may behave nicely in both settings.

This sublevel and discrepancies between this and the sublevel of presentation are obtained at second hand, from clinical case reports. Many clients, especially couples and families, want to project a public image of respectable conformity and superficial adjustment, which is often belied by the symptom carrier. They present themselves as if they were "normal" were it not for the identified patient, the symptom carrier, who behaves in negative ways that may destroy any positive public image the couple or family may want to portray. Often, individuals, couples, and families, in their attempt to appear normal, may hide patterns of sexual, verbal, and physical abuse, either from their families of origin or in their families of procreation.

Explanatory Levels of Interpretation

How do we explain such consistencies and inconsistencies between the two descriptive sublevels? Both descriptive sublevels, presentational and phenotypical, are explained by two additional sublevels, one structural and the other historical. These sublevels are inferential or hypothetical, in the sense that, in contrast to the preceding sublevels, they are not available to the naked eye or to direct observation. The descriptive level tried to answer the questions "What?" and "How?" Whereas the explanatory level tried to answer the question: "Why do individuals behave the way they do?" Consequently, whatever explanation is given on the basis of internal causes, it is inferred from the two previous levels and how individuals conceptualize their own selves.

Genotype: The Structure of Self. Structural explanation is given by the genotype, how an individual defines him- or herself with or without being aware of it. It is represented by the self-view or concept underlying the structure of self. How is this view consistent–inconsistent or congruent–incongruent with descriptive levels? Some theorists would like to retain intrapsychic traits, inferred concepts (e.g., self-esteem), as explanatory genotypes. Chapter 3, presents the argument that we construct ourselves according to an automatic, unconscious if you will, but relational psychophysical continuum of likeness (L'Abate, 1976, 1986) consisting of a continuous comparison with other relevant individuals, first parents and siblings, then peers, and sometimes later on, mentors, lovers, and partners. In addition to this internal but relational continuum of likeness, the genotype is made up also by our sense of importance, that is, how we learn to attribute importance to ourselves and to significant others (Chapter 6). These two dimensions of likeness and of importance are not sufficient to make up the self-concept. There is still a residual component of self-construal found in self-determination (Deci & Ryan, 1985) (Chapter 3). Very likely, our genotype may be the outcome of all three sources of definition.

Historical, Developmental, or Situational? The genotype is explained historically, in how the individual has learned to define self from his or her family of origin, that is, generationally. Developmentally, the genotype grows according to peculiarly individual lines that may or may not repeat generational patterns. Situationally, the genotype may be free from historical and developmental factors and respond instead to immediate situational constraints or demands (L'Abate, 1964).

This level tries to answer the question: "How did the individual develop such a genotype?" To understand the nature of the genotype fully, we need to look at the transgenerational transmission of the attribution of importance, the self-differentiation of likeness, and the level of intrinsic motivation from the family of origin as seen in parental practices. In addition to this transgenerational transmission, we must examine the situational determinants of the genotype from the family of procreation, which may involve the nature of the marriage of the individual's parents. Finally, we need to consider the relationship of this sublevel with the three preceding sublevels (L'Abate, 1964, 1976).

The Experiencing-Expressing Continuum and Levels of Interpretation

Levels of interpretation and the continuum of experiencing–expressing are linked together to the extent that each component of the ERAAwC model needs to be considered at different levels of interpretation, as shown schematically in Table 1.3. From this tentative scheme, we can derive an understanding of functionality as the full use of all five components of the ERAAwC model at various levels of interpretation. Dysfunctionality means using or overusing one or two of the five components of the model at the expense of the remaining others. For instance, if a person were to overuse E at the expense of R, the outcome would be unbridled and uncontrolled emotions. Or, if A were used in the extreme without relying on E, R, Aw, or C, the outcome would be hyperactivity and impulsivity. The avoidance of hurtful affect in E would produce either an enlargement of R, leading to obsessions, or to an enlargement of A, leading to character disorders.

While Chapters 1 and 2 deal with what a theory and personality are, E at various levels of interpretation starts with feelings of hurt-happiness at the genotypical sublevel (Chapter 4), shown phenotypically through either approach or avoidance and their verbal or nonverbal presentation. R starts with the self-concept, which governs and controls discharge-delay functions at the phenotypical sublevel. These functions are shown in delay and overuse of control or "illogically" in discharge and the inability to control the self (Chapter 5). A finds its sources in the continuum of likeness, which shows itself phenotypically through three styles in intimate relationships, the ARC model (Chapter 3) as well as through Doing (Chapter 7) and Having (Chapter 8). Aw will not be considered in this volume because its nature and functions were covered in a previous work (L'Abate, 1986). The nature of the context, which can be used or denied

TABLE 1.3. Levels of Interpretation and the Experiencing–Expressing Continuum

Levels of Interpretation	Experiencing		(Processing)	Expressing	
	Emotionality	Rationality	Activity	Awareness	Context
Description — Presentational	Verbal–Nonverbal	Logical	Impulsive Balanced Compulsive (driven) Obsessional	Restricted (external) Wide Constricted (internal) Reality- or fantasy-oriented (L'Abate, 1988)	Used–Denied
Phenotypical	Approach–Avoidance (Chapter 4)	Discharge–Delay (Chapter 5)	Abusive–Apathetic Reactive–Repetitive Conductive–Creative (Chapter 3)		Used–Denied
Explanation — Genotypical	Hurt–Happiness (Chapters 4 and 6)	Self-Concept (Chapter 5)	Likeness continuum (Chapter 3)	Dialogue–Monologue (L'Abate, 1986)	Used–Denied (Part Four)

Historical antecedents

Generational: Family of origin, grandparental influence.
Developmental: Parental practices, sibling influences, traumas.
Situational: Financial, occupational, societal reverses.

(Dumas, 1989; Scharfstein, 1989), will be specified in Part Four (Chapters 9, 10, 11, and 12).

What Are the Units of
Personality Development?

This theory's third point of emphasis pertains to choice and selection of the most relevant and important *units* of behavior for observation, understanding, prediction, and control. In the past, a variety of distinctions were used to distinguish and select units of behavior, such as molar–molecular, proximal–distal, internal–external or public–private, observable–inferred, and more recently, vacuum/nonrelational versus relational. Among these distinctions, this theory stresses molar–relational behavior that is both proximal and distal, public and private, observable and inferred, not in an either-or fashion but in a both-and fashion. As stated earlier, the theory represents a rejection of the vacuum view of personality development suggested by most theories of personality (Dunne & L'Abate, 1978; Pervin, 1990). Thus, *the units of behavior of interest for personality development are relationships with, between, and among other human beings and the settings in which they live and function, primarily the family.* These relationships are the outcome of interactions and transactions between and among people. They are the product and the producers of other relationships in an infinite spiral.

In stressing the importance of relationships, therefore, we cannot have a theory of personality development for individuals that is not valid or applicable also to dyads. Nor can be have a theory just for dyads that is not valid and also applicable to families. We need an all-encompassing theory that is applicable to individuals, couples, and families in relationship to their most relevant settings. We need to distinguish also between intimate (close, committed, and prolonged) versus superficial, short-lived, or trivial relationships. Most of monadic psychology and many personality theories, at least in the United States, consist of the psychology of the college sophomore in a vacuum or in trivial, short-lived, and contrived experimental situations. Nonetheless, I will use the evidence from that research to apply, whenever relevant, to personality development in the family and other settings. Personality does not develop in isolation from other personalities. For instance, we need to consider marriage, the most intimate relationship between adults, from which we could derive a great deal of information about personality development, if we were to focus on it. But most personality theorists have not and do not. Marriage is followed in order of importance by parent–child–siblings relationships and the individual's relationships with his or her family of origin, in-laws, relatives, friends, neighbors, co-workers, and, finally, strangers.

Antecedents-Consequences: The Causes of Personality Development

The fourth point of emphasis of a theory of personality development lies in stating relationships between cause(s) (antecedents) and effect(s) (consequences) of behavior. By now, we are all aware of the complexity of personality development and of the inadequacy of past and simplistic S-R (stimulus–response), or S-R reinforcement paradigms that would fit into the action-reaction stages in Dewey and Bentley's (1949) classification of evolution in thinking. A more complex, difficult, and transactional view of causality can be found in the two concepts of *equipotentiality* (the same cause can have many outcomes), and *equifinality* (different causes may have or arrive at the same outcome). An example of how these two concepts work together can be seen in Figure 1.2. Here, the central construct of personality, to be elaborated further in Chapter 6, consists of the attribution of importance. Such an attribution is the outcome of various historical antecedents as well as the cause of various consequences in the person's life cycle.

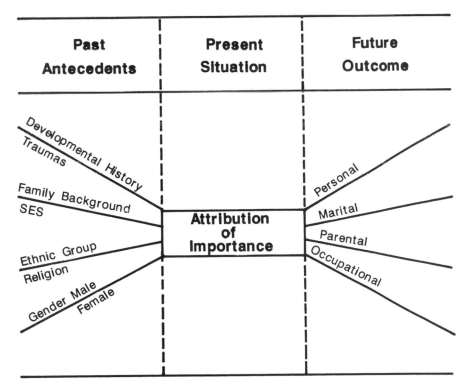

Figure 1.2. Antecedents and consequences of attribution of importance in development.

Independent Variables in Personality Development

The fifth point of emphasis for this theory is to choose the most relevant independent variables that affect behavior. Even though they may not be elaborated in this manuscript, their undeniable and ever-present influence will qualify whatever conclusions we may reach about personality development. Most determinants of personality development in the first five to six years are based on family interactions. Even beyond those years, through the individual's life cycle, the family of origin or of procreation remains always one of the major determinants of personality development. For instance:

1. *Age.* Age is the most important variable in determining relationships. Intimate relationships vary as a function of age and stage of personality development over the life cycle. Chronological age, however, cannot be equated with emotional and interpersonal stages of development, as discussed in greater detail in Chapter 3.

2. *Gender Differences.* We actually need to have three theories of personality development, one for women, one for men, and the third for how we interact with each other. Issues of sex differences in how we are socialized will be discussed in Chapter 6. Any theory of personality development needs to consider two different types of personality according to gender characteristics that reflect and are determined by differential socialization practices (Clausen, 1968; McNeil, 1969). In fact, the role of gender differences has received more and more attention in the psychological literature (Al-Issa, 1980; Baker, 1987; Lee & Stewart, 1976; Lips & Colwill, 1978; Pleck, 1981; Shaver & Hendrick, 1987). There are many other sources, too many to mention. As described in greater detail later on, from early childhood, more boys than girls are socialized for instrumental roles, consisting of performance (Doing, Chapter 7), production (Having, Chapter 8), and functional problem-solving; whereas more girls than boys are socialized for giving love and status to others rather than to themselves (Being, Chapter 6), which is the behavior stressed in the socialization of women (Belle, 1987).

3. *Socioeconomic Status* (SES). This status can be a powerful influence on personality development. Unfortunately, only passing references will be made about its influence, except to generalize from the outset that very low and very high SES levels may unduly restrict personality development.

4. *Ethnic Origin or Race.* We are becoming more and more aware that, at least in the United States, we are the outcome of a mosaic of different nationalities, cultures, and ethnic groups that have played a powerful role in shaping personality development.

5. *Education.* This variable may be the result of the intermingling of the other variables listed here.

6. *Religion.* Religious beliefs and practices, ranging from the liberal to the conservative and from the fundamentalistic to the free-thinking agnosticism or atheism, relate to how a person thinks and behaves in other contexts (L'Abate & Swindell, 1970).

7. *Physical Status or Health.* How an individual functions physically may have a powerful effect on how that individual functions emotionally and interpersonally.

8. *Parental Practices.* Child-raising practices by parents or caretakers and their relationships (marital abuse and conflict, divorce, single-parent family) will determine the emotional and intellectual adjustment of the developing child. This adjustment is the major dependent variable of direct relevance to a theory of personality development. The role of deviations from functional personality development will be considered throughout this volume. Emotional adjustment was already elaborated elsewhere (L'Abate, 1986) from (1) the viewpoint of the ERAAwC model considered earlier; (2) the ARC model to be considered in Chapter 3; and (3) the various theoretical assumptions (Part Two), competencies and skills (Part Three), in interaction with and settings (Part Four).

9. *Sibling Relationships and Rivalry.* In a way, these relationships would be one of the dependent variables determined by parental practices. We must keep in mind that sibling relationships are the longest ones in a lifetime, longer than the parental relationship and almost always longer than the individual's marriage. This longevity, in addition to its intensity in the early years of development, is bound to make an impact on personality development.

Further complexity is achieved when these variables are combined. For instance, one of the most important issues in personality development deals with gender differences in psychopathology. Already in childhood, clear gender differences are apparent in the prevalence of antisocial behavior among boys (Richman, Stevenson, & Graham, 1985). Two generations ago, Pasamanick, Roberts, Lemkau, and Krueger (1959) reported that twice as many men as women were being diagnosed as "psychotics" (p. 188), and almost twice as many women as men were being diagnosed as "psychoneurotic" or as suffering from "psychophysiologic, autonomic, and visceral disorders." In dating, there is a greater tendency for girls to internalize stresses and tension and for boys to externalize them. Cultural changes, however, may decrease the validity of these generalizations, which will be considered again in the various chapters.

These independent variables interact with settings in determining a specific outcome (the dependent variables) in each setting (home, work, leisure, transit, and transitory). There may be cross-setting consistency between and among settings. The value of each variable for personality development may vary from one individual to another. However, their inevitable influence on personality development cannot be denied.

CRITERIA TO EVALUATE FOR THEORY BUILDING AND TESTING

A theory of personality development needs to be evaluated both empirically as well as applicatively. A theory cannot be valid in the laboratory and not valid in real-life situations. It needs to be valid in the home as well as in the hospital, in the clinic, and in the laboratory. However, we cannot expect personality to be manifested in the same manner from one setting to another: An irresponsible marriage partner may be a terrific tennis player, and by the same token, a terrible driver during peak transit hours may be a relaxed manager. We expect a certain amount of cross-situational consistency from one setting to another, but as discussed at length in Chapter 12, a person's priorities determine how he or she will behave in any one setting and from one setting to another.

To be deemed acceptable, a theory of personality development must satisfy the various criteria or requirements that are described next.

Specificity

This criterion could be stated as follows: *"Better be specific and wrong than general and right."* As long as a theory is stated in general and vague terms, as in the case of so-called systems theory, it becomes practically impossible to evaluate it. There are many appealing and seductive theories of personality development and psychotherapy. However, their level of abstraction and generality is so great that they cannot be verified easily. Being specific and wrong is preferable to being general and right without any criterion for evaluating the adequacy of hypotheses stemming from the theory.

Concreteness

A theory needs to be *concrete* enough to meet all the other requirements. This particular theory is built in part on six resource classes developed by Foà and Foà (1974), in which at least four resources—information, services, money, and possessions—are particular and concrete enough to be defined in and by themselves. Two other resource classes in their theory—status and love—perhaps are not as concrete as we would like them to be. In this work, however, both resources will be defined and refined as concretely as possible. Why is concreteness so important? It is important because to evaluate and validate a theory, we should be able to define each construct of the theory, or each term of the theory in an operationalized way (e.g., constructs need to be reduced to operations). Consequently, concreteness is the primary prerequisite for all the other requirements of theory building and testing. If the theory were to be so abstract that it could not be defined operationally, it would create many problems. This is essentially the problem with humanistic, psychoanalytic, and systems theories, which have many terms that are extremely difficult to define and therefore to validate.

Simplicity or Parsimony

A theory needs to encompass and explain the widest ranges of personality development with the least number of assumptions. The present theory, for instance, makes two basic assumptions about personality development—space (Chapter 4) and time (Chapter 5).

Testability

A theory needs to be concrete enough to be evaluated and validated through both *accountability* and *verifiability*. These two criteria imply that a theory of personality development may or may not lead to applications. Applications can take place in experimental situations (in the laboratory) or in less controlled and controllable conditions, (clinical situations).

Accountability relates to the measurement of results through pre- and postevaluations and follow-up of interventions based on a particular theory. The first criterion, accountability, is independent from the second criterion, verifiability, which implies a component analysis of the various aspects of the theory to account for the process. Accountability deals with the results of an intervention, whereas verifiability deals with how and why the various components in the overall intervention process obtained certain results or lack of results in that intervention. If a theory cannot be verified in its component parts, it will be highly difficult to validate *as a whole*.

Verifiability is the criterion that tries to answer the question: "If a theory cannot be evaluated, how good is it?" Many personality and psychotherapy theories, are untestable because verifiability and demonstrativeness are not criteria for professional applications. Usefulness, aesthetic appeal, and ease of dialectic applicability are the earmarks of a profession that seeks to discover rather than to demonstrate or prove anything. Demonstrativeness and the context of justification are the earmarks of science. We need both criteria without assuming mutually exclusive, extreme positions in either direction (L'Abate, 1986). As shall be discussed in Chapters 13 and 14, a theory can be evaluated through self-report, paper-and-pencil tests, and observations of interactions; or it can be verified through specific, theory-derived interventions.

Applicability

This criterion tries to answer the question: "If a theory cannot be applied to a variety of situations, how good is it?" A theory could produce interventional results and yet not be verifiable, because we could not look at the components of the interventions. By the same token, a theory could be verifiable and not produce interventional results. This distinction is the reason the concepts of accountability and verifiability are independent of each other. Therefore we need them both. In this particular theory, we will develop models that can be verified either through paper-and-pencil evaluations (Chapter 13) or through component analysis of the process of intervention (Chapter 14). The theory produces a variety of models. Each model can be verified independently of the others (L'Abate, 1986).

Reducibility

A theory needs constructs that are *reducible* as much as possible to known and established psychological concepts. If, for instance, we choose to explain personality development in a family, there must be constructs that are relevant to the realm of the family and at the interactional level among family members. Part of this interaction cannot always be reduced to individual determinants. There are dyadic and multiperson family interactions that are supraordinate to the individual but in which the individual has a definite influence. By the same token, individual determinants may have been produced by past family *interactions* that still affect present interactions. Family interactions, in part, reflect how various family members interact with each other, which creates variance in these interactions. Some of the variance is due to dyadic interactions—the relationship between husband and wife, or parent and child—who would be part of that interaction. Coalitions and conflicts, dyadic or otherwise, may influence the interaction. As stated earlier, some of the variance in family interaction is also due to individual determinants that are the result of previous family interactions. Personality development (as discussed in Chapters 3 and 6) is determined, for the most part, by how the infant and the child is socialized in the family.

Consistency and Validity

If a theory does not relate to the realm it purports to describe and understand, how good is it? There should be a certain degree of isomorphism between theory and personality development. This criterion needs to be *relevant,* applicable, and verifiable at all three levels of prevention—primary, secondary, and tertiary—as will be reiterated in Chapter 14.

Complexity

A theory of personality development needs to recognize that behavior is too complex to be understood solely on the basis of the study of independent variables. A theory needs to speak to the nature of *causes.* To understand the complex nature of causality, we need to use the butterfly or bow-tie model that validates (a) the importance of equifinality (different causes can produce the same results), and (b) the principle of equipotentiality (one cause may have different results), as illustrated in Figure 1.2. This complexity may seem to contradict the previous requirement of simplicity. This apparent contradiction may be clarified by stating that a theory needs to reduce complex behavior to simple verifiable constructs.

This model may be called systemic in that people who interact for long periods in close relationships have the largest amount of influence on each other. Therefore, we can say that different behaviors can produce different results varying from individual to individual, from family to family, and from setting to setting. The principles of equifinality and equipotentiality discussed earlier represent a requirement of systemic influence that acknowledges the complexity and contextuality of personality development as well as the continuous give-and-take exchanges in human relationships.

Integration

If at all possible, a theory of personality development needs to be *integrative* of existing theories. In addition to being developmental, this theory is also integrative: It attempts to integrate systematically and to go beyond a variety of past theoretical viewpoints such as humanism, psychoanalysis, behaviorism, Gestalt, and contextualism. The two theories that seem to be more relevant and that can be integrated from this approach are humanism, with its emphasis on the subjective experience of feeling on the input side of behavior, and behaviorism, with its emphasis on objectivity on the output side of behavior and its consequences. By the same token, a theory of personality development needs to integrate psychoanalytic views about the nature and cognitive aspects of the self. The ERAAwC model, summarized earlier, attempts to integrate these theories (L'Abate, 1986). The present theory will attempt to integrate, or it could be said that this book is part of an attempt at integration already started (L'Abate, 1976, 1986) years ago (Table 1.1).

Fruitfulness

This criterion attempts to answer the question: "If a theory does not influence others, how good is it?" A theory or model does not need to be valid to be fruitful. For instance, the whole concept of complementarity in marriage produced a great deal of research (L'Abate, Weinstein, Fraizer, & Russ, 1989). Ultimately, very little empirical evidence was found for this concept as long as it was couched in inadequate terms. By the same token, the notion of a double bind in the genesis of schizophrenia found few consistent results that could be supported and accepted wholesale. This hypothesis has produced many studies but little if any confirmation. Thus, fruitfulness is an independent criterion because a theory or a model could be invalid but be extremely influential in promoting research. Although it is preferable for a model to be valid and fruitful, sometimes, we may have to follow blind alleys to find the most effective route through the theoretical maze.

Vacuum versus Relational Orientation

Another issue that is relevant to the present theory deals with the question: "If a theory of personality development does not deal with relationships and does not see that this development is the outcome of continuous, intense, forceful interactions in the family, how good is it?" This question will be addressed throughout this volume.

SUMMARY AND CONCLUSION

In this introductory chapter, I have attempted to delineate five different epistemological issues in theory definition: (a) the width and range of personality development as represented by the experiencing–expressing continuum; (b) the depth of personality at various levels and sublevels of description and explanation; (c) the units of personality development, which are seen as relationships between and among individuals in close, committed, and prolonged relationships; (d) complex cause–effect, antecedents–consequences relationships as understood through the principles of equifinality and equipotentiality; and (e) the independent variables of personality development through the life cycle, age, gender, SES, ethnic origin or race, religion, physical and mental health, parental practices, and sibling relationships. In conclusion, as Kurt Lewin was fond of saying: "There is nothing as practical as a good theory."

CHAPTER 2

What Is Personality?

Relationships cannot become a reality by which life is lived until there is a vocabulary through which they are realized. This vocabulary is slowly beginning to emerge, and with it a sensibility that should render relationships as palpable and objective as the individual selves of previous eras.

(GERGEN, 1991, p. 160)

This chapter proposes a definition of personality that is consistent with the development of competencies (Part Three) in the home (Chapter 9), at work (Chapter 10), at nonwork, discretionary activities (Chapter 11), and in the interrelationships among these competencies and three settings as assessed by priorities (Chapter 12). Instead of a vague and untestable person × situation interaction, which has influenced and colored personality theories in the previous generation, this definition posits specific, competence × setting transactions that are indigenous to the three, sometimes overlapping, settings already mentioned—home, work, and leisure. Personality expresses itself in terms of how competent individuals are to meet the task demands and requirements of each setting. Some individuals can fulfill those requirements in all three settings, and other individuals do well in one or two, but not in the third. Finally, there are individuals who are unable to fulfill the demands of any of them. A continuum of competencies, therefore, suggests itself, where in each setting, we may set up criteria of success and failure with gradations of competence in between those extremes. Thus, each setting will be considered in terms of the minimal task requirements, or responsibilities, demanded of each individual in that setting (Phillips, 1968). This definition posits a developmental competence × setting interaction in the three settings that account for most of our waking time.

We need to specify the contexts where these sets of capabilities, effectiveness, and skills are manifested and used. Competence can be specified and even assessed in a specific setting much more easily than "personality." Furthermore, whereas personality seems to encompass a wide range of traits and states, most of them internal and difficult to measure, competence is limited to a finite and definite number of settings. Although competence is a more restricted term than personality, it may be easier to define and to measure, because competence $\times$ setting is a more specific interaction than just person $\times$ situation.

PROBLEMS IN THE DEFINITION OF PERSONALITY

The history of personality definitions presents a troubling trajectory. Since the days of James (1890) and Allport (1968), who summarized various extant definitions, to the present (Pervin, 1990), no satisfactory definition has received widespread acceptance in the psychological community. Before I offer a proposal for this definition, we need to examine the reasons for this unsatisfactory state of affairs. This chapter reviews some of the major problems with previous definitions and closes with a definition that I will elaborate in the rest of this book.

Person or Personality?

We can become so embroiled in picky definitions that we forget there are persons behind the term *personality,* and that our definition should acknowledge this distinction. For instance, Helson and Mitchell (1978) suggested that issues of identity, knowledge, Cartesian dichotomies (disguised as dialectics), time, space, traits and environment, and genetics have confounded research in personality development. The meaning of being a person—personhood—cannot be delineated without clarifying these issues. Nevertheless, they concluded that "personality psychology is the fundamental discipline, because the psyche comes before any of its more specialized activities" (p. 580). Later, Carson (1989) pointed out that the genetic and environmental issues of personality development and their meaning for the (mental and physical) health of the individual still have not been worked out. These fundamental problems have implications for the health and well-being of individuals and for therapeutic interventions, thus requiring further exploration. Information processing, genetics, and environment are the areas he suggested need further exploration. He gave no succinct description of person or personhood. Crosby (1985), on the other hand, described the person as a being made up of a multiplicity of "ego states." He asserted that each person must accept and include all his or her "various faces, moods, and feelings" to be a "meaningful whole" person (p. 201).

From various conceptualizations and problems inherent in understanding what a person is, there arises the sense that being a person—personhood—is more than simply the sum of the genetic and social environmental endowments of a human being. These two key background elements are brought to the experiences in the life of every human. Through their interaction with the elements of each experience or with other people, the person emerges as a unique being. The way an individual processes information may partially be determined by genetic and past environmental influences (history) but also may be influenced by issues in the present situation. How others perceive an individual in social situations (social appearance) and in private (phenotype) is affected by the individual's history, and it affects in turn genotypic attributions by others.

Multiplicity of Definitions

Personality, thus far, has been undefinable or difficult to define because most definitions are either too general and vague or too abstract to link them with actual and specific behavior. Past definitions have traditionally focused on internal, intrapsychic, and monadic states or traits that bypassed specific, concrete, and observable behaviors (Abramson, 1981; Cartwright, 1979; Ewen, 1984; Gatchel & Mears, 1982; Hall & Lindsey, 1978; Mischel, 1981; Monte, 1980; Pervin, 1980; Schultz, 1981; Singer, 1984). For instance, how are we going to distinguish among "self," "identity," "person," or "personhood," or even more esoteric terms such as "ego," "self-esteem," "self-concept," or "I-ness"? Even if we could distinguish these terms from each other, how are we going to link them to discriminably different behaviors? Endler's (1983) conclusion is even harsher than the one reached here: "What the field of personality has pretentiously called theories of personality are not really theories at all, but are merely models pretending to be theories" (p. 155). As Pervin (1985) noted in reviewing theory and research on personality: ". . . most recent reviews have been relatively critical and pessimistic (p. 84) . . . progress is being made, but not as much as some might expect" (p. 104). We need to ask, then, why progress has not met reasonable expectations? One answer would point to definitional difficulties that do not allow the linkage of specific constructs (traits, dispositions, inferred, attributed, or hypothetical internal states) to specific behaviors.

A critical review of the literature on personality assessment and theory supports this position. Most of the classical references on personality assessment, starting with Allport (1968), going on to Kleinmuntz (1967), Mischel (1968), McReynolds (1968, 1971), Pervin (1990), and ending up with Vernon (1964) focus on measuring personality in a vacuum, abstracted from the natural settings where personality development, experience, expression, and competencies take place. These theories and practices are, therefore, *acontextual,* avoiding consideration of personality in the very settings where personality expresses itself. Many of the dilemmas about personality—the state versus trait controversy (Mischel, 1968); objective versus projective methods of personality assessment (Pervin, 1985); emphasis on questionably useful and generally vague traits or states, such as anxiety (Pervin, 1990); and the difficulties in measuring personality change as a result of psychotherapeutic interventions (Garfield & Bergin, 1986)—fail to focus on specific and relevantly concrete matters. All these references have a distinct and basic short-coming: They disregard the natural settings where personality competencies develop and ultimately take place. At best, the person × situation interaction is invoked as a way out, as a solution for definitional difficulties inherent in terms, personality, and environment. But these constructs and their alleged interaction remain vague, ill-defined, and difficult to operationalize because of their high level of abstraction and the absence of specificity about where and how such an interaction is to take place.

Lack of Agreement and Consensus among Theorists

The shortcoming of acontextuality in the definition and description of personality is not limited to the theoretical literature; clinical references (Jessor & Feshbach, 1967; Megargee, 1966; Woody & Woody, 1972) avoid this topic as well. Although these references may be somewhat out of date, it is doubtful whether any definition even in the clinical literature, has considered the three contexts, settings, or domains where personality competencies are transacted every day. One more recent reference (Woody, 1980) does cite three (out of 91 chapters for the three preceding sources) chapters on marital adjustment, family functioning, and parenting assessment. None of the other sources cite either home, work, or leisure as potential settings where assessment could take place. All the traits, or states, or dimensions detailed in the remaining 88 chapters contained in those references were described as coming out magically from a contextual vacuum.

In addition to these difficulties, personality theorists have ignored the work of researchers such as Moos (1974, 1976), on the importance of the "human context," and of Phillips (1968), who made interpersonal competence a measurable and researchable subject. Competence is a much more specific (and hopeful) concept than personality. It can be broken down into specific, finite, and definite roles. Each role has a specific set of skills that can be assessed and evaluated as part of transactions among individuals in their natural settings and observers. The individuals who are part of such transactions will influence those events, whether they like it or not.

Borofsky (1974), in dealing with issues of diagnosis and classification in personality functioning, suggested five major objections to current systems of classification:

> . . . (1) most systems of diagnosis tend to focus on pathology and weakness rather than on adaptive functioning and ego strengths; (2) most systems view psychopathology as being discontinuous with adaptive psychological functioning; accordingly they classify disturbed individuals into one of several discrete types, rather than viewing

emotional disturbance as an exaggeration or disruption of normal adaptive functioning; (3) most classification systems tend to ignore the individual personality and the possibility of individuality and uniqueness in the search for adaptation; they tend to focus on a nomothetic approach to deviancy and adaptation; (4) diagnostic systems use typologies rather than traits; and (5) diagnostic classifications are used to make value judgments in legal or moral matters. (p. 25)

The present proposal, therefore, suggests a continuum of setting-specific competencies that bypasses the traditionally attributed traits, the hypothetical, nonrelational states, and the vague and inferred intrapsychic entities that have produced many of the controversies alluded to by Borofsky. If there is to be a classification, it needs to consider the settings where these competencies take place every day. If there are to be intrapsychically inferred constructs, as with any other source (Chapters 3 and 6), they need to be relational.

In this regard, Moos (1976) quoted Barker (1968), who suggested the concept of "circuits" for goals, programs, deviation-countering, and vetoing activities that specify person × setting interactions (pp. 222–223): "The reality and nature of behavior setting of eco-behavioral entities do not reside in psychological processes of the inhabitants, but in the circuitry that interconnects behavior settings, inhabitants, and other behavior setting components" (p. 74). As Moos concluded from the preceding quotation: "Thus, the 'essence' of behavior settings is not just people, nor is it just places. It is instead a complex network of *relationships* between individual psychological processes and setting components" (p. 224). Moos also cited Holland's model (1973) at length to classify personalities and environments. Last but not least, Phillips' (1968) contribution allows a complete classification of competencies at home, work, and leisure-time activities. This classification, combined with Moos's (1976) methods of assessing settings, would go a long way toward understanding competencies × setting transactions.

In spite of the many differences, the various proposals may have common factors or dimensions conceived as polarities, such as uniqueness versus normativeness, stability versus change, normality versus abnormality. Can a theory reconcile these polarities giving equal value to each extreme?

DEFINITIONAL DIFFICULTIES

Difficulties in the Definition of Environment

Thus far, the term *environment* has been thought of either as internal states, such as privacy, personal space, territoriality, and crowding (Altman, 1975); or, in most personality theory, as context (Levy, 1970), culture (Pervin, 1980), or social influences (Schultz, 1981). In most cases (Gatchel & Mears, 1982; Maddi, 1980; Mischel, 1981), it has been referred to as "situation." Efforts to pin down the specific meaning of *situation* draw a blank. It seems to be a blanket, or generic, term for anything outside of the personality.

In this regard Mischel (1981) concluded:

> . . . in current debates on this topic, "situations" are often treated like entities that supposedly exert either major or only minor control over behavior, without specifying what, psychologically, they are and how they function. But while some situations may be powerful determinants of behavior, others are trivial. The relative importance of individual differences and situation will depend on the situation selected, the type of behavior assessed, the particular individual differences sampled, and the purpose of the assessment. (p. 525)

Mischel (1981) then proceeded to distinguish six dimensions of human environments based on Moos's work (1973): ecological, behavior settings, organizational, characteristics of inhabitants, perceived social climate, and functional properties. Of relevance to the thesis of this chapter are the dimensions of behavioral settings in the home, work, and leisure, their perceived social climates, and their functional properties. Once these settings are identified, we need to distinguish between setting and situation. The former is strictly the physical and objective place where behavior can be photographed, recorded, and reproduced (Endler, 1983; Maddi, 1980). Its characteristics can be described minutely down to the last brick. Situation, on the other hand, refers to the phenomenological interpretation that each of us gives to a particular setting—what Moos (and Mischel) call "perceived social climate" as well as its attributed functional properties with their subjective and symbolic meaning and value to the individual.

A review of the literature on personality to determine whether situation covers home and family (where most of us spend two-thirds to three-fourths of our time), indicated that family-related terms, such as family, father, marriage, mother, maternal, parental, and parent-child relationships, are only mentioned, at the most, on the average in one page out of a hundred (Dunne & L'Abate, 1978). Years later, a check through more recent personality textbooks (Abramson, 1981; Cartwright, 1979; Gatchel & Mears, 1982; Hall & Lindsey, 1978; Maddi, 1980; Mischel, 1981; Monte, 1980; Page, 1983; Pervin, 1980; Schultz, 1981; Singer, 1984) to search for any changes in this trend shows that on the average less than half a page in one hundred is devoted to terms denoting family and home. Home and the family have not been considered in either the preceding personality assessment references or by most personality theorists. One notable exception to this melancholy appraisal is Massey (1981), who devoted 258 out of 532 pages of text to topics relevant to the family, such as culture (41), context (23), family (44), marriage (11), parent ego strength (10), situation (8), social influence (72), parenting conditions for growth (17), and socialization (32).

Unfortunately, such a trend is not limited to psychological texts. One anthropological text (LeVine, 1973) devoted less than 3 pages of text out of 293 pages to the family. Yet, we spend most of our time in it. How can we justify talking about personality development outside the home? The same kind of analysis for work and leisure shows an even smaller number of pages devoted to the influence of these settings on personality. No wonder that the field of personality theory is in trouble.

Thus far, apparently, we would want students, as well as the average person off the streets (and the proverbial, visiting Martian), to believe that personality development takes place in either a vacuum, or as a complete product of genetic influences. Fortunately, this belief is being challenged, and evidence has been presented to indicate not only that personality development starts from the cradle (Kaye & Furstenberg, 1985; L'Abate, 1985b) but that personality development continues over the life cycle (Levinson, 1986). This development occurs first, and primarily, in the family context, then at work, and third, in discretionary, leisurely pursuits. Lee and Kanungo's work (1984b) lends support to this argument by providing methodologies and research relevant to the influence of all three settings.

Consequently, the terms personality and environment, either alone or in combination as interaction, have not produced a distinct conceptual or practical improvement. Environment has been just as difficult to define as personality or their interaction.

Difficulties in the Definition of Person × Situation Interaction

Both terms in the personality-environment interaction, seen by many (Ekehammar, 1974; Endler & Magnusson, 1976a,b; Magnusson & Allen, 1984; Magnusson & Endler, 1977; Mischel, 1981) as a solution to the various difficulties inherent in defining personality from a traditionally intrapsychic and monadic viewpoint, remain just as difficult to define. Both terms, either by themselves or together, have remained vague, general, and too abstract to define operationally. Nor has their combination led to any dramatic advances and breakthroughs in personality theory or research (Endler, 1983; Mischel, 1979; Mischel & Peake, 1983; Pervin, 1985). A possible solution for the dilemmas posed by definitional difficulties, in personality, environment, or their combination, could be to consider personality in terms of sets of competencies in three different and diverse settings. Personality expresses itself 100% of the time (except for time spent in transit from one to another setting): (a) at home, (b) at work, and (c) at leisure. In addition to the three sets of competencies, a fourth concept of priorities is needed to evaluate how these three sets are ranked and organized in each setting in relationship to the other two.

The personality–environment interaction supposedly was brought forth as a solution to past definitional problems (Ekehammar, 1974; Endler, 1983; Endler & Magnusson, 1976a,b; Magnusson & Endler, 1977). However, the term *interaction* proved just as difficult to define, as either personality or environment (Maddi, 1980; Mischel, 1981, 1983; Pervin, 1985). Hence, whereas the situational–interactional view may have been a distinct acknowledgment of a more dynamic relationship between the two constructs than either one alone, it remained stymied in its seeming inability to specify the parameters of this interaction (Bowers, 1973; Endler, 1983). In dealing with this issue, Pervin (1985) concluded:

> The person–situation controversy continues to dominate the attention of personality psychologist (p. 85). . . . Despite years of debate and numerous investigations, the person–situation issue has not yet been resolved. Nor, one might venture to guess, will it be in terms of the current framing of the issue. (p. 91)

He felt that interactionism:

> . . . does not begin to provide us with answers concerning what and how—what in the person interacts how, with what in the environment (p. 104) . . . A critical question here is whether it will be useful to try to develop a taxonomy of situations relevant to personality. (p. 103)

The answer to Pervin's critical question should be clear by now: Personality consists of sets of competencies in different and diverse settings. Critical to this answer is the definition of competence or sets of competencies, which we will discuss after we consider the concept of self as a substitute term for personality.

THE CONCEPT OF SELF AS A SUBSTITUTE
FOR PERSONALITY

Recently, the concept of self, rather than the concept of personality, has achieved a greater frequency of citation (Gergen, 1971, 1991). This frequency still begs the question: "What is the self?" Among the many investigators postulating the importance of a self-concept in personality theory, Levin (1987), discussed the concept of self as described by psychoanalytic writers like Kohut, or by humanistic writers like Rogers (1961). We tend to think of the self as an organizing, integrating concept that is related to our conscious sense of guidance, planning, and responsibility, the "I" of our identification as human beings and as persons. This sense of self is necessary but is insufficient to understand, describe, and explain personality development.

Functions of the Self

The concept of *self* is an attribution that allows us to describe and explain behavior. The central construct that we call "self" fulfills many functions: (a) regulation and integration of the different parts or roles we play; (b) regulation of the internal experience of affect with its outward expression (emotionality), going from one extreme of approach to another extreme of avoidance, and from an extreme of discharge to another extreme of delay (Chapters 4 and 5); (c) balancing of affect experience with affect expression can take place when one is able to use other personal components, like rationality, activity, awareness, and context, as in the ERAAwC model (see Chapter 1), to aid toward a more appropriate and constructive expression of affect; (d) balancing of different priorities (Chapter 12); and (e) integration among levels of description (presentational and phenotypical) and of explanation (genotypical and historical), discussed in Chapter 1.

Personality, Selfhood, and Self-Concept

We need to look at the concept of the self and explore some of its definitions. Kegan (1982) proposed that the self is an intrapersonal matrix where events are received, interpreted, and responded to—"the zone of mediation where meaning is made" (p. 3). Kegan's view is that the development of self begins at birth, and we might consider even the fetal experience as significant to development in terms of predisposition. For Jung (1983), the self was a hypothetical point between the conscious and the unconscious from which we make decisions and receive guidance. According to Kierkegaard, the process of individuation—the birth of self—begins when the individual starts making choices (Cole, 1971). Outler (1987) saw the self as a unique unity that must be transcended for the individual to develop fully. Considering these points, we may say *the self is the central point of the individual that processes and evaluates information and experience and guides the individual in meaning making, decision making, and attributions to the self and others.* Out of this central core of the self, personality and identity arise. Self-awareness and exploration distinguish humanity from lower animals (Bennett, 1984) and are necessary for the subtle process of the acquisition of self-importance. Consciousness of self depends on the individual's ability to distinguish him- or herself from others (Jung, 1954).

Although the self is a subsystem of the family (Crosby, 1985), we must learn and experience differentiation from our family of origin to develop selfhood (Bowen, 1978). According to Freud (Hergenhahn, 1984), the first step in individuation is for the child to begin a bonding to his or her major caretaker. May (1953) pointed out, however, that this bonding does not always occur, and it is through development of the intellect and by making choices that an individual begins to separate. Bowen's theory (1978) would agree with this position to some extent. He believed individuals must develop objectivity through rationality to avoid a maladaptive pattern of triangulation with other family members. According to Bowen, family tensions usually found in the parental dyad fuse children emotionally with their parents, creating an undifferentiated ego mass and preventing selfhood from developing. Crosby (1985) believed that many intrapsychic conflicts begin in the family of origin and manifest themselves later in interpersonal relationships, especially in spousal conflicts. To avoid bringing these conflicts into new relationships, individuals must become aware of their reactions to past family experiences and work toward resolution of that past.

Some distancing may be required in current relationships, but this goal can be accomplished by cognitive mediation and not by a complete withdrawal (Chapter 4). Bowen's theory stands in hope that a person may be differentiated yet remain connected with the family of origin and to significant others. Self-discovery does not occur in the absence of others, but only in interaction with others. Furthermore, attempts at individuation ideally should not lead to extreme individualism (Waanders, 1987). Individualism must be transcended to give the self meaning and value. Selfhood has meaning and value only in a context of relationships.

The ability to think and to make independent decisions is important for selfhood in that decision making is the point of departure for individuation (May, 1953). Although it is important to recognize ambiguity through awareness of self according to Jung's theory, without decision making, the individual stagnates or is controlled by external events. Through decision making, we overcome traumatic experiences and personal deficiencies. Decisions must be self-conscious and not from compulsion; they must be responsive to the total picture (May, 1953). Individuation as a decision-making process is often confused with rebelliousness. As we shall see in Chapter 3, a choice made in rebellion to someone else is reactive and becomes an externally controlled choice. Individuation-related choices do not exclude compliance with authority. Decision making toward selfhood involves clarification of personal goals and values, which depend on self-awareness (Crosby, 1985).

Self has often been equated with self-concept, how and what we think of ourselves, or how well we think of ourselves (self-esteem). The literature on self-esteem (Guidano, 1987; Hamachek, 1978; Lynch, Norem-Hebeisen, & Gergen, 1981) has been as a whole a theoretical and methodological dead end. Wylie (1974) has shown that self-esteem is an extremely murky and difficult concept to define. Another way of looking at the self-concept, which was considered by Rogers (1957), has been the differentiation, and degree of discrepancy, between the actual self-concept and the desired or ideal self-concept. The discrepancy between actual and ideal is matched in some way or another by how the self is presented externally and how the self is viewed privately, which would represent the dimension of self-esteem.

Self-esteem is an internal representation, the intrapsychic outcome of interpersonal counting and discounting from important others. These others include caretakers, siblings, and loved ones who have participated in the individual's rearing from inception through close and prolonged exchanges. The process of counting or discounting in intimate relationships involves the attribution and exchange of importance or nonimportance. Self-esteem, therefore, is the internal outcome of such an interpersonal exchange. Self-esteem does not develop in a vacuum. It develops from close and prolonged intimate exchanges, usually with and from family members, friends, and co-workers. We do not fall in love on the basis of another person's self-esteem, nor do we marry that person on such a basis. Instead, we fall in love and marry on the basis of our attribution of importance to that person. That we may match that person in the level of self-esteem (Murstein, 1976) speaks to the point that we tend to marry persons whom we perceive to be as important as we are. Similarly, we mourn someone on the basis of his or her importance to us and not on the basis of that person's self esteem.

The self-concept, therefore, means a view of our identity, of our personhood, as implicit in how we view the self. Under this rubric, at least three different topics of relevance to the self will be reviewed critically, from a relational viewpoint: (a) self-esteem, (b) self-interest, and (c) personal responsibility. Since the concepts are interrelated, they will be subsumed under the rubric of self-esteem.

Rosenberg (1979), in discussing self-concept, essentially indicated that the self-concept represents "the totality of the individual's thoughts and feelings having referenced to himself as an object" (p. 7). The self-concept, however, needs to be discriminated and differentiated from (a) how the individual's self comes off to others, (b) how the individual presents his or her self, and (c) how and what the individual feels underneath the facade of self-presentation. Rosenberg considered the content of self-concept as determined by social identity, which is based on labels defining what were called (Chapter 1) the independent variables (sex, age, race, nationality, religion, family status, and name). From all these labels arises the definition of an individual's identity.

Social identity arises from the process of social labeling. This process is based on deviant behavior that characterizes an individual. Someone who drinks heavily would be characterized as an alcoholic. Someone who takes drugs is labeled as an addict. Another form of classification for social identity is on the basis on an individual's biography, for example, a war veteran, an emeritus professor, a divorcee. The part of the social identity that Rosenberg called personal identity is whatever qualities the individual ascribes to the self. Rosenberg considered at least nine different dimensions of the self-concept that make up the structure of the self-concept: (a) content, which represents social identity; (b) direction, especially in terms of positive or negative self-esteem; (c) intensity, the strength or weakness of a person's feelings about certain issues; (d) salience, which represents the importance of one particular identity compared with others; (e) consistency, how consistent or contradictory an individual is about the self; (f) stability, which represents the individual's firmness and unchanging opinions about self and others; (g) clarity, which represents how unambiguous the individual might be about his or herself; (h) accuracy, which represents the validity of the individual's perceptions of self and others; and (i) verifiability, whether the opinions of the individual can be matched by an external reality. Another aspect of the self-concept considered by Rosenberg is self-confidence and individuality, how confidently an individual sees his or herself as being different from others.

Rosenberg's view considered what he called significant others, the people who have personal significance to us. To clarify this concept, Rosenberg described (a) global self-esteem, (b) perceived self, and (c) interpersonal evaluation, which represents essentially an individual's concern with the others' opinion of the self. He commented: ". . . self-esteem . . . does not show a linear progression with severity of mental illness, as ordinarily conceived" (p. 77). Rosenberg quoted both Wylie (1974, 1978) and Kaplan (1975) that the self-esteem of psychotics is as high as, or even higher, than the self-esteem of neurotics. However, he does not concede how the self-esteem of neurotics is different from the self-esteem of "functional individuals."

In a chapter devoted to "Beyond Self-Esteem" (Chapter 11, pp. 260–289), Rosenberg invoked four principles that relate to the self and go beyond self-esteem: (a) deflected appraisals, how an individual learns to change the appraisal of self on the basis of what others think about him or her; (b) psychological centrality, the dimensions of self that are important to the individual, such as honesty or dishonesty, strength or weakness; (c) self-attribution, the qualities that are bestowed on the self; and (d) social comparison processes, which are related to a continuum of likeness in the development of self and self-appraisal (as discussed in

Chapter 3). This introduction to Rosenberg's views as well as research with adolescents' self-concepts is relevant to the concepts used here as well as in Chapter 6.

PERSONALITY, SELF, AND SELF-ESTEEM

Self-esteem is important to selfhood as a motivation factor for growth. If a person's thoughts are full of depreciatory cognitions, his or her feelings will follow suit (Beck, 1976), and the person may act in such a way that most likely will not benefit self or others. The attribution of value, either to the self or to another, is not merely an intellectual event, but is seen in attitude and behavior. Recognition of the value of that self influences the decision-making process and the way that individuals interact with others. Devaluation is seen in choices where an individual chooses substances or engages in behaviors that inhibit or preclude relationships. Compulsive and addictive behaviors place value on things or experiences, not only on persons. Although the individual is born with a potential for selfhood, without nurturance and healthy interactions or corrections of past unhealthy interactions, the self may not grow. The lack of growth creates an emptiness or void that may be readily filled with any available substitutes. In this sense, selfhood is seen as a cycle; the individual must have something of value to give value, and it is only through corrective experience that deviations in personality development may develop into rewarding selfhood. The corrective experience, for instance, may be the decision to begin to attach value to the self by seeking treatment.

Branden (1969) and Coopersmith (1967) have been among the early proponents of the importance of self-esteem, as well as the importance of emotions in the individual's consciousness. Branden also emphasized the importance of "rational being" and "being of volitional consciousness." In further consideration of self-esteem, beyond the work of Wylie (1961), Steffenhagen and Burns (1987) related the whole psychology of self-esteem to (a) Adler's concept of inferiority versus superiority; (b) realistic versus unrealistic goals; and (c) the Adlerian concepts, such as lifestyles (pampered versus neglected, and social interest versus self-interest). These topics are relevant to the present theory because, as we will see in Chapter 6, a pampered lifestyle essentially produces egocentrism and selfishness whereas a neglected lifestyle probably produces selflessness, and extremes or contradictions in both would probably produce no self. Steffenhagen and Burns affirmed: "Human behavior can be understood only in terms of self-esteem. Self-esteem can be achieved through social action . . . and through movement from inferior to the superior" (p. 10). They differentiated between social interest, which we will call "selfulness" (Chapter 6), and selfishness, which they call "self-interest" (p. 13):

> . . . what we call selfish or self-centered behavior, lacking social interest, is not behavior independent of community norms but behavior inconsistent with those norms. . . . When we speak of behavior lacking in social interest we are referring to behavior that results from inadequate socialization or reflection. . . . The converse of social interest is self interest, that is, self-grandizement at the expense of others (p. 14). . . . Self-esteem, [Adler argued] is the basic motivating force of behavior; the goal of the individual is to build, or at least, protect, self-esteem (pp. 19–20). . . . We cannot understand self-esteem intrapsychically, but only within the parameters of the individual's immediate social milieu. (p. 23)

Self-esteem was defined by Steffenhagen and Burns as "the totality of the individual's constructs of self: self concept (mental), self image (physical), and social concept (cultural)" (p. 28). Of relevance to the present formulation of selfhood, Steffenhagen and Burns commented:

> Self acceptance is an important dimension of self-esteem (a part of it but not synonymous with it) and accrues from . . . difficulty dealing with interpersonal relations. . . . People who cannot accept themselves cannot develop good self-esteem. . . . [Self-acceptance] . . . is a distinct but not an isolated level of self esteem. (p. 32)

These authors (pp. 34–45) relate self-esteem to the status of the individual, including courage as an important component of self-esteem. Thus, their model is a Star of David figure in which three of the corners of one triangle are self-image, self-concept, and self social-concept.

The three parts of the other triangle are status, courage, and flexibility. Steffenhagen and Burns, contrary to Rosenberg's and Wylie's positions, argue that ". . . low self-esteem is the basis, or the etiology, of the deviance, not the resultant of the deviance" (p. 54). The model developed by Steffenhagen and Burns "places self-esteem at the apex of personality," and assumes that individuals of any personality type may vary in self-esteem, and that self-esteem itself, as well as distinctive styles of coping with the need for or lack of it, develops out of the social context in which individuals are embedded.

A lack of self-esteem, thus, is seen as:

> the most important psychological variable in the etiology of deviance and/or personality maladjustment; the nurturance and development of an individual's self-esteem are the key factors in the rehabilitative process (p. 56). . . . Self-esteem develops in the individual through repeated experiences of mastery, that is, repeated experiences in which efforts to achieve a goal are met with subjectively perceived success. As such, an

individual's self-esteem is the reflection of both the level of aspiration and of self-confidence. (p. 90)

Although these authors stress the social context, they fail to specify what makes up this social context. (I want to specify that the most immediate social context is the family.) According to these authors, self-esteem is not sufficient to predict what kind of deviant behavior an individual will learn. Lifestyle is another important concept in Adler's theory that will explain specific choices of pathology. They discriminate (p. 84) between (a) psychological correlates of self-esteem, which can be high or low, (b) goal orientation, which can be socially useful or useless, (c) personality traits, either normal or neurotic, (d) sociological correlates of lifestyle, which can be self-centered or contributive, (e) family groups, which can be supportive or nonsupportive, and (f) social milieu— friendly or hostile.

To explain further the relationship of love and self-esteem to behavior, Steffenhagen and Burns used the concept of compensation (pp. 95–118) as the link between low self-esteem and ways of compensating for that low self-esteem. "An individual with high self-esteem is able to deal with personal and interpersonal conflict has no need to resolve it by deviant coping mechanisms (p. 97) . . . We will define compensation as a safeguarding mechanism, ultimately, when self-esteem becomes too low, the organism will think in terms of termination, suicide being the most devastating and final compensatory mechanism. Compensatory mechanisms are the individual's attempt to achieve a psychological balance of felt needs, although what is actually created is a pseudobalance. The compensatory mechanism is used to resolve a conflict" (p. 97). Steffenhagen and Burns related psychopathology to low self-esteem in general and did not differentiate between different kinds of self-esteem and different kinds of compensatory mechanisms.

Why has the contribution of these authors received so much attention here? It represents to a high degree the view shared by many authors and theorists who assume or make self-esteem a basic determinant of behavior (Bednar, Wells, & Peterson, 1989). I would argue, instead, that self-esteem as a hypothetical, inferred construct is relationally irrelevant. It has outlived its usefulness and failed to show a nomological network to support its centrality. We do not construe ourselves or others on the basis of self-esteem. We construe ourselves on the basis of the attribution of importance to ourselves and to relevant others—what Steffenhagen and Burns called "self-acceptance" and "status." We do not value people on the basis of their self-esteem. We value them in terms of their importance to us. We do not mourn the loss of people we love on the basis of their self-esteem. We mourn their loss on the basis of their perceived or attributed importance to us. We may even attribute self-esteem to ourselves, but we cannot make this attribution to others unless we ask them. Without this fundamental attribution of importance, it is difficult, if not impossible, to become a responsible, deviation-free, and competent adult. Status (Foà & Foà, 1974), which I define as the attribution of importance to self and to intimate others, is the most fundamental resource that is continuously exchanged among people. Furthermore, the concept of self-esteem has received cogent criticisms about difficulties in defining it as well as about the inadequacy of many empirical findings (Scheff, Retzinger, & Ryan, 1989).

The Problem of Boundaries

Boundaries that define ourselves, others, and our relationships spatiotemporally are just as relevant as the knowledge of and sensitivity to context. In fact, boundary setting is part of the definition of ourselves and of context. Notions of privacy, territoriality, punctuality, accuracy, and negotiability pertain to the drawing of lines, both concrete and imaginary, for our behavior and the behavior of others. Without boundaries, there would be no context. Up to the present time, traditional psychological notions have drawn strong lines between individual intrapsychic traits and their interrelationships to contextual factors. These lines have been drawn by ignoring or failing to acknowledge the family, work, and leisure contexts. Furthermore, the notion of a context is too fuzzy and hence uncontrollable to be methodologically included when conceptualizing personality development *in a vacuum*. Thus, the notion of boundaries is just as relevant as that of context continuity and contiguity. Boundary difficulties start with distinguishing between self and nonself, between self and others, and among parts of the self and nonself, early on in single dichotomies (good–bad), by more complex definitions, or even by a rejection of labels or dichotomies in more advanced development.

Boundary definition is relevant to the setting of priorities among self and components of the individual's nuclear and original family (marriage, children, in-laws) and between the individual's family and extrafamilial resources (work, status, information, etc.). Boundary definition is relevant to the setting of implicit and explicit interpersonal contracts; hence it is through a setting of boundaries that the individual defines his or her relationship to self, others, and the physical world. Definition of boundaries is an acknowledgment of the person's awareness and sensitivity to the relationship of self to the immediate and relevant context.

The Concept of Competence

Ever since White (1959) brought forth this concept, it has captured considerable currency in motivational and even personality theories

(Brody, 1980; Ford, 1985; Marlowe & Weinberg, 1985; Phillips, 1968; Wine & Smye, 1980). It seems to be more specific, more concrete, and more definable than personality, environment, or both. In itself, the concept of competence implies an interaction with something or somebody. It is impossible to talk about competence without specifying the context in which such a competence is manifested. Ford (1985), in reviewing past and present definitions of competence, referred to it as (a) "capabilities" for formulating and "producing effortful, persistent, goal-directed activity" (p. 4); (b) the individual's behavioral repertoire of specified and specifiable skills and abilities; and (c) effectiveness in relevant contexts.

Consequently, we need to specify the contexts where these sets of capabilities, effectiveness, and skills are manifested and used. Competence can be specified and even assessed in a specific setting. On the other hand, self-esteem or similar constructs seem to encompass a wide range of traits and states, most of them internal and difficult to measure. Competence is limited to a finite and definite number of settings.

As a conclusion to the foregoing discussion, *personality* is henceforth defined *as the sum total of an individual's competencies in various settings*. These competencies consist of the individual's ability to love and the ability to negotiate. The abilities are transmitted developmentally from and through families of origin to individuals and from them back to families intergenerationally, according to a *continuum of likeness* (see Chapter 3). The process of developmental transformation goes through transition points that may produce conflicts, fixations, and failures to advance and to go forward normatively, progressively, and sequentially.

As a result of this definition, the ability to love the self (personhood) relates most significantly to the individual's ability to love a partner in a committed, prolonged, and close relationship and to love the children resulting from that partnership.

PARTNERSHIP

Personhood, the ability to love the self, is necessary for partnership, which involves the ability to love another in a reciprocal and mutual fashion. The relationship between two persons in a marriage is predicated on their personhood. If either or both are lacking in genotypical characteristics necessary for full expression of independent personhood (attributions of self-importance), then the partnership is made more difficult. Indeed, under these circumstances, true partnership, with intimacy and mutual respect between the members, may be impossible.

Partnership implies acknowledging the importance of gender differences in personality definition and development. Gender is an important determinant of personality development. Differences in socialization practices for the two genders, which will be considered in greater detail in Chapter 6, determine what kind of partnership arises from the union of two persons. In this regard, we cannot ignore the importance of ethnic origin, religion, and socioeconomic level in personality definition and partnership development.

The process of becoming partners is based on the first step of mate selection. The selection of a mate is part of a complex process that involves not only the current circumstances of the two individuals but all the genetic, family, educational, economic, social, and cultural influences each has experienced (Otto, 1979). This conceptualization of the mate-seeking process does not explicitly address the complex personality of each individual. It does not address the attributes of love, intimacy, negotiation, empowerment, and forgiveness without which a marriage is simply a legal contract.

From this selection, we can predict the marital quality and stability. Once a mate has been selected, marital stability (whether a marriage lasts) is affected by marital quality. Marital quality, in turn, is affected first by the premarital factors of homogamy, resources exchanged, role models, and support from significant others (Lewis & Spanier, 1979). It also is affected by social and economic factors including the husband's occupational status, whether the wife works outside the home, the composition of the household, and how embedded a couple is in the community. Finally, marital quality is affected by interpersonal and dyadic factors of positive regard, emotional gratification, communication, role fit, and interaction. Marital quality is the totality of subjective qualities and dimensions commonly and traditionally used in research about this factor (Lewis & Spanier, 1979). Thus, the marital relationship, as the prototype of a committed, prolonged, and close relationship is predicated on personal characteristics and the interaction of these characteristics with each other.

Clark and Mills (1979, 1986), Clark and Reis (1988), and Clark and Wassell (1985) studied interpersonal processes deemed to be important and to affect close interpersonal relationships, such as marriage. They considered interdependence, emotion, intimacy, and love to be the important building blocks of close relationships. Clark defined a relationship to be close if it "endures and involves strong, frequent, and diverse causal interconnections" (displays interdependence of the two involved). This interdependence progresses (changes) over time and eventually transcends the quantity of the benefits each partner receives from the relationship. In this conceptualization, the whole of partnership exceeds its parts, as does personhood. Emotions are involved in any interdependent relationship (Clark & Reis, 1988; Clark, Mills, & Powell, 1986). Several emotions may be involved in close relationships including joy, happiness, attraction, moods, sadness, satisfaction, fear, anger, jealousy, depression, anxiety, and love. Reflection and self-evaluation are relevant to the maintenance of interdependence. Although interdependence is seen as a whole, intimacy is reduced to components such as disclosure, sexuality, and cohesiveness. Emotional openness is considered a key component for intimacy (Clark & Reis, 1988, p. 629). Intimacy, like interdependence, is a process that develops over time in a close relationship.

Partnership may be defined as the union formed by the coming together of two individuals to work toward a common goal or set of goals. The understanding of marriage motivation has changed in recent history from a need for security, physically and economically, to a need for growth and personal fulfillment (Barnett, 1981; Stauffer, 1987). However, couples come together with a variety of goals and expectations, conscious or unconscious, that have dramatic bearing on the direction, intensity, and outcome of the marriage. Many goals and expectancies are unrealistic and lead to disillusion and generational dysfunction (Crosby, 1985). Entering into a partnership in marriage provides a great opportunity for growth and continued development (Blanck & Blanck, 1968). It is important to consider the level of psychological readiness and relationship competency of a couple.

Some basic abilities are necessary to establish a healthy relationship: "The ability to share love, negotiate power, and establish an intimate foundation are three of the necessary and sufficient conditions for a satisfactory and fulfilling marital and sexual relationship . . ." (L'Abate, 1983a, p. 51). These abilities are affected by our family of origin experiences and physical health. Love and intimacy must be shared unconditionally within the relationship and not exchanged or bartered—they are givens. Roles and power can be negotiated. The ability to negotiate power in relationships depends on the level of the couple's functionality.

The couple's initial goal in courtship may be seen as a desire for physical and emotional closeness (Beck, 1988). The desire for closeness has several facets, among which are needs for pleasure, acceptance, companionship, and belongingness. Beck asserts that the reality of attraction for partners is that they are drawn together by things other than functional skills. Individuals are drawn together by similar levels of competency, and Bowen (1978) addressed attraction on the basis of differentiation of family or origin similarities. Barnett (1981) discussed attraction as a combination of similarities and differences from the individual's family of origin. There is a balance of enough similarities to be comfortable, yet enough differences to allow tension to continue to individuate.

Adams (1979) followed a process of mate selection that includes a series of deepening attractions beginning with physical attraction, valued behaviors, and interest similarity progressing toward a deepening intimacy through barriers to breakup. Critical points in the sequence may lead to termination or deepening of the relationship depending on a variety of factors such as support of significant others, heterogeneity, and role compatibility. Lewis and Spanier (1979) theorize about marital stability predictors based on similar factors but expand them to include homogamy, wealth of resources, parental models, value congruence with behavior, conventionality, and motivational factors. It would be important to consider these factors in examining marital stability and partnership potential, but also to realize that individuals continue to develop in adulthood and correction of previous individual or familial patterns is possible, even if limited (Blanck & Blanck, 1968).

Individuals who come to marriage usually have unrealistic expectations to varying degrees of what the marriage will provide and what they will need to do (Crosby, 1985). Individuals may expect the marriage partnership to meet all their needs and may become frustrated and angry when they begin to realize that this is not so. According to Crosby, individuals often have an illusion of what marriage entails, and it is only by becoming disillusioned and choosing to give up the illusion of marriage that they are able to grow. Barnett (1981) proposes that in courtship an individual begins to have an increased experience of self providing a taste of the potentials of personal growth in marriage.

It is important, however, to consider that the individual may begin to see the self in light of his or her limitations and expectations of self and other. Barnett's theory of marriage as a development process asserts that each marriage partner goes through an extended honeymoon period of 5 to 7 years that ends with a crisis that may be dealt with in three ways: (a) to reject the partner in hopes of maintaining a fantasized ideal or illusion; (b) to allow apathy to prevail, ending growth and satisfaction; or (c) to demythologize the relationship and allow acceptance of each other's true selves. Barnett refers to the third choice as "creative turmoil" (p. 12). To engage in this turmoil depends on the individual's ability to self-explore, to be honest to self and others about his or her actual state of being, and to seek and allow growth. This process sounds similar to Kierkegaard's theory of the development of selfhood through resolution of sequential crises (Cole, 1971).

Partnership is dependent on several relationship skills that are manifested in personhood. Among these are communication skills, but additional to these is the ability to be loving:

> The ability to be loving is made up at least four different skills; (a) caring and commitment . . . ; (b) seeing the good . . . to disregard negative aspects; (c) forgiveness or decision to accept or tolerate and forget one's demands for perfection, performance, problem solving, or production;

(d) intimacy, or the ability to share one's self and a loved one's hurts and fears of being hurt, which, in turn, requires the ability to be available emotionally to self and other. (L'Abate, 1986, p. 138)

The development of effective communication skills allows openness and honesty without unnecessary abrasiveness. Unpleasant emotions and reactions are often triggered by our perceptions and cognitions as we apply meanings to events (Beck, 1988). Exploring personalized meanings of events and communicating with a partner by offering self-disclosure of feelings and owning those feelings and perceptions (Beck, 1988; L'Abate, 1986) allow resolution of misperceptions and negative or unpleasant feelings toward the self and other.

PARENTHOOD

A competent partnership is crucial to the development of competent parenthood. Both partnership and parenthood are awesome responsibilities for which very few of us are socialized (L'Abate, 1990). Hence, we cannot separate how we function as a person from how we function as a partner and as a parent. In a partnership as well as in parenthood, the ability to love is necessary but it is not sufficient. In addition to that ability we need the ability to negotiate, bargain, problem solve, and make decisions in a way that acknowledges the importance of everybody in the family. To think simply that personality develops, without paying attention to how that personality functions as a partner and as a parent, means regressing to a vacuum view of personality that is no longer valid and acceptable. In spite of intact families becoming a smaller and smaller percentage in relation to singles, cohabitants, and single-parent families, most of us lived in one family and created another one. Whether that family is intact or not, the outcome of personality and partnership factors cannot be denied or avoided. Personality in its phenotypical and genotypical manifestations is shown in the heat of the passions and emotions that surround intimate relationships. A self-presentational facade may last for external, social consumption, but it becomes irrelevant and actually destructive within the privacy of home. Personality shows its true colors, not in the marketplace, but in the privacy of a person's bedroom, livingroom, and kitchen.

Parenthood is more than just the production of children; it is a stage of development based on selfhood and partnership. Partnership is built on the relationship abilities of selfhood; if the partnership is not functioning, parenting will be adversely affected. Parents define themselves in ways other than job or role so that there is an equal distribution between work and availability to the child. The only way of learning to be

partners and parents is to experience relationships, to allow for introspection and reflection, to facilitate communication, and to have a commitment to personal growth and the growth of the relationship. We need
to prioritize in terms of self and relationships as well as roles. Partners
who have decided to enter into the world of parenthood need to develop
a highly functional relationship to promote the healthiest environment
for child rearing.

The reasons for having children and the value placed on them has
changed as societies have changed through the ages (Jensen & Kingston,
1986). Some motivation is internal; whereas other motivation comes
from societal or religious pressure. There may even be selfish reasons
such as compensation for deficits in the personality or marriage. Motivation and valuation may have intense effects on the development of the
child and the child's self-concept. Historically, children have been seen in
a combination of images with a largely negative connotation. Currently,
there is a focus to see children as unique individuals with potentialities
that insightful caregivers may develop in a healthy fashion.

Newman and Newman (1988) view parenthood as an extension of personal growth. Although parents must have reached an appropriate level of
maturity to facilitate a healthy family environment, the new role of parent also prompts further cognitive and emotional growth. Parents encounter new roles and situations that require divergent thinking and that
challenge them to new depths of commitment, care, and the balancing of
personal needs with the needs of their partner and their dependents. Just
as with the transition of personhood to partnership, the transition of
partnership to parenthood involves building on past development and experience.

The transition to parenthood may be marked by increased anxiety and
decreased marital satisfaction (Jensen & Kingston, 1986). The advent of
a child brings about a number of changes that may stress the relationship.
Although some stress is inevitable, the preparedness of parents may have
an effect on the amount of stress and disruption. Parental readiness involves education in child development, both emotional and physical. A
period of planning and study together may facilitate a smoother transition and increase the couple's coping skills. Ideally, much of the discussion on individual outlooks on parenting should be a part of premarital
planning and exploration. Children are visitors or guests to the marital
relationship. As such, priorities, expectations, and demands must be adjusted. Parents who have developed a good working relationship may
spend less time in their own conflicts and have time and energy to be
available to child rearing without a great loss of marital satisfaction.

As children become older, they may be included in family negotiations
and decision making. Jensen and Kingston (1986) cited numerous studies

on parenting styles that suggest a democratic approach for family decisions encourages healthy development and independence. Authoritarian styles of parenting may produce maladaptive behavior in children. Compliance in families is often difficult to achieve. Jensen and Kingston (1986) reviewed major theories of discipline and broke discipline theories into three levels of power: (a) high power techniques such as behavior modification; (b) moderate power techniques, such as reality therapy and logical consequences; and (c) low power techniques such as active listening and reasoning with use of induction.

Steinmetz (1979) brought to the forefront the importance of child-rearing techniques not only as an individual issue, but also as a societal issue. She pointed out that the major determining factor in shaping history is psychogenic change. The manner in which a parent disciplines the child affects levels of dependency, conscience, and aggression. Although more complex than can be adequately dealt with here, Steinmetz reported a positive correlation between aggressiveness and physical punishment. Variables include the age and sex of the child and which parent is the administrator of the punishment. Steinmetz describes a sequence of identification with parent, dependency, frustration, and aggressiveness that is involved in the normal developmental process. Aggressiveness changes in expression as the child matures and is related positively with both punishment and rewards. Identification with the parent is also related to the development of conscience. Low and moderate power techniques may be the interventions of choice with childhood aggression.

Understanding a child's cognitive and moral development may help parents to adjust their own expectation of child performance. Children have developing but limited cognitive and moral abilities (Jensen & Kingston, 1986). Children are unique in perceptions and understandings of events. We all have perceptual and processing idiosyncrasies. Accepting children as individuals in their own right can encourage healthy individuation. Being able to listen objectively, asking appropriate questions, providing feedback, and reflecting can enhance the parent–child relationship and facilitate reality testing.

On the basis of the foregoing consideration, this chapter concludes with a defensible definition of personality that derives from the earlier definition: Personality comprises what a person is, what a person does, and what a person has. Personality is how a person reconciles the three preceding modalities, Being, Doing, and Having. Chapter 6 explores what a person is. Chapter 7 describes in detail what a person does. Chapter 8 considers in depth what a person has. How these competencies interact with settings is elaborated in Chapter 9 (home), Chapter 10 (work), and Chapter 11 (leisure). How a person reconciles and integrates these three aspects is covered in Chapter 12.

CONCLUSION

A definition of personality competencies according to Being, Doing, Having, settings, and priorities will be elaborated, and a program of verification for this definition will occupy the rest of this book. Instead of a vague, general, and unspecified person × situation interaction, this definition posits developmental competence × setting transactions in three specific settings that account for most of our waking time: home, work, and leisure. Drawing from disparate sources, this definition integrates the work of social, environmental, and family theories in a coherent and convergent whole.

CHAPTER 3

What Is Development?

. . . to understand human behavior it is necessary to examine close, romantic relationships which are fundamental in our society.
(STAFFORD & CANARY, 1991, p. 221)

Development implies two completely different meanings. One meaning applies to development over the life span of an individual qua individual, as a marriage partner, as a parent, and as a worker. The other meaning applies to development as a sequential differentiation of stages that may or may not be reached by everybody. This second meaning will be considered under the rubric of self-differentiation. The thesis of this chapter is that development in the sense of personal competence, that is, Being, or the ability to love (Chapter 6); Doing, or the ability to negotiate (Chapter 7); and Having (Chapter 8) are a function of (a) the sense of personal importance achieved by the child from attributions made by caretakers since birth, and even before birth, and lasting for the rest of the child's life; (b) the process of differentiation of self from caretakers and other important persons in the child's life that affirms how he or she is different and unique from important others; and (c) the process of self-determination that is the outcome deriving from the first two processes. Self-determination will be left to the elaboration of Deci and Ryan (1985a,b).

Personality development and growth is a sequential process that follows certain emotional, cognitive, social, and contextual changes, phases, and stages over time. This process views development in terms of three major *phases* in skill achievement: (a) nonverbal, (b) verbal, and (c) written; and four major *stages:* (a) dependence, or childhood; (b) denial of dependence, or adolescence; (c) autonomous interdependence, or adulthood; and, finally (d) a return to dependence in old age. Adulthood means achieving three different goals: (a) personhood, (b) partnership, and (c) parenthood, not always in this sequence. Phases will be considered in Chapter 14 as different modalities of treatment, whereas stages will be subsumed here under the rubric of self-differentiation. The process of attribution of importance will be discussed in Chapter 6.

DEVELOPMENT AT WHAT LEVEL?

Development takes place at different levels of interpretation. It is possible to magnify self-presentational appearance at the expense of phenotypical sublevel (how the individual functions in intimate relationships) or to spend a great deal of energy functioning at descriptive sublevels, without paying attention to the genotypical and historical sublevels. Hence, before we deal with various aspects of development, we will need to answer the question, Development at what level? The answer is: At the genotypical sublevel. This sublevel was characterized in Chapter 1 as being hypothetical and inferred. The only difference between past theoretical views about the nature of the genotype (self-esteem, ego, mastery, etc.) and the one proposed here lies in its relational nature. We need to come up with a conceptualization that will relate the genotype to contextual factors. Personal and interpersonal development at the genotypical sublevel, as defined in the first chapter, therefore, takes place along three different dimensions: of importance, differentiation, and self-determination.

Because development occurs at various levels of description and explanation, it is too complex to be reviewed in one chapter. In fact, this whole manuscript could be considered as revolving around the process of personality development over the life cycle. The three major life cycles, individual, marital, and familial, are summarized in Tables 3.1, 3.2, and 3.3. These life cycle perspectives are theory-independent and describe what happens observationally on a normative basis at the descriptive level, even though I am perfectly aware that normative at this point means *idealized* or even *hypothetical*. The term *normative*, developmentally speaking, applies to so few people that its meaning has to be changed accordingly. Nonetheless, these summaries will serve as background to the question, How does development take place? We know what takes place and we can summarize it fairly accurately. But, what kind of processes underlie it? Here is where explanatory theoretical hypotheses about the nature of the genotype enter into the picture.

We need to distinguish also among various types of personality development. Some types may overlap with others. Some other types may be completely separate from the others. For instance, *chronological* development means strictly age—how old a person is—a datum that may or may not be directly related to the other types of development. Then there is *intellectual* development—how bright a person is and how this brightness is expressed or nonexpressed familially, occupationally, interpersonally, and in leisure pursuits. As Gardner (1983) has argued, there are different types of intelligence, and most of us are endowed by multiple intelligences in different degrees: linguistic, musical, logical-mathematical, spatial, bodily-kinesthetic, personal, and interpersonal. Some of these intelligences when put together would lead to *occupational* intelligence. Among

TABLE 3.1. The Normative Individual Life Cycle*

A. Infancy—Years 1–4: Overcoming dependency and establishing self-awareness.

B. Childhood—Years 5–8: Physical independence-emotional dependence.

C. Latency—Years 9–12: Learning to give and to receive.

D. Adolescence—Years 13–19: Developing individuality.

E. Early adulthood—Years 23–30:

    1. Intimacy-isolation—Years 18–30:

        a. Pulling up roots—Years 17–20.

        b. Leaving the family—Years 17–24.

        c. Trying out various life courses—Years 20–28.

    2. Marriage—The trying twenties:

        a. Childbearing.

        b. Work.

        c. Choosing and establishing a life cycle.

        d. Involvement into adulthood.

F. Middle adulthood—Years 31–50:

    1. Generativity versus stagnation—Years 30–55:

        a. Deciding about life goals in personal and in work relationships— Years 28–43.

        b. Management of household tasks.

        c. Management of a career.

        d. Transition—Around age 30.

        e. Settling down—Years 32–38.

    2. Late adulthood—Years 43–48:

        a. Evaluation of past achievement and/or failures.

        b. Becoming one's own person—Years 35–39.

        c. Catch thirties—Years 30–40.

        d. Mid-life transition—Years 40–45.

        e. Entering late adulthood, building a new life structure—Years 45–50.

        f. Mid-life crisis—Years 40–50.

G. Integrity versus despair—Years 55–death:

    1. Late adulthood—Years 51–65

        a. Redirection of energy.

        b. Acceptance of one's life.

        c. Developing a point of view.

    2. Age 50 transition—Years 50–55.

    3. Second middle-age structure—Years 55–60.

    4. Late adulthood transition.

    5. Late adulthood and retirement—Years 60+

        a. Activity versus passivity.

        b. Involvement versus isolation.

        c. Getting on versus giving up.

* From L'Abate (1994).

TABLE 3.2.   The Normative Stages of the Marital Life Cycle*

Stages	Issues
1. Courtship and marriage	Isolation versus intimacy
	Freedom versus commitment
	Individuality versus merging
	Family loyalties versus old and new
2. Childbearing and early parenting	From dyad to triad
	Shifting generations-realignment of loyalties
	Nurturance: giving versus receiving
	Symbiosis: health versus pathology
	Possession versus sharing
	Cooperation versus competition
	Conductivity versus reactivity
3. Childbearing socialization	Parenting as singles or as partners
	(Separateness versus integration)
	Patterns of parenting:
	Authoritarian versus laissez-faire
	Authoritative versus democratic
	Rigid versus flexible
	Abusive–reactive versus conductive–creative
	Permeability of boundaries
	Individuals versus dyads
	Family versus society
4. Middle age and adolescence	Separation versus symbiosis
	Crisis and menopause
	Intimacy-individuality renegotiated
	Facing nonbeing
5. Old age	Retirement:
	Fulfillment versus emptiness
	Generativity versus despair
	Coping with increased dependence
	Physical impairment, illness, death

* From L'Abate (1994).

these types, the personal and interpersonal development, differentiated into *psychosexual* and the *psychosocial,* is of specific interest and focus to the present theory, without denying the importance of the other types in overall psychological development.

THE CONCEPT OF DIFFERENTIATION IN DEVELOPMENT

Differentiation is the ability of an individual to separate from his or her family and to form a personal identity as well as to strengthen different parts of the self. Within this process of personal identity differentiation, the various components of the self develop into an integrated whole. In terms of the ERAAwC model summarized in Chapter 1, differentiation

TABLE 3.3. Various Aspects of the Normative Family Life Cycle*

Age	Marital	Parental	Sibling	Educational	Occupational
1–16			Competition versus collaboration between and within generations with role models of other siblings	Finished–unfinished	
17–25	Marriage role differentiation	Childbearing and childrearing	Voluntary versus involuntary competition with other priorities	Continuation–discontinuation College Professional school	Labor–blue collar
26–35	Lessening of satisfaction	Birth of last child Greatest feelings of inadequacy in parental role Increasing demands		Decreasing job satisfaction	White collar
35–45	Lowest point of satisfaction	Beginning of empty nest	Declining contacts	Peaking	Blue and white collar income
46–59	Return to couple relations, increase in satisfaction, greater need for companionship	Empty nest completed Marriage of children Grandparenthood	Reinstatement of contacts		Peaking of professional income
60+	Death of one spouse	Parents return to their children for advice and help Children become parents to their parents			Retirement

*From L'Abate (1994).

means setting boundaries among various parts so that one part will not interfere with the functions of another part. Whenever emotionality interferes with rationality, or whenever rationality interferes with activity, we have inadequate differentiation of parts. An adequate differentiation would mean emotionality, rationality, and activity working together in an integrated whole. Differentiation, therefore, represents the progressive breakdown into parts that develop their own functions, separate from but interdependent with the other parts. The individual's capacity to keep the self separate from another, to distinguish internal from external experience, fantasy from reality, animate from inanimate experience, physical from nonphysical experience, emotions from actions, personality from performance, traits from overall personality, and all the many other differentiations we must make constantly throughout our lives involves an awareness and appreciation of boundary line distribution. The setting of personal boundaries is important to self-formation and development as well as to the formulation and development of any relationship.

What a person believes about self is the guiding factor for success or failure in life. This belief may be rather simple and undifferentiated along rather primitive concepts (good–bad) or it may be highly differentiated and complex. This concept is different from other definitions of differentiation, as previously discussed (L'Abate, 1976). The one researcher who was not reviewed previously was Witkin (1965), whose definition of differentiation is quite different from the one used here. For him, differentiation was a perceptual process with objects, while the present definition stresses the relevance of distinguishing among affective, cognitive, and behavioral process. Therefore, this distinction ultimately has an interpersonal outcome, especially with intimate others.

Witkin's definition was reviewed by Lewis (1971) in connection with her concept of differentiation in neurotic shame and guilt. As she observed:

Psychological differentiation is a construct that has been developed over the past quarter of a century to encompass a wide range of observed differences among people in terms of "person and style." A stable, characteristic style of functioning has been shown to connect perception, cognitive and social behavior, choice of defenses, and organization of the self in a pattern of congruent behavior. (p. 47)

In regard to psychopathology, Lewis concluded:

The differentiation construct, derived from observation mainly on normal persons and on children, has also been connected to differences in kind of pathology (Witkin, 1965). Psychiatric and normal populations do not differ from each other in extent of psychological differentiation. Within a psychiatric population, however, there are differences in kind of pathology, predictably associated with patients' personal style. (p. 126)

Witkin's own words and Lewis's review show that his definition of differentiation is different conceptually and operationally from the one used here and elsewhere (L'Abate, 1976) even though some overlap between these two concepts may be present. The main characteristics of differentiation are specialization of functions, clear separation between self and nonself, and among congruent parts of the self (integration, cognition and affect, defense mechanisms, etc.). This conceptualization, however, emphasizes the relationship of the individual's differentiation with past and present family members and intimate others. Witkin, instead, emphasized the perceptual intellectual and cognitive aspects of differentiation in terms of ahistorical field-dependence–independence. The present definition stresses the relevance of the self to the family of origin and present intimates. The self is an affective domain that influences other parts of one's personality—that is, rationality and activity (as summarized in the ERAAwC model).

The emotional climate in the family is an important factor in personality development and differentiation. The manner in which parents deal with their own emotions will affect directly childhood development as well as provide a role model. Not only visible emotions, such as depression and despair, but also deep-seated emotions, such as shame, guilt, envy, and pain, may have a negative impact on the child. Uncontrolled expression of emotions by caretakers can have detrimental effects on the offspring. Both direct and indirect expressions of anger, hatred, and rage can traumatize the child. Chronic displays of intense emotions, such as verbal abuse, let alone physical or sexual abuse, can set up dysfunctional behaviors that persist throughout life (Jensen & Kingston, 1986).

Winnicott (1965) approached the effect of relationships with the previous generation on current relationships from object-relations theory. According to this theory, the infant's first relationship is with a part-object, the mother's breast. As the infant's personality integrates, the part-object is recognized as a part of a whole object; this recognition of an independent whole object gives rise to the beginnings of a sense of dependence and therefore of a conflicting need for independence for the infant. This conflict is most satisfactorily resolved when the mother is perceived as dependable, thus meeting the infant's need for a secure base from which to leave. Winnicott (p. 18) categorized the functions of the "good-enough" mother in the early stages of an infant's life into (a) holding, (b) handling, and (c) object-presenting. The mother's holding function is strongly related to her capacity to identify with the infant so that a mother–infant partnership emerges in which the mother by one kind of identification meets the infant's original state of undifferentiation (p. 19). The infant's personality and capacities for future relationships emerge from the relationship provided by both parents.

In addition to object-relations theory deriving from an individual perspective (Bowlby, 1970, 1973, 1981, 1988), the importance and influence of the family context from the very outset of development has been stressed by family therapists, such as Bowen (1978) (see review; L'Abate, 1976). The family context also includes intergenerational influences. As explained by Boszormenyi-Nagy and Krasner (1986): ". . . context implies consequences that flow from person to person, from generation to generation, and from one system to its successive system" (p. 8). An individual's psychological organization and ability to enter into relationships are derived from ". . . the consequences of past relationships, and hold consequences for future relationships" (p. 9). *Transgenerational consequences* are asymmetrical with the parent generation and have a greater influence on the offspring than vice versa. Characteristically "a person offers the next generation the same quality of unilateral caring that one received as a child" (p. 118). Consequently, according to the theories of Bowen (1978), Winnicott (1965), and Boszormenyi-Nagy and Krasner (1986), the kind of relation that a child develops with his or her parents will strongly influence the kind of relation that he or she will have with spouse and children as an adult.

The effect of maternal bonding on later emotional stability is laden with controversy (Rutter, 1974): "Bowlby has gone so far as to suggest that individuals suffering from any type of psychiatric disorder always show an impairment of the capacity for affectional bonding" (p. 13). Current research is showing that bonding occurs not only with the mother but to a significant degree with the father as well (Jensen & Kingston, 1986). Bonding has more to do with emotional sensitivity and responsiveness of parents than to feeding, dressing, and playing with the infant. Also, there is a positive correlation between bonding, emotional availability, and adult depression. The parent's emotional state as anxious or depressed has an effect on bonding (Rutter, 1981).

This definition of the individual's differentiation not only alone but as an *individual in relationships* is important for the achievement of partnership and parenthood. The understanding of personhood and partnership in relation to marriage is based on several assumptions. Among these are (a) to be or become a competent partner, the individual must first be a differentiated person or have the potential to become such; (b) to be a person, the individual must be able to love, to be intimate with another human being, and to negotiate power issues in relationship with another intimate; (c) partnership, therefore, cannot be understood without an understanding of personhood; and (d) partnership is a process, not a state, which involves a variety of processes basic to the development of competent parenting. Without such a partnership, parenting will be impaired or at best incomplete.

A differentiated person, therefore, is one who functions with a considerable degree of separation from the immediate social context, who is tolerant of and comfortable with ambiguity, who may function well in loosely structured, intimate relationships, who is self-reliant, and who is unlikely to need the opinions of others, without discounting those opinions. The familial antecedents for such differentiation may include parental clarity and firmness tempered by tolerance for and encouragement of differentness and individuality.

Imitation, Identity, and the Continuum of Likeness

Through imitation, the child follows in the footsteps of caretakers to form an identification from watching and mimicking the models provided by significant others. Originally, the concept of imitation was accepted as a given and not elaborated in all its implications. Imitation, based on observation of important people, is a natural and effective learning process for children. Parents or caretakers are powerful role models. Imitation is the external process that eventually becomes internalized as identification—the child's sense of self-identity. Indeed, Kagan (1958) originally defined identification as "perceived similarity in attributes between the person and the model" (p. 304). Thus, a great deal of similarity is based on perception rather than on actual behavior—it is subjective in this regard. On the other hand, Bronfenbrenner (1958, 1960, 1986), as well as Lynn (1969), considered real and assumed similarity both in patterns and traits as important to the growth of identification. Identification, therefore, is considered an extreme form of likeness or similarity to a model. This similarity is most often shown in attributes that may be real or assumed, traits that may be inferred or attributed, and behavior that can be overt or covert.

The roots of identification lie in the child's ability to discriminate different types of similarity in those closest and most similar to him or her. If identification is based on learning to be similar to a model, the child could just as well underidentify as overidentify to the point that either extreme becomes deleterious to a sense of identity. How is optimal similarity and, therefore, identification to be sought? The original conceptualization of identification remains limited to the extent that a model is either followed according to the norm of similarity or not followed according to the norm of dissimilarity. This restriction makes the process of imitation or identification dichotomous. The child either does imitate or does not. Such dichotomy is insufficient to describe how the process of identification takes place. Consequently, similarity is perceived, like beauty, in the eyes of the beholder. Furthermore, the major shortcoming of most theory and research on similarity is the restricted range of behaviors that the term itself connotes (L'Abate, Weinstein, Fraizer, & Russ, 1989 manuscript). This restricted range does not allow the user to distinguish between similarity and sameness. By the same token, the use of *dissimilar* as an antonym to *similar* makes it difficult to distinguish between differentness and oppositeness.

Consequently, this simple dichotomy was expanded and extended to a psychophysical, dialectical continuum of likeness by adding the ranges of sameness–oppositeness and symbiosis–autism, as shown in Figure 3.1 (L'Abate, 1976, 1983a). The range of sameness–oppositeness was derived from the work of Taylor (1960), who showed how extreme "left" attitudes are similar in structure to extreme "right" ones. The extreme symbiotic–autistic range was derived from the work of Mahler (1968), whose observations and studies of deviant mothers indicated the presence of these two extreme patterns of mothering. The dialectical characteristic was applied to the whole continuum of likeness, to the point that similarity has no meaning without dissimilarity or differentness. Sameness has no meaning without oppositeness, and symbiosis has no meaning without autism (Figure 3.1).

Personality develops, internally or genotypically, according to this psychophysical continuum of likeness, a process that is automatic and basic to a lifelong modeling process of differentiation in comparison to significant (important) others. We model, compare, and contrast ourselves after significant others. We grow up as social comparison agents (Festinger, 1954), constantly comparing and contrasting ourselves with or against important others (parents, siblings, relatives, peers, lovers, mates, friends, acquaintances, enemies, employers, employees) according to six definable ranges of likeness on a bell-shaped frequency distribution (Figure 3.1). Thus, differentiation of identity (genotype) is achieved according to the continuum of likeness ranging from symbiosis = "I am you,"

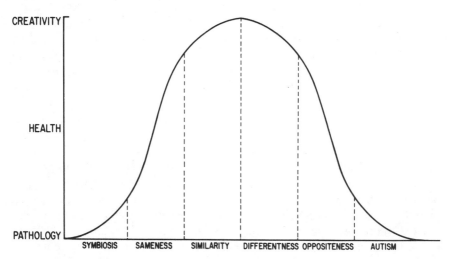

Figure 3.1. The continuum of likeness in personality development.

sameness = "I am like you," similarity = "I am somewhat like you," differentness = "I am not like you," oppositeness = "I am the opposite of you," and autism = "I am not." Actually, in the two extreme positions, symbiosis and autism, the personal pronoun "I" may not even be present (L'Abate, 1983b, 1986).

This lifelong comparison of self against others is a continuous process indicating that we all compare and contrast ourselves with loved ones as well as unloved ones, friends or foes, throughout our lives. The self is defined according to its degree of likeness or unlikeness to other selves. On the basis of this definition, an individual may be located at a given point on the continuum. For example, a person who defines himself or herself as "just exactly like" a significant other in his or her life would fall in the "sameness" range. Individuals who approach the ends of the continuum are seen as exhibiting more pathology; those in the middle are more likely to be healthy, creative, self-actualizing individuals. Individuals who fall in the middle of the likeness continuum define themselves through their essential similarities and unique differences from other individuals and are flexible, interpersonally creative, confident, and exhibit a high degree of congruence between affect and behavior. Individuals in the middle ranges of the continuum, similarity and differentness, will be referred to as differentiated individuals. Those who fall in either the sameness–oppositeness or symbiosis–autism ranges will be referred to as undifferentiated.

As Figure 3.1 shows, change for the better, emotional, cognitive, and behavioral, is easier and greater for differentiated than for undifferentiated individuals. Hence, likeness as a continuum is multidimensional, that is, the judgment of likeness can be based on a variety of grounds— physical, emotional, cognitive, objective, and subjective.

Differentiation and Undifferentiation

Inner-directed criteria for self-definition according to an integration of similarity–differentness from others lead to a much greater degree of flexibility and openness to change than the ranges of sameness and oppositeness. Differentiated individuals, therefore, would possess greater ability to tolerate less structure and greater ambiguity. Furthermore, within the middle of the continuum, similarities and differences become negotiable and blend into a new solution specific to the individual. Differentiated individuals are more creative in problem solving and in interpersonal relations. Creative here means the ability to transact with intimate others in a new and differentiated fashion, in a self–other enhancing fashion. This aspect does not refer to the intellectually creative but instead to the interpersonally creative, especially in closely intimate family dyads. The genotype, how we define ourselves in comparison with others, is evidenced in how we behave within the stress of intimate relationships, not under the facade of how we present ourselves in short-lived and superficial relationships outside the home.

Qualities of differentiated and undifferentiated thinking can be found in the work of Harvey and co-workers (1966), who studied information processing according to levels of integration along the conceptual-complexity dimension. Low integration levels are characterized by fixed rules and programs without alternatives and in a static fashion. Higher integration levels, on the other hand, have more connections among rules with alternatives to generate solutions, greater degrees of freedom or more options, and are more subject to change as changes take place in the environment. Low levels of information processing are characterized by (a) categorical, black–white thinking; (b) minimization of conflict in which situations either fit into a category or are excluded from consideration with no conceptual apparatus to generate alternatives; (c) anchoring of behavior on external conditions and causes; and (d) absolutist rules and generalizations within a limited range forcing change to be abrupt or compartmentalized. Conflicting information is either misperceived or "warded off" because of the absoluteness of categorization in dichotomies.

At moderately low levels of organization, a conceptual repertoire is present to generate alternatives and choices even though there is no conceptual apparatus to relate and differentiate rules. This level has a degree of ambivalence not found in the preceding level, where choice is minimal. Under these conditions: (a) there is a movement away from absolutism; (b) a primitive view of internal control and causes emerges (versus external causes under low levels); (c) instability and noncommitment are present with lack of consistency in decision making and judgment; (d) rigidity is still present but not to the extent found under low levels; and (e) pushing against or negativistic orientation is evident. Roughly, therefore, these two levels respectively describe sameness and oppositeness, whereas the next two levels of moderately high and high organization would seem to describe similarity and differentness. In the former, the thinking is deterministic with a simultaneous utilization of two schemata and the presence of choices generated by internal processes of control and causation. At high levels of organization, greater complexity and diversity can handle a variety of problem solutions, generating also alternative pathways inside the system and without intervention from the outside.

Most important decisions in our lives are of a digital nature, like to marry (or not), to have children (or not), to stay married (or not), to seek professional help (or not), or to change jobs (or not). One of the most destructive aspects of decision making relevant to the differentiation-undifferentiation distinction pertains to the individual's admission of personal responsibility for inappropriate or contradictory behavior. The major difference between being hospitalized or incarcerated lies in being aware of self-destructive behavior and making the consequent decision to seek professional help in order to change. The individual's first step in the change is admission of failure. Unfortunately, making such an admission is a difficult process especially if the individual is personally hooked to a two-valued logic of perfectionism (to be perfect means to be "good" and to be less than perfect means automatically that the person is "bad"). Consequently, people become alienated from their own humanity as well as from the proof that to err is human and that being less than perfect only demonstrates our humanity.

Denial, therefore, of admission of personal responsibility is a digital decision. Whom to see professionally, how often, when, and how much are mostly analogic decisions if a variety of options are available to us. Among individuals hooked on sameness and oppositeness are those who can make constructive digital decisions ("I am sick," "I need help"), and those who make destructive digital decisions ("I am not sick," "I do not need help") that will only alienate them further from themselves and others. Consequently, both differentiated and undifferentiated individuals need to make digital decisions. However, differentiated individuals tending toward similarity and difference will tend to make positive, constructive decisions, whereas undifferentiated individuals hooked on sameness–oppositeness or symbiosis–autism will tend to make negative, destructive decisions.

Similarity–Differentness

Differentiated individuals' self-concept is different from that of undifferentiated individuals. The former define themselves through their essential similarities and unique differences from other individuals. For these persons, the social support of dissimilar others is more influential in increasing a person's confidence that his or her judgments are accurate and decisions are correct. Differentiated individuals are more likely to appreciate and enjoy differentness without any threat to their own sense of self. Differentiated individuals are hypothesized as being inner directed, flexible, open to change, tolerant of less structure and greater ambiguity, able to negotiate similarities and differences, creative, capable of greater intimacy, confident (even in the face of disagreement), autonomous, assertive, original, and relatively free of pathology. The more differentiated the individual, the less the attribution of his or her own characteristics to others and vice versa.

Sameness–Oppositeness

Undifferentiated individuals are characterized by a homeostatic repetition and an inability to change because sameness and oppositeness are defined by others and not by the self. Sameness represents the require-ment for a person to be like and conform to another person who demands blind and unquestioning conformity to his or her wishes. For example, parents may ask the child to behave as they want the child to behave with-out questions or choices. Or, one partner may want the other partner to do exactly what the first partner wants. Under these conditions, opposite-ness is the expected outcome in forms of outright rebellion or passive re-sistance. Oppositeness can remove perceived injustices and promote the possibility of change:

> Opposition is a regenerative force that introjects new vitality into a so-cial structure and becomes the basis of social expression to latent dis-agreements and hostilities, but it also helps to remove the sources of these conflicts. It is a disturbing and divisive force that ultimately con-tributes to . . . stability and cohesion. For major cleavages are more likely to occur precisely when recurrent oppositions have been sup-pressed and conflicts have smoldered. (Blau, 1964, pp. 301–306)

Conflict is greater between people defined by sameness–oppositeness and even greater between people characterized by symbiosis–autism:

> Conflict is based on an opposition to identities, such that whatever en-hances the identity of one combatant damages the other's, and damaging alters identity becomes a way in which ego can enhance his own identity. (Scanzoni, 1972, p. 72)

One of the major qualities of inadequate differentiation is digital thinking, that is, the tendency to think (and act) in terms of dichotomies: all–none; true–false; bad–good; right–wrong; always–never. This ten-dency, which polarizes issues and individuals toward extremes, could be related to pathology as well as to meaninglessness in the individual's life. Inappropriate or pathological rigidity in an individual, however, is most apparent in how the individual behaves in two different situations. The differentiated individual may use extreme responses selectively, whereas the inadequately differentiated individual uses extreme responses indis-criminately or behaves consistently regardless of changes in the situation or setting.

The multifarious ways in which oppositeness can show its negative head can be direct or indirect, passive or active, evident or subtle. None-theless, the most obvious and relevant ones are as follows: (a) opposite-ness in job or occupational choice, such as selecting a job that is the opposite from the employment the parents desire or expect (choice of a blue-collar job, whereas the parents have white-collar occupations); (b) oppositeness in religious choice or lack of it (children from funda-mentally religious parents may choose either atheism or extremely liberal religious sects); (c) oppositeness in marital choice, that is, selecting a mate who has most of the opposite characteristics desired or exemplified by the individual's parents; and (d) oppositeness in fear or avoidance of success, as in the child who loves to fail as a reaction to his or her parents' excessive preoccupation with success. This last pattern of oppositeness can take at least three different forms: (i) downward mobility in financial earning and income; (ii) underemployment, in view of the person's educational level; (iii) failure in jobs or frequent changes in jobs.

Whereas boys may tend to rebel against the mother's requests for unquestioning compliance leading to a disproportionate number of requests for help from mental health professions (Forehand, Walley, & Furery, 1984), girls may show their oppositeness by becoming prematurely pregnant. The girl who is unable to define herself in any way except her sexuality is essentially opposing parental demands for conformity to avoid intercourse and pregnancy. In some cases, pregnancy and motherhood may be seen as an easy way to receive monthly welfare checks. More often than not, pregnancy is the only act of rebellion and of self-determination that many teenagers low in a sense of self-importance may see as available to them. Through their pregnancy, they will proclaim their independence and their self-determination. Where any such intent is denied, the outcome is still the opposite of what the parental figures desire. Whether pregnancy is a passive or active outcome, it may be one way for girls to define themselves as being separate from their own parents. Sexual acting out may be to girls what juvenile delinquency is to boys, just a different way of being opposite to parental wishes and demands. For girls, the outcome of such behavior is pregnancy. For boys, the outcome of this oppositeness is apprehension or confinement. Either way, both boys and girls become constricted in the very freedom they claim so much to want. How can a person be more confined than in pregnancy or in jail?

Symbiosis–Autism: Abrupt Role Reversals

From the symbiotic matrix of mother–child interaction, most individuals develop into steps of greater and greater differentiation. Those who fail to reach toward the center of the likeness continuum are slowed down in the process of change and growth or remain stuck where they were, either at a symbiotic or at an autistic stage. One aspect of inadequate differentiation can be seen in abrupt role reversals such as a change from criminal to informer and the nasty–nice reversals evidenced by many (beasts at home and nice outside or less often, vice versa). This nasty–nice pattern is but one aspect of the compliance–defiance polarity model by Brehm (1966) and Brehm and Jones (1970) which, as noted earlier, does not leave room, however, for the various shades of similarity–differentness available in the likeness continuum. These role reversals were seen as hawks and doves by Raush, Barry, Hertel, and Swain (1974). Another instance of abrupt role reversal is found in descriptions of reversals in authoritarian versus permissive models of parenting. Contradiction as found in the double bind, either within a mode of expression such as language or between verbal and nonverbal modes. Contradiction, although present in adequate differentiation, is less frequent, intense, or evident; and when present, it is acknowledged and corrected. Symbiotic love affairs, characterized by immediate, fast "falling in love" with a parallel euphoria and loss of self ("I want to make you happy") fizzle very quickly when the individuals must face the responsibilities of marriage and parenthood.

THE CONTINUUM OF LIKENESS AND STYLES IN INTIMATE RELATIONSHIPS

The first two extremes of symbiosis–autism are extremely dysfunctional. The second two ranges of sameness–oppositeness are dysfunctional but extremely frequent, to the point that many, at least 50% if not 60%, of the most intimate human interactions are of a reactive nature. Only the two ranges of similarity–differentness are functional (L'Abate, 1976; 1986). Many forms of psychopathology, as well as addictions, for instance, derive from symbiotic–autistic and same–opposite styles of interaction in families of origin. For instance, as the work of Stewart and Livson (1966) suggests, a great many addictions, especially smoking, may derive from a developmental pattern of rebelliousness, which would equate to oppositeness on the continuum of likeness.

There may be an isomorphism between internal ranges of differentiation in likeness and external manifestations of that continuum in styles that are especially evident in intimate relationships (L'Abate, Weinstein, Fraizer, & Russ, 1989). Very few (and only mild) psychopathologies and addictions may derive from past family interactions based on similarity–differentness. External characteristics of symbiosis–autism are emotional, physical, chemical, liquid, and material dependencies, as well as sexual abuse, apathy, or emotional atrophy/neglect (AA). External characteristics of sameness–oppositeness are rigid and blind conformity on one hand, or explosive rebellion to conformity, on the other hand, as shown by repeatedly reactive patterns of behavior (RR). Similarity and differentness, when differentiated and integrated, produce autonomous interdependence and a conductively creative style of living (CC).

The qualities of reactive–abusive relationships are shown verbally through the following repetitive exchanges (L'Abate, 1991): (a) preeminent use of the "you" pronoun in a blaming fashion ("It's all your fault"), with rare use of the "I" or "we" pronouns, using generalizations, such as "never" and "always"; (b) mind reading, that is, knowing what the other person (partner or offspring) feels, thinks, or plans; (c) bringing up the past at the expense of the present and the future; (d) threats of abandonment, rejection, revenge, retaliation, and betrayal ("I will see my lawyer"); (e) emotional bribery and blackmail as seen in ultimatums, which represent conditions for continuation of the relationship ("If you do not do such and such by this date . . . I will leave you"); (f) excuses to justify one partner's behavior but not to justify the other's behavior ("I am a grown-up, you are still a teenager"); and (g) distracting behavior, going away from the problem at hand, and bringing in irrelevant topics ("What is the price of eggs in China?").

To summarize the reactive style, the person responds by either exploding or withdrawing from the situation. The reactive explosion would be mostly verbal, like an immediate response, or could take a long time, like an individual who chooses a mate on the basis of oppositeness to one's parents. Instead of responding, the person may abandon the situation, but this withdrawal would not improve the situation any better than a reactive response, keeping the interaction the same. Hence, the repetitive nature of reactive responses. The main difference between abusive and reactive styles is the intensity of the response. In the abusive style, for instance, a verbal response would be additionally characterized by curse words and derogatory expletives. In addition, there would be the possibility of physical or sexual assault. In the abusive style, the other side is apathy or neglect, by either giving up, dealing with the situation incompetently, inconsistently, or contradictorily, or not dealing with the situation at all, as in neglect. Hence, repetition is characteristic of reactivity, while neglect is the other side of abuse. One style could not exist without the other. While in the reactive style one supposedly wins at the other's expense, in the abusive–apathetic style both self and other lose. While in the reactive style there may be some attention paid to external correction and feedback to change the situation, in the abusive–apathetic style there is resistance to any external correction or feedback. While the reactive style may be amenable to psychotherapeutic intervention, the abusive-apathetic style is not.

To summarize the conductive–creative style, the term "conductor" is used to represent two metaphors—electrical and musical—to indicate some one who is in charge of self and situation. The conductor understands that no one can be in charge of another except through oppression and coercion. Thus, *the conductor keeps cool* by following a score, plan, or script, that includes nonreacting, delaying action by gathering relevant information by asking questions, and if and when action is necessary, following a positive and thoughtful course of action that will enhance self and other. In this style, both self and other win because they are both acknowledged as important to the situation. Further elaborations of these three styles will be made in Chapter 6.

TABLE 3.4. Hypothetical Relationships among Different Developmental Approaches

Interpersonal Relationships L'Abate (1986)	Parental Styles Baumrind (1975)	Attachment Patterns Ainsworth et al. (1978)	Cognitive Stages Piaget (1970)	Moral Development Kohlberg (1968)	Self-Definition L'Abate (See Chapter 6)	Play L'Abate (1979)	Identity Status Erikson (1954)	Legal Thinking Tapp and Kohlberg (1971)	Popularity Patterns Peery (1979)
Abusive	Abusive Neglectful	Avoidant	Sensorimotor and preoperational	Preconventional	No-Self	Exploration	Moratorium and I.D. diffusion	Prohibitive	Rejects
Reactive	Authoritarian Permissive	Insecure Ambivalent	Concrete Operational	Conventional	Selfish/Selfless	Aggression	Foreclosure	Prescriptive	Isolates
Conductive	Authoritative	Secure	Formal Operational	Postconventional	Selfulness	Construction	Identity Achievement	Beneficial Rational	Stars

The three patterns (AA, RR, CC) that form the ARC model (L'Abate, 1986) are hypothetically related (Table 3.4) to different parental styles (Baumrind, 1975), attachment patterns (Ainsworth, Blehar, Waters, & Wall, 1978), cognitive stages (Piaget, 1970), moral development (Kohlberg, 1968), self-definition (Chapter 6), stages of play, differentiated into exploration, aggression, and construction (L'Abate, 1979), identity status (Erikson, 1954), legal thinking (Tapp & Kohlberg, 1971), and popularity patterns (Peery, 1979). These three patterns can be seen also in children's understanding and developmental differentiation according to Selman and his co-workers (Yeates, Schultz, & Selman, 1990). The latter posited four levels of social-perspective coordination, from the lowest to the highest: (a) egocentric and undifferentiated; (b) subjective and unilateral; (c) self-reflective and reciprocal; and (d) third-person perspective and mutuality. The first level would be generated by and generate an abusive–apathetic (AA) style in intimate relationships. The second level would be generated by and generate a reactive–repetitive (RR) style in intimate relationships. The last two levels would be generated by and generate a conductive–creative (CC) style in intimate relationships. Ulrici (1984) has distinguished hypothetically among three different levels of cognitive differentiation that would parallel these three styles in intimate relationships (Table 3.5).

These three styles relate also to how dependency is dealt with (Table 3.6). In the abusive–apathetic style (neglectful) (AA), regardless of what the individual may say, the outcome (as in the addictions) is dependence on others, whether with intimates or with public welfare, with possible hospitalizations or incarcerations. No intimacy, as defined by the sharing of hurts, is possible here (L'Abate, 1986). In the reactive–repetitive style (RR), there is either an admission or a denial of dependency, with power

TABLE 3.5. **Levels of Cognitive Differentiation and Styles in Intimate Relationships***

Level I: Perceptual Differentiation—Apathetic–Abusive
    Stage 0 Pure symbiosis–autism
    Stage 1 Awareness of subjectivity
    Stage 2 Differentiation of self from others
    Stage 3 Differentiation of individuals

Level II: Conceptual Differentiation—Reactive–Repetitive
    Stage 4 Advent of thought and awareness of person permanence
    Stage 5 Differentiation of self-perspective and awareness of internal states
    Stage 6 Differentiation of self-perspective from the perspective of others

Level III: Analytical Differentiation—Conductive–Creative
    Stage 7 Awareness of another's view of self
    Stage 8 Differentiation of third-person perspective

* Adapted from Ulrici (1984), with permission of the author.

TABLE 3.6.   Continuum of Likeness, Styles in Intimate Relationships, Dependency, and Their Outcomes

Ranges of Likeness	Styles in Intimate Relationships	Levels of Dependency	Outcomes
Symbiotic–autistic	Abusive–apathetic Emotional atrophy	Extreme	Regression, chaos, and instability in personal, marital, parental, and occupational arenas (psychosis, murder, suicide, homelessness)
			Addictions
			Dissociations
			Intimacy nonexistant
Sameness–oppositeness	Reactive–repetitive Competitive Manipulative	Denial and conflicts over admission versus denial of dependency	Status quo at risk for conflict and stress in marital, parental, and occupational arenas
			Intimacy sporadic
Similarity–differentness	Conductive–creative Cooperative Synergistic	Awareness and acceptance of autonomies and interdependencies	Progression and resiliency in intimate relationships and occupation
			Intimacy present

and control conflicts over who is dependent on whom. Intimacy, if and when present, is sporadic and short-lived. In the conductive–creative style (CC), there is an awareness, acknowledgment, and admission of interdependence, based on equality of importance, leading to intimacy as an ever-present process in the intimate relationships (Cusinato & L'Abate, 1994).

The same three styles of differentiation in intimate relationships take place in marriages, as shown in Table 3.7. Even though there may be at least five levels of differentiation in marriage, the first two levels may fit into the abusive–apathetic style, the third level may fit into the reactive–repetitive styles, and the last two levels may fit into the conductive–creative style. Hence, the style a person learns from his or her family of origin may well be transmitted and repeated in the family of procreation. As the Rossis have amply demonstrated, these styles are transmitted from one generation to another, (Rossi & Rossi, 1990). A child who is born and raised in a household where an abusive–apathetic style is most common and frequent will very likely use the same style in future intimate relationships. A child born and raised in a household where a reactive–repetitive style is often present will very likely use the same style in other intimate relationships. A household with a predominant conductive–creative style very likely will produce children who tend to use that

TABLE 3.7. Developmental Levels in Marriage

Authors	Levels of Development				
	1	2	3	4	5
Nichol (1977)	Autistic–symbiotic	Projective–omnipotent			Autonomous–homonomous
Tamashiro (1976)	Magical	Idealized–conventional	Individualistic	Affirmative	Relationship-oriented
Bernal and Baker (1980)	Object-oriented	Individualistic	Transactiona		Contextual
Jurkovic and Ulrici (1980)	One-sided	Two-way partnership		Mutual sharing	Creative–conductive
L'Abate (1986)	Abusive–apathetic	Reactive–repetitive	Cooperative	Reciprocal	Mutual
Bader and Pearson (1988)	Symbiosis	Differentiation	Practicing	Reapproachment	Mutual interdependence

style in future intimate relationships. We inherit (through observation, modeling, and practice, not through genes) the primary style used in our family of origin and we usually carry it in our family of procreation.

This view is supported by the work of Simons, Whitbeck, Conger, and Chyi-In (1991), who used a sample of 451 two-parent families with a 7th grader in each. They used self-report questionnaires to evaluate harsh parenting from the previous generation to the present. Using structural equation modeling, these researchers found: ". . . grandparents who had engaged in aggressive parenting produced present-day parents who were likely to use similar parenting practices. The effect was stronger for mothers than for fathers" (p. 159). Socioeconomic status (SES) was also a factor in this transmission. For instance, these three styles may be also related to social class differences (Orthner, 1991; Trickett, Aber, Carlson, & Cicchetti, 1991). Whereas the RR style may be more normative in working-class families, the CC style may be more normative for middle-class families. The AA style may be present at all levels of SES, with some possible differences between physical and verbal abuse.

Thus, either from the classification of marriages according to stages of development (see Table 3.7), the normative work of the Rossis, or studies of abusive patterns of parenting, we can distinguish among styles of parenting that derive from at least three styles of individual differentiation. For an elaboration of these three styles to various theories of basic stages in psychological development, the reader is referred to Mahoney (1991, p. 150).

GENDER ISSUES IN DIFFERENTIATION

Compared with the 1930s and 1940s, women are increasing their levels of education and postponing marriage and childbearing as well as having fewer children (Van Dusen & Sheldon, 1976). Despite these changes, patterns of employment for women have not changed as quickly. Women are still mainly employed by service industries or in professions such as health, medical, or educational fields. These fields are thought to use stereotypic skills attributed to women, manual dexterity, and patience in caring for children or others. Women's pay still is not commensurate with the skill and the tasks performed, and rarely are women found in supervisory positions over men. In many ways, things have not changed greatly in the past decade. Gilligan (1982) argued that theories of psychological development that are presumedly neutral are actually gender-biased in favor of men. She noted that according to psychodynamic theory, the woman's failure to resolve the Oedipus complex compromises the development of the superego. It follows that women have little chance at developing to stages considered more desirable by male theorists. The present formulation avoids stereotyping, as far as possible, the likelihood that most girls will tend to mature in ways that yield similarities to their mothers, whereas boys will tend to behave in ways that resemble their fathers' behavior. From this generalization, however, there are other gender-specific differences that will be elaborated in Chapter 6.

Of interest to a review on differentiation are the differences in socialization of sons and daughters by their mothers and fathers (Block, 1978; Gjerde, 1986). Stereotypically, from an early age, girls are socialized to be more family oriented than boys. Chodorow (1978) observed that mothers perceive more similarities with their newborn daughters than with their newborn sons, who are seen as sexual opposites. This distinction is the first push toward differentiation and encouragement of independence in boys. Conversely, mothers feel that their daughters are like themselves, and they encourage closeness with them. The process of encouraging boys to be independent from their mothers while encouraging girls to be dependent comes to a head during the Oedipal stage. Boys resolve this stage by identifying with their fathers and rebelling against their mothers, but girls resolve it by identifying with their mothers and behaving like them. Chodorow (1978) argued that gender differentiation from the mother is not biological. Rather these differences stem from differential socialization patterns of sons and daughters that continue throughout childhood. Girls are encouraged to stay within the family. Boys are encouraged to venture forth outside the family. Household chores reflect these differences: Girls are given cleaning and cooking tasks to do within the house; mowing the lawn, servicing cars, and taking out the garbage are boyhood chores. Chores that involve physically leaving the home, increase the likelihood of exposure to interaction with people outside the family (Block, 1982; Hoffman, 1977).

The notion of staying within family confines is reinforced more for daughters than for sons. Daughters are also encouraged to seek help in problem solving from family members. Requests by daughters for family help in solving problems receive more support than requests by sons (Rothbart, 1971; Rothbart & Rothbart, 1976). Young adolescent girls have closer emotional ties with parents than do they with friends (Niles, 1979). Young adolescent girls rate another immediate family member as a significant other in their lives. In contrast, young adolescent boys will tend to rate somebody outside the immediate family as significant in their lives. Girls may become more independent and autonomous, however, when their mothers are employed outside the home. The mother who works outside the home serves as a role model and encourages independence in her daughter (Hoffman, 1977; Stein & Bailey, 1973).

Boys are encouraged to achieve, to explore outside the family, and to experiment with different solutions. They are, however, discouraged from becoming aware of and expressing affect (Block, 1978). It can be hard for them to learn to establish an identity within a relationship. Girls, on the other hand, are less encouraged to explore outside the family. Instead, they are encouraged to embrace the family's value system (Bernard, 1981). It is more difficult for girls to develop the adequate skills or confidence to be independent. Indeed, moves toward independence by girls are discouraged because they threaten the family affiliation that has been continuously reinforced (Hoffman, 1972).

Traditional male traits are more valued in the present culture than traditional female traits. In one study, mental health professionals, to describe a healthy adult, selected adjectives that previously had been rated as more characteristic of men (Broverman, Vogel, Broverman, Clarkson, & Rosencrantz, 1972). Not surprisingly, women who are achievers consistently show high masculine role identities (Stein & Bailey, 1973). Traditional masculine traits emphasize exploring opportunities and being independent from the family. Women with nontraditional sex role views achieve a clearer sense of identity than women with traditional views. Because nontraditional views go against societal norms, these women would require a healthy sense of who they are (Stein & Weston, 1982).

Thus, although some women can achieve self-differentiation through traditional male routes of exploring and developing unique occupational, religious, and moral identities, most may not. Women are reinforced for achieving their identity in the context of interpersonal relationships. Because of the profound difference in how men and women are socialized in this culture, Gilligan (1982) questioned whether much of our developmental research uses instruments that capture the stages of identity development in women. Rather than using scales that emphasize traits reinforced in men, she proposed incorporating assessment of the individual's identity in the context of relationships.

CONCLUSION

This chapter has argued that genotypical development, or differentiation, takes place along a psychophysical continuum of likeness distinguished by three major dialectical ranges: symbiosis–autism, sameness–oppositeness, and similarity–differentness. From this continuum and its three ranges, I have derived three behavioral styles observed in intimate relationships: abusive–apathetic, reactive–repetitive, and conductive–creative. I have related these three styles to various patterns of attachment, cognition, morality, play, identity status, legal thinking, popularity, social perspectives, marriage, parenting, and the transmission of these styles from the individual's family of origin to the family of procreation. I have hypothesized an isomorphism between a continuum of likeness and these three styles and patterns. Future chapters will elaborate how these patterns are interrelated to patterns of approach–avoidance in space, discharge–delay in time, self-definition, and priorities.

PART TWO

Theoretical Assumptions

CHAPTER 4

The First Assumption of Space: Approach–Avoidance

Emotionality is fundamental to beliefs and behavior.
(MAHONEY, 1991, p. 176)

This theory makes two assumptions that are basic to personality development. Space, the first assumption, deals with what eventually becomes the ability to love. Time, the second assumption, deals with what eventually becomes the ability to negotiate and problem solve; it will be discussed in Chapter 5. Both assumptions have been part of the present theory from its inception (L'Abate, 1964, pp. 64–86) and in its more recent revision (L'Abate, 1976, pp. 31–44). Then as now, it was argued that space subsumes distance and distance subsumes movement and nonverbal behavior. This volume will not repeat the arguments in the two previous sources concerning the importance and primacy of space over time for personality development. Briefly, the infant is born in a world of space and only later on does the child become aware of a world of time. Instead, I shall elaborate on this assumption and on its previous presentations by relating space to the ability to love and to be intimate, a development not touched upon in previous publications. The original assumption, however, that space subsumes a dimension of distance, defined by extremes in approach and avoidance, remains unchanged.

The dimension of distance deals with how close or how distant we keep from loved ones, superiors, inferiors, friends, neighbors, and strangers. Elsewhere (L'Abate, 1986), I have linked this dimension to emotions and emotional development. Feelings and emotions are developed in space, as represented by the emotional distance between the child and his or her caretaker (Biringen & Robinson, 1991), or the emotional distance among loved ones in the family. Emotions and feelings, on the receptive side, modulate and modify whom and how we approach and whom and how we avoid on the expressive side. Usually, but not always, we approach people we like and we avoid people we do not like.

The ability to love and to be close is based on feelings and emotions and not on strict rational bases. What space subsumes, therefore, is movement, nonverbal behavior, and, eventually, emotional availability. The whole area of spatial approach-avoidance is relevant to interpersonal attraction, mate selection, heterosexual relationships inside and outside marriage, friendship formation, and parent–child relationships (L'Abate, 1976).

Ultimately, we need to differentiate among various types of distance. For instance, physical distance is not synonymous with emotional distance. We can be very close emotionally to someone who is very distant from us physically. By the same token, we may be close spatially to some people, such as the next-door neighbors, and be extremely distant emotionally from them, as if they were strangers.

- **Physical Distance.**   This distance is the easiest to see, to measure, and to evaluate in space: how close two or more individuals are, from the closeness of sexual intercourse to the sharing of each other's losses and crying together, all the way to the distance between strangers who do not know and care relatively little about what happens to one another. The important aspect about physical distance is that two or more people could be at great physical distances but closely legally or emotionally, such as the wife of a soldier serving abroad or the families remaining in the native lands of immigrants.

- **Legal Distance.**   This distance refers to legal bonds or contracts that exist between various people, such as the bond of matrimony, the bond of parenthood, or the bond of family ties and loyalties from birth to death and afterward.

- **Emotional Distance.**   Neither of the first two types of distance, as easy as they are to quantify, are as important as a third type of distance. A person could be physically close, but legally and emotionally distant, as in one-night stands or in the relationship between the prostitute and the john. It is also possible to be physically distant but legally and emotionally close as in the relationship between parents and child or husband and wife. Distance, therefore, as Kantor and Lehr (1975) have shown, is the basic aspect of functioning among family members. This dimension determines, modulates, and controls a family's ability to love, which admittedly, is by itself an even more complex concept than distance. Yet, the ability to love is expressed and shown by how close and how far we keep from people who claim the same positive sentiments toward us as we do toward them, that is, emotional availability.

THE IMPORTANCE OF SPACE

We all need body-buffer zones that provide a certain amount of personal space. When someone invades or interferes with this space, we usually move away, although in some situations (e.g., in a line for food stamps or employment), we may defend our space and react in a more aggressive and even violent fashion. Somers (1987) related spatial behavior to privacy, spatial invasion of territories, small-group ecology and arrangements, and environmental programming. The major implication of Somers' work in relation to personality development pertains to the effects of living arrangements (apartment, house, etc.), crowding, density, moving around, freedom of exploration, and the whole of what Levin (1935) conceptualized as the "life space" of the individual.

Space and the Physical Environment

In an important review of the effects of physical environment on behavior, Moos (1976) considered how the weather, temperature, noise, and atmosphere affect all of us. Among physical qualities are distance factors that seem to determine mate selection (as propinquity) and friendship formation. Moos distinguished between physical and functional distance. The former measures linear distance in terms of sheer physical space. The latter refers to the actual time it takes to go from one point to another. To the physical and functional distinction, we need to add the concept of psychological (emotional) distance, that is, how close or how far we feel to somebody and how often and how much we contact that person and spend time with her or him. This latter variable is of greater importance here, even though there is a developmental sequence that goes from initially physical, then to functional, and ultimately to emotional or psychological distance, with or without legal distance. What is relevant about Moos's presentation is that design and spatial arrangements affect behavior. We cannot separate personality development from its physical context, that is, whether a child grows up in a rural, sparsely populated prairie or in a crowded, teeming ghetto; whether a child is raised in a shack or in a mansion, with plenty of space and privacy or without either.

Another concept brought out by Moos relates to environmental consequences with cultural and social characteristics. Most of us try to shape or match our physical environment to be congruent with expectations about ourselves and others. Whereas a machine worker can get used to a large, noisy factory, that kind of setting would not be congruent to activities requiring concentration, such as reading or even composing or creating, in spite of what we are told about J. S. Bach composing his

Brandenburg concertos in a room full of screaming children. A different environment is needed for different activities. As Moos concluded:

> The physical environment we create affects our behavior. By recognizing this relationship and by closely examining both our objectives and the ways in which our designs function, we can create environments that are more congruent with our goals . . . The crowding phenomenon can be conceptualized as a continuum that ranges from perceptions of spatial inadequacy (crowded) to perception of spatial adequacy (uncrowded) to perceptions of spatial excess (undercrowded or isolated). Cognizance of spatial inadequacy or spatial excess evokes psychological and physiological stress in the individual. Although the present model primarily conceives crowding stress, there is evidence that isolation (undercrowding) may not be associated with various symptoms, including mental illness. The perception of space as inadequate, adequate, or excessive is mediated by the interaction of the physical milieu, social milieu, and personal factors. The most important qualities of the physical environment are the amount and arrangement of space. As space becomes scarce, the individual is behaviorally constricted; however, various arrangements of available space can allay or heighten the feeling of constriction (e.g., surrounding a small room with mirrored walls and/or careful arrangement of furniture may make the room appear larger). (p. 145)

In reviewing some of the studies on individual and cross-cultural differences in the uses of space to establish proxemics and territoriality, Moos (1976) summarized his arguments as follows:

> . . . groups differ in their personal space expectations according to their sex, their physical health, their mental health, and their tendency toward violence . . . personal space requirements or expectations are situation-specific (i.e., individual space expectations expand and contract depending on the overall situation) and individual-specific (i.e., individuals in identical situations will differ in the amount of space they expect). (pp. 166–167)

In this regard, Moos gave a great deal of credit and regard to the ecological psychology of Barker (1968). In dealing with distance, Moos commented:

> Distance is related to friendship formation and the use of recreational, social and other possible facilities. It is important to distinguish between physical and functional distance, but it is clear that distance is a prime variable in determining whether people will meet and whether they will develop and continue a friendship. Mediating variables must be taken into account. For example, the life cycle phase of the individual is important and

friendship formation in special interest groups (e.g., a gourmet society) may transcend distance variables. (p. 111)

Space and Body Experience

How we deal with space is very likely shown by how we deal with our bodies. Spatially, the body represents the demarcation between the self and the outside space. It represents how we define, delineate, and defend ourselves. Spatial boundaries begin with the body. These boundaries are apparent in how we care for our body through personal hygiene, exercise, and proper nutrition; and whether we exhibit it or shy away from showing it at all, even to our mate. How much we eat and how little we care for maintaining a proper weight are all examples of how we care for our body and what boundaries we set to separate it from the outside world. Fisher (1970) illustrated and showed how important body perception is for an understanding of normal and disturbed behavior. Body boundaries represent the demarcation of a person's body limits from his or her world. More specifically, Fisher related body boundaries to various psychophysiological, autonomic levels of behavior with interior–exterior differences in the demarcation of body boundaries, as assessed through Rorschach inkblots, body focus, and body distortion questionnaires. Body awareness varies sharply between men and women and it is related to various types of normal, psychosomatic, and psychopathological states.

Body boundaries important to the development of personality are defined in many ways, from how a child is taught to sleep in his or her own bed rather than in the parents' bed to how both sexes protect themselves and each other during intercourse. These boundaries are relevant to how we define ourselves to others. The setting of body boundaries is just as relevant to the setting of personal and interpersonal boundaries and relationships, such as kissing on the first date and intercourse on the second.

This definition of body boundaries is relevant also to the definition of context. Setting body and spatial boundaries is part of a definition of context. Notions of privacy, territoriality, punctuality, accuracy, and negotiability pertain to the drawing of lines, both concrete and metaphorical, to our body, to our behavior, and to the behavior of others. Without this definition and setting of spatial boundaries, there would be no context. Difficulties in setting personal boundaries start with distinguishing between self and nonself in a simple, dichotomous fashion (good–bad, right–wrong), eventually with age, more complex definitions, and ultimately a rejection of labels to define the self, as suggested in Table 4.1.

There is a whole field of body language and kinesis that looks at the relationship between the body and how body movements, including and especially facial cues, are related to nonverbal behavior and to emotions.

TABLE 4.1.   Modalities and Space: Distance from the Body*

Modalities	Internal (to the body)		External	
Below Awareness	Psychosomatic	Visceral	Proximal	Distal
Kinesthetic	Stomach pains	"Butterflies in stomach"	Mannerisms Tics	Running
Auditory			Hallucinations	
Visual			Hallucinations	Projections
Tactile			"Bugs crawling on the skin"	

* From L'Abate (1964, p. 76).

From kinesis to movement, we expand the use of body language into non-verbal actions consisting of movements described by the field of proxemics (L'Abate, 1976). This continuum applies not only to external movements but also to what we choose or need to avoid or approach within our internal space. Do we choose to develop an internal dialogue for feedback so we can learn from our experiences or do we choose or need to avoid looking at ourselves for fear of what we are going to find out? Thus, we need to consider that this continuum represents both our internal (inside the body) and external (outside the body) space. Hypothetically, the greater the avoidance of internal pain (grief, unpleasantness, displeasure, disappointments, frustrations, tensions of any kind, stress) the greater the probability of external, interpersonal avoidance.

SPACE AND LEVELS OF INTERPRETATION

The amount and use of space by family members in the home (crowded–uncrowded, large–small, clean–dirty, organized–disorganized) can be interpreted at various levels. For instance, at the presentational level, a house may be kept for strictly business reasons, as appearance, or as something separate from external considerations of appearance and worth. By the same token, parts of the house may be kept in immaculate condition for guests, to make a good impression, while the rest of the house may be in shambles. At the phenotypical level, we need to see how a house is used by those who inhabit it, collaboratively–competitively, constructively–destructively, caringly–uncaringly, and so on. How is this place viewed by the family members at the genotypical level? As a refuge from the pressures of the outside world, or merely as a place to eat and sleep? As a place to come back to, or to avoid and never come back to at any cost? How do inhabitants of the house conceptualize themselves in their movements around the house, freely or furtively, joyously or anxiously, relaxed or tense? As Duhl, Kantor, and Duhl (1973) stated:

> . . . all systems not only inhabit space but are surrounded by a functional space and an invisible though meaningful boundary (p. 50) . . . We, too, often forget that the children we once were lived in a nonverbal world in which spatial perceptions and affect were intimately connected. We have renounced the physical aspects of our early learning, although we still respond to them unconsciously. Making this dimension of learning live again intensifies the experience (p. 52) . . . Think "space" and "action" until it comes naturally, like a second language, or, more realistically, like a primary language regained. After all, action in space is the child's original way of learning. (p. 63)

Approach–Avoidance: The Basic Dimension of Behavior

The approach–avoidance dimension defines *where and with whom* we spend our time. With whom do we live? How do we live with people who have freely and mutually chosen and agreed to live with us? The infant develops approach–avoidance tendencies from the day of birth, if not earlier. How does the caretaker approach that child? With a smile? With a snarl? With soothing words or with screaming tantrums? Abusively, angrily, and reactively or apathetically and neglectfully? Will the caretaker keep in charge and control of him- or herself in a conductive–creative manner or lose control and react to the child not out of the child's needs but on the basis of the caretaker's unmet needs?

Even though approach and avoidance are two sides of the same continuum of distance, it is more useful, for purposes of exposition, to consider them separately. As shown in Table 4.2, from this basic dimension of behavior can develop extremes with pathological characteristics.

The Continuum of Approach: Approach and the Development of Self-Importance

How often do we approach someone and for what reason? Whom do we approach? What does this approach mean? Does it mean dependency to love or to support another? Usually, the infant is approached in the crib; only later, when the child is mobile, does he or she learn to approach. This mobility will then indicate how much the child depends on the caretaker for physical survival, emotional support, social and intellectual stimulation, and learning. Hence, we equate approach with attachment and dependency. The more a child approaches someone, usually a caretaker, for fulfillment of survival and succorance, the more he or she is or becomes dependent on the other. In some cases of symbiosis, both

TABLE 4.2.   Possible Pathological Consequences of
Extreme Deviations in Movement*

Pain (Punishment)	Pleasure (Reward)
Avoidance (withdrawal)	Approach
Turning within and/or against	Overdependency
Flight into action or fantasy	Turning to others
Evasion (and deception)	Symbiosis + approach to others
Seclusion	Hyperactivity
Isolation (personal)	Sexual deviations (paraphylias)
Mistrust–rejection	Overacceptance
Isolation (social)	Diffusion (codependency)
Social contact minimal	Social contact maximal
(Denial of dependency)	(Extreme dependency)

* From L'Abate (1964, p. 69). Concepts in parentheses have been added
recently.

members, caretaker and dependent child, become dependent on each
other for mutual support and succorance. Attachment, therefore, is
based on approach tendencies that are rewarded by the caretaker.
Whether this attachment becomes appropriate, as interdependence, on
one hand, or inappropriate, as extreme dependency or isolation, on the
other hand, are all examples of frequent or infrequent, but usually intense, approach tendencies. Functional attachments, especially in marriage and committed relationships, as well as between children and
parents, are based on mutuality and interdependence. Dysfunctional attachments are based on inconsistent, or contradictory approach–avoidance characterized by abuse–apathy and repetitive reactivity. Abusive
relationships, for example, frequently involve overdependence, which
is now fashionably called *codependency* (Kitchens, 1991; Kokin &
Walker, 1989).

Once we equate approach with attachment and dependency, we then
need to link this dimension to Attachment Theory (Bowlby, 1970, 1973,
1988) and how this theory has been tested through the Strange Situation
methodology (Ainsworth et al., 1978). As Fox, Kimmerly, and Schafer
(1991) found in their meta-analysis of 11 studies using this methodology:

> . . . security of attachment to one parent was dependent upon security to
> the other parent . . . type of insecurity (avoidant/resistant) to one parent
> was dependent upon type of insecurity to the other, and . . . subcategory
> classification within the secure category to one parent was dependent upon
> subcategory classification to the other. (p. 210)

We shall come back to how attachment theory and the present theory
are related in Chapter 6.

As already indicated in Chapter 1, the sense of self importance is the cornerstone of personality development. This sense is communicated by caretakers well before the child is born, since the sense of importance of the parents and caretakers is transmitted to the child in myriad ways, directly–indirectly, verbally–nonverbally, consistently–inconsistently, caringly–uncaringly, abusively–apathetically, reactively–repetitively, or conductively–creatively. Many family rituals, such as holiday celebrations, birthdays, family reunions, and vacations, are ways of affirming the importance of the family and of its individual members.

The Continuum of Avoidance: Approach–Avoidance and Levels of Interpretation

The act of approach is usually accompanied by a parallel act of avoidance. As we go toward someone, we may also go away from somebody else. In many cases, conflict is the outcome of being unable to choose between whom to approach and whom to avoid. We may avoid unpleasant and painful situations, sweeping them under the rug, postponing their solutions, or we may confront them to solve and resolve them.

Functional avoidance may be necessary and sufficient in the sense that all of us try to avoid situations as well as the people who may represent unnecessarily unpleasant or painful consequences for us. We avoid danger or risks, unless, of course, we enjoy them. As the work of Pennebaker (1990) has shown, most of us tend to avoid dealing with many past traumatic experiences unless we are required to bring them back up into our awareness. In fact, a great deal of pathology may derive from our avoidance of painful feelings (L'Abate, 1986). This conclusion has been strengthened by the arguments of Hayes and Melancon (1989):

> We argue that a single common denominator, namely, emotional avoidance, underlies many of the diagnostic classifications, client expectations, and therapeutic interventions in clinical psychology. Emotional avoidance, we argue, is often the "problem" our clients are dealing with, and clinical psychology is a major supporter of the difficulty (p. 185) . . . client's real problem is not his feelings of guilt, depressed mood, or suicidal thoughts, but his unwillingness to feel depressed feelings as they are (not as what they *say* they are). The problem is his unwillingness to think guilty thoughts (again, as they are, not as they say they are). Suicide is the ultimate attempt to avoid feeling "bad," but many other classic depressive behaviors can also be viewed as attempts to avoid experiencing unpleasant thoughts and emotions . . . to keep from feeling the emotional pain that accompanies rejection by a loved one, the depressive may avoid forming intimate relationships, or avoid confronting problems in existing ones . . . the depressive's attempts to escape from

what he is feeling and thinking create a type of anticipatory cycle of depression that is self-sustaining. Trying hard not to be depressed is itself depressing (p. 186) . . . Although the potential for psychological disturbance inherent in avoidance of unpleasant private experiences has long been recognized, the breadth and depth of the sources of this avoidance seem greatly unappreciated. (p. 187)

This position could be also extended and expanded to include multiple personality disorders, as well as impulsive and acting-out individuals, usually diagnosed as character disorders. We all tend to avoid unpleasant and painful feelings just as much as depressive personalities, as shall be expanded in Chapter 6. In all of us, there is a dissociation of past, painful experiences. What is dissociation but the ultimate, extreme form of avoidance? Dissociation is a process whereby painful experiences or events are separated from awareness and repressed, suppressed, and ultimately left somewhere in the self, where energy is expended to keep them hidden and hopefully forgotten (i.e., avoided).

The basic issue that may explain individual differences in amount of avoidance of painful experiences and events may be their extent and intensity and their being counterbalanced by pleasurable ones. Dysfunctional avoidance, therefore, consists of anxieties, fears, and phobias (Denny, 1991) that are the outcome of defenses such as suppression, denial, repression, and eventual dissociation from painful and hurtful experiences, as in the case of physical, sexual, and verbal abuse. Thus, these defenses are the outcome of a process of internal as well as external avoidance, even though it is possible for a person to be inconsistent and contradictory in approaching someone who should be avoided, especially in abusive–apathetic relationships.

Thus, approach–avoidance tendencies are complementary, both dialectically and metaphorically. These tendencies vary on the basis of individual differences. We may avoid someone whom somebody else may find worthy of approach.

Extremes of approach and avoidance at a phenotypical level, visible after prolonged observation and after the initial effects of the presentational level have worn off, so to speak, suggest the need for further explanatory levels underlying this continuum. That we have continuous conflicts in our approach–avoidance tendencies indicates that other factors, often hidden to observation, either superficial, casual, or prolonged and controlled, are present. These underlying factors relate to the nature of the genotype in the self and to its relationship to approach–avoidance tendencies. Underlying approach–avoidance tendencies is an internal, almost hidden characteristic that will be responsible for the prolongation or the shortening of any approach or avoidance. Why do people attract each other, marry, have children, build homes, and then divorce? Why do people commit murder, suicide, and other destructive acts (extreme avoidance) after an initial approach? Visibility of constructs may be necessary but insufficient to encompass the complexity of human interaction. Our approach–avoidance tendencies at a descriptive level are the result of external, situational as well as internal genotypical and developmental factors. In turn, environmental and genotypical factors need to be viewed from an historical perspective, that is, time. Past history and future goals influence why we approach or avoid the way we do, just as individual-setting transactions—whom and what we approach and avoid—form the structure of personality development.

Approach–avoidance tendencies are relevant to the development of defensive and coping reactions or styles of coping. For instance, admission either to self and others would represent a form of approach, whereas denial would represent a form of avoidance. In Chapter 5, we shall see how admission and denial may be related to certain personality defenses; and in Chapter 6, how admission and denial are related to certain personality types in intimate relationships.

DISTANCE AND LIKENESS

The concept of distance and its polarities (close–far) have often been understood as being isomorphic with likeness, equating similarity with contiguity. In many cases, similarity has been made synonymous with contiguity and propinquity. For instance, the principle of contiguity essentially suggests that variables with an increasingly similar facet structure will also show a stronger empirical relationship by contiguity, proximity, or similarity.

Similarity in differentiation is not, however, synonymous with distance per se. As previously stated, we can be physically distant but emotionally very close. That closeness would be revealed in any self-rating or self-description of one individual in comparison with another. Just as different ranges of likeness represent various distances between two or more individuals, we need to differentiate among a continuum of likeness versus continua of distance, proximity, and contiguity. All the latter are spatial concepts whereas the notion of likeness as a continuum does not share this spatial quality. Hence, it is important to separate the dimension of likeness from any other spatial dimension even though the overlap may be great. As Gregson (1975) noted:

Increasing similarity implies decreasing distance and the solution of the problem of measuring this distance implies a psychological space. It is important to note that psychological space thus defined is a representation of behavior, not a model of something inside the subject's head that generates observable behavior. (p. 93)

Nahemow and Lawdon (1983) also equated similarity with propinquity, whereby "attractiveness increases as a function of perceived similarity" (p. 282). These authors found that proximity was a critical factor in the selection of friends: "Thus the proximity effect appears to be a powerful force in friendship formation and operates for people of all ages, races, and for both sexes . . . Similarity proved to be an equally powerful predictor of friendship formation" (p. 286). Factors that defined similarity were "status" in age, sex, and race: "People's tendency to choose friends of their 'own kind' is so pronounced that it would be easy to lose sight of the important fact that a substantial minority of friendships did cross age and racial lines" (p. 286). Thus, these authors concluded that there is a significant *interaction* between similarity and proximity. However, interaction does not mean identity. We may discover that we are very similar to one of our parents, but that does not mean we like it or want to be close to them.

In intimate relationships, conductive–creative styles express distance flexibly and positively, whereas abusive–apathetic and reactive–repetitive styles express it rigidly, contradictorily, and inconsistently. We learn how to be close or distant, intimate or isolated, from our family of origin. We transfer and transmit these tendencies from our family of origin to our family of procreation. Eventually, our ability to be emotionally available to ourselves and to intimate others indicates the level of personality development we have reached. What are the mechanisms of transmission within individuals in families and from one generation to the other? We observe and experience the kind of attachments our caretakers form, how they accept or reject other people, how they come together and separate from intimate others. This learning and modeling takes place on the receptive side (input), to the point that we are not aware of how we may mimic or even avoid the mimicry of our caretakers according to a continuum of likeness (Chapter 3). This transmission also becomes a function of how caretakers attribute and contribute to the child's sense of importance. This process will impinge on and influence the child's self-definition, sense of self, and how the child chooses to define him- or herself according to the continuum of likeness in the processing of inputs (i.e., experiences). The sense of self is basic to the development of self-definition and self-importance. Hence, in cases of extreme symbiosis–autism, abuse and apathy, we are going to obtain extreme dysfunctionality in approach–avoidance tendencies. There will be extreme and abrupt reversals in approach–avoidance. In cases of sameness–oppositeness, we are going to obtain borderline functionality in the same tendencies, perhaps not as abrupt or as extreme as with symbiosis–autism, but still repetitively reactive. Integration of similarities and differences, as in a constructive-creative style, will lead to functionality in approach–avoidance.

APPROACH–AVOIDANCE AND THE DEVELOPMENT OF EMOTIONALITY

Emotions are a framework on which to hang personality development. Four basic and fundamental emotional reactions are available to children by age three (Harter, 1986): happiness, sadness, anger, and fear. As Mahoney suggested in his review of theories of emotionality (1991, p. 187), most investigators agree that fear, anger, joy, and sadness are the four basic emotions in development, which become differentiated into more complex, derived emotions (disgust, surprise, contempt, shame, and guilt). Although all emotions are real, proper, and necessary for an appropriately functional personality, we need to differentiate functional from dysfunctional expression of emotions. A person who feels fear and anger may hurt the self or hurt others, and happiness may be used as a false euphoria to cover up other true emotions. Happiness becomes dysfunctional when it is stressed at the expense of other feeling states and is expressed almost exclusively to avoid other feelings. Whenever any one of the four basic emotions is expressed almost exclusively to avoid dealing with the other three feelings, or their derivatives, it produces a dysfunctional process and outcome.

The normative, functional expression of feelings and emotions relies on using a wide repertoire of them and their derivatives without exclusion, so that each state, primary or secondary, can be expressed appropriately according to each specific situation. Under these conditions, happiness expressed as joy, a temporary state rather than a permanent one, would be as suitable and real an emotion as the other three. It would be meaningless to speak of using an inappropriate emotion in an appropriate way. Surely there is a proper level of contentment or happiness for humans to feel. Happiness, anger, sadness, and fear are all necessary emotions if a person experiences and expresses them appropriately. Dysfunctionality may be the result of substituting counterfeit feelings for one or more of the "true" emotions: euphoria or mania for happiness, resentment or envy for anger, shame or despair for sadness, and worry or need to control for fear. If this conclusion is valid, then all four basic feelings would be appropriate and could never be out of balance. It would never be inappropriate to be truly happy, angry, sad, or fearful, for each feeling would manifest itself at a suitable time and in a suitable manner.

The concept of deviant personality development would then be modified by stressing that although normative development is based on the appropriate use of all four feeling states and their derivatives according to specific situations, deviations in personality development consist of the extreme and inappropriate *expression* of these four feelings states (i.e., an amplification of these feelings). For instance, when euphoria or mania become the dominant dysfunctional emotions, as an avoidance of painful feelings, drivenness would be the resulting outcome or symptom. When resentment or envy are the dominant dysfunctional emotions, impulsivity and most character disorders may be the result. When shame or despair are the dominant dysfunctional emotions, depression or even suicide may result. When worry or need to control are the dominant dysfunctional emotions, anxiety or obsession may result. When dysfunctional states are combined with each other, different personality patterns may be possible. For instance, (a) euphoria/mania + shame/despair may produce bipolar manic depressive disorders; (b) euphoria/mania + resentment/envy may produce character disorders; (c) euphoria/mania + worry/need to control may produce narcissistic personalities; (d) resentment/envy + worry/need to control may produce passive–aggressive personalities; (e) resentment/envy + shame/despair may produce paranoia; (f) worry/need to control + shame/despair may produce obsessive–compulsive disorders; and (g) excessive guilt and shame may produce feelings of worthlessness and hopelessness.

A model for emotionality that includes some of the foregoing considerations is shown in Figure 4.1. The relationship between grief and pain, on the left, intimacy in the middle, and pleasure or ecstasy on the right of the figure, is quite complex and not as straightforward as it appears to be in this figure. Most of us like to avoid pain and grief and approach pleasure and excitement. A few find excitement in physical pain, and even fewer enjoy inflicting emotional pain. Some people are able to approach and achieve intimacy with another loved one. Some others want, crave, and seek intimacy but are afraid of it at the same time, producing an approach–avoidance conflict that may last all their lives. Others avoid intimacy and closeness like the plague. The issue here involves reconciling individual differences with emotionality. We will be able to attempt such a reconciliation after taking a few more steps in the next chapter and eventually in Chapter 6.

SPACE AND THE ABILITY TO LOVE

The ability to love is expressed spatially in nonverbal behavior, not only by how close or far emotionally or physically we are from those we love, but also through what we do for them. The ability to love is expressed in

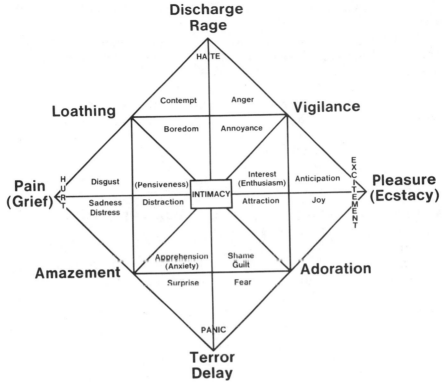

Figure 4.1. A model for emotionality (E). From L'Abate (1986).

nonverbal behavior, through what we do, what services we perform for someone, and what we expect the person to perform for us in a reciprocal fashion (Aron & Aron, 1986). Early attachments become the paradigm for future ones. How a child learns to depend on the caretaker and how that child weans away gradually or traumatically from the same caretaker may be repeated in future relationships, later on in life.

How does the child learn the concept of conditional or unconditional love? A child learns it by how parents model that love in the marital relationship and eventually how they show that love toward the child in terms of his or her performance in the home, on the playground, and eventually in school and academic performance. Learning conditional rather than unconditional love means that the child learns that he or she is lovable to the extent that love is equated with performance ("I love you to the extent that you follow what I tell you"), which would be equated with uncritical and blind obedience (sameness). Rebellion, on the other hand, would indicate that the child has not been given a choice and has been forced or coerced to choose digitally between blind obedience on one hand or the opposite of what he or she has been told to do ("You either follow what I tell you or you are rejected").

Thus, love becomes equated with how the child responds to parental or caretaker demands, that is, conditionally. Only when the parent is able to assume a conductive–creative position, which includes unconditional love, can the child choose among alternatives, as suggested by many parent training manuals. The sense of unconditional love is communicated by caretakers to the child from the day of birth. Conditional love will stem from abusive–apathetic and reactive–repetitive parent–child relationships, while unconditional love will be present in most conductive–creative parent–child relationships.

SOLIDARITY: SPACE, PERSONALITY DEVELOPMENT, AND FAMILY SOLIDARITY

Consequently, extremes in approach–avoidance tendencies would develop over time, starting with the three possibilities outlined from the Stranger Situation (Ainsworth et al., 1978): insecurely attached, avoidantly attached, and ambivalently attached. From these three extremes, there develops different extremes of dependency on one hand and of denial of dependency on the other. These patterns culminate in adulthood, where there is the well-known triad of Pursuer, seeking closeness; Distancer, avoidant of closeness; and Regulator, ambivalently torn between avoidance and approach ("Come here, I need your help. Go away, you did not help me!) summarized by L'Abate (1986) as a characteristic of depressed individuals. At greater extremes, we would find the symbiotic relationship, exemplified by folie à deux on one hand and the autistic alienated person on the other hand, with the Alternator representing the person who vacillates inconsistently between the two extremes (Table 4.3).

TABLE 4.3.   Extremes in Approach–Avoidance and Conflict over Attachment and Dependency

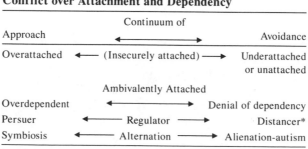

	Continuum of	
Approach	←———————→	Avoidance
Overattached	←— (Insecurely attached) —→	Underattached or unattached
	Ambivalently Attached	
Overdependent	←————→	Denial of dependency
Persuer	←— Regulator —→	Distancer*
Symbiosis	←— Alternation —→	Alienation-autism

* This dimension was described in greater detail in L'Abate (1986).

How close or distant a person learns to be in relation to other human beings develops from the child's family context and first of all from the infant's caretaker(s). How close caretaker(s) will be to the infant will depend on how they themselves learned to deal with distance in their families of origin. Thus, how close or distant a family is will affect how its members will learn to deal with distance in their families of procreation. This distance may relate to the loyalty family members feel toward each other (family solidarity).

To explain social solidarity, which is the concept used to deal with intergenerational gaps, Bengtson, Olander, and Haddad (1976) borrowed from Homans' (1950) three basic processes: (a) similarity, (b) sentiment, and (c) activity. Similarity is defined as "those elements of behavior that interacting persons carry out in similar ways, and on which they feel some consensus of opinion," or "the extent of agreement or similarity in personal and social values, opinions, and beliefs, between family members" (p. 245). Activity "deals with associative behavior, the interactional patterns between members of the family" (p. 245). Sentiment "has to do with the expressions of emotional feeling affect, or the nature and extent of positive sentiment toward members of the other generations in the family" (p. 245).

These processes are related to other sociological theories and are covered by Bengtson, Olander, and Haddad (1976), who also summarized the factors associated with each of these processes. As far as consensus similarity is concerned, education, occupation, and peer group experience would be negatively correlated with intergenerational similarities, whereas being of native or foreign-born origin, family traditions, and acceptance of changed norms would be positively correlated with intergenerational similarities. As far as associational activities between members of the middle and older generations (where there seems to be the greatest degree of conflict) are concerned, residential propinquity (not only defined by distance but also by mail and telephone communication) and types of sex linkages are reliable indicators of association between members of the same generations:

> The chief indicator of affectional solidarity appears to be the amount of helping behavior, especially of the non-essential kind, that occurs within the family. This is influenced, however, by dependency needs, residential propinquity, and the type of sex linkages and the degree of filial responsibility. (p. 255)

On the basis of these processes, Bengtson, Olander, and Haddad (1976) suggested seven propositions and corollaries that would account for intergenerational solidarity: (a) residential propinquity; (b) helping behavior; (c) dependency needs of the elderly; (d) place of birth; (e) acceptance of changed social mores; (f) filial responsibility; and (g) education, occupation, and peer group experiences. These are all factors that affect how family members love each other. We cannot forget, however, that how close we are to someone is also defined by how much time we spend with that person. Hence, space without time may be meaningless. If we like or love someone, we like or want to spend as much time as possible with the person.

CONCLUSION

Space is the primary context for development in the ability to love and to be close and intimate or their opposites, being unable to love, being isolated and distant from intimate others. Approach–avoidance tendencies are also basic to the development of personality to the point that balanced, flexible, appropriate, and consistent tendencies will lead toward functionality, whereas rigid, extreme, and contradictory tendencies will lead toward dysfunctionality. The balanced, appropriate approach needs to be complementary to balanced, appropriate avoidance as found in the conductive–creative style. Balanced approach–avoidance tendencies will produce a wide and flexible repertoire of feelings and emotions. Imbalanced or extreme approach–avoidance tendencies will produce a narrow and limited emotional repertoire, as in the reactive–repetitive and abusive–apathetic styles.

We cannot, however, separate spatial tendencies from issues of time. We cannot describe where we go and whom we are with unless we know *how long* we stay. Hence, issues of space are orthogonal to issues of time. We need both space and time to more accurately describe personality development.

CHAPTER 5

The Second Assumption of Time: Discharge–Delay

All movement may be conceptualized in terms of social time.
                                        (LAUER, 1981, p. 42)

Going from one person to another or from one setting to another takes time. How long we spend with someone is a measure of how important that someone is for us. How fast we do what we are told to do indicates the importance of what we have been told to do. We choose to marry someone with the idea of spending the rest of our life with that person. The assumption of time has been part of the present theory from its inception (L'Abate, 1964, pp. 87–104) and in its more recent revision (L'Abate, 1976, pp. 45–69). This volume will not repeat the information in the two previous sources about the importance of time. I shall try, instead, to add to this assumption and to its previous presentations by relating and linking time to the ability to negotiate power, as made up by performance (Chapter 7) and production (Chapter 8). This linkage is related also to the control and management of feelings and emotions, since the ability to negotiate is related to the ability to think appropriately and constructively and to use rational resources for bargaining, problem solving, and decision making, in short, negotiating.

The dimension subsumed by time deals with how we control ourselves, whether we tend to *discharge* and explode on one extreme, or whether we tend to *delay*, wait, and control what we are going to say or do, sometimes not saying or doing anything, on the other extreme. Thus, the basic dimension of control, subsumed by time, as defined by extremes in discharge and in delay, verbally, nonverbally, or in writing, as contained in previous versions of this theory, remains unchanged. Ausloos (1986) maintained that families, and presumably the individuals constituting them, do not "live" time in the same way. For instance, in families with rigid transactions, time is arrested. For families with chaotic transactions, time is eventful. Thus, for some individuals, awareness of time may be nonexistent, while at the other extreme, for other individuals, time may be of the utmost concern. The issue here is one of individual differences. How do we learn to control or be controlled by time? From this assumption, we shall try to relate and link self-control to the process of negotiation and problem solving.

THE IMPORTANCE OF TIME AS A FUNDAMENTAL PSYCHOLOGICAL ASSUMPTION

Interest in the study of time has continued unabated. References in previous publications (L'Abate, 1964, 1976) attest to its importance. The most recent generation has not diminished its interest, as many additional references deal with time within the context of scientific, psychological inquiry (Block, 1990; Kelly & McGrath, 1988; Lauer, 1981; McGrath, 1988; McGrath & Kelly, 1986), within a developmental viewpoint (Friedman, 1982), within a multidisciplinary perspective (Fraser, 1989), within the viewpoint of psychopathology (Ausloos, 1986; Hartocollis, 1983; Melges, 1982) and ultimately within a strictly functional, normative viewpoint (Juster & Stafford, 1985). These references are not exhaustive but they are representative of how the study of time is still of major concern to theorists, researchers, and clinicians. The reader is directed to those sources for a more detailed rendering than is possible here (for reasons of space).

THE TEMPORAL PERSPECTIVE OF PAST THEORIES

Theories differ in the ways they emphasize the influence of time. For instance, psychoanalysis stresses the retrospective importance of past influences. The level of explanation in psychoanalysis resides in past traumatic and repressed experiences. Humanism stresses the prospective importance of the present view and of future goals. In humanism, explanation resides in how an individual perceives the present situation subjectively and ahistorically, often in abstract and long-range projections and expectations. Behaviorism stresses the present, objective situation, its immediate antecedents and its immediate consequences. In behaviorism, explanation is found in the objective relationship between behavior as it takes place and its immediate contingencies. Thus, theories of behavior differ in their temporal focus of understanding and interpretation and, hence, in their approaches to explanation.

The present theory views the temporal perspective as being all important, covering the whole complementary range of past and present, events and experiences as well as expectations for the future. Harner (1982) commented on temporal perspective thusly:

The notions of past, present, and future are central to the ways we organize our lives and how we think and talk about events, experiences, and ourselves. Some of us are more influenced by past events in terms of what we think and talk about. Others live largely for the future, always planning, waiting, or dreaming. Still others have a "now" orientation and are mainly concerned with the present moment's experiences. We all vary in our temporal orientations and in our subjective interpretations of time and the ideas of past, present, and future. (p. 141)

From this comment, it seems clear that we cannot separate temporal perspective from issues of personality definition and development, functional or dysfunctional.

CHARACTERISTICS OF TIME

There are many lists characterizing time. McGrath (1988), for instance, classified time according to five temporal facets, both internal and external: (a) *pace of life,* measured in subseconds and seconds; (b) *rhythms of behavior,* measured in seconds and minutes; (c) *allocation* and enjoyment of time, measured in minutes and hours; (d) *developmental cycles,* measured in hours, days, and weeks; and (e) *continuity and change processes,* measured in weeks, months, and years. These temporal facets were used by McGrath to organize diverse contributions in the psychology of time. Jones (1988) made pace of life a matter of temporal perspective of past, present, and future that varies from culture to culture and within a culture from one individual to another.

Other definitions of time are usually made on the basis of linear, objectively physical time versus psychologically subjective time. For instance, physical time can be measured by (a) *frequency of occurrence,* the frequency and repetition of behavior occurrence (How *often* does it take place?); (b) *rate of occurrence,* the interval between occurrences that could be seconds to years (How *fast* does it take place?); (c) *duration* (How *long* does it last?); (d) *intensity* (How *strong* is it?); and (e) *latency,* the difference and interval between a stimulus and the occurrence of the behavior elicited by the stimulus, like reaction time. This reaction time at a very simple level of analysis is strictly measured in seconds and minutes. In hyperactivity and impulsivity (discharge), for instance, reaction time is shown by acting out unthinkingly, acting before thinking. At the other end of the dimension, obsessive individuals are extremely slow in responding (delay). Thinking takes precedence over action.

Cycles and cyclical patterns as well as temporal perspective are examples of psychological time. The emphasis we give to past, present, or

TABLE 5.1.   Possible Pathological Consequences of Deviations in Controls*

Excitation ◄─────────────►	Inhibition
Discharge of impulses	Delay of impulses
Expression	Suppression
Expulsion	Retention
Alloplasticity	Autoplasticity
Externalization	Internalization
Extrapunitiveness	Intrapunitiveness
Extraversion + approach against	Introversion
Impulsivity	Compulsivity
Foreplanning limited	Foreplanning extreme
Acting out	Acting in or intellectualization
Internal controls minimal	Internal controls maximal (daydreaming)
Action maximal	Action minimal
Fantasy minimal	Fantasy maximal
Maximal facilitation of impulse discharge	Maximal interference of impulse discharge
Criminality	Thought disturbance

* From L'Abate (1964, p. 89).

future events can be influential in the following ways: (a) Overemphasizing the past at the expense of the present will affect the future and may produce dysfunctionality, such as depression or other psychopathological conditions; (b) overemphasizing the present without regard to the future will tend to produce impulsivity and acting out; and (c) overemphasis on the future without regard for the present and disregard for the past may produce drivenness (Table 5.1).

THE ELUSIVE NATURE OF TIME

The elusiveness of time is evident in biological rhythms, calendar subdivisions, macro- and microscopic views of time, and views of the past, present, and future. Like every living organism, we are governed by time. Because we exist at the mercy of thousands of intricately synchronized rhythms, time influences not only our activities, but our very being. Our hearts beat and the tempo of our pulse is in tune with our environment—tranquil or agitated. Likewise, the rhythm of the electrical waves of the brain adjust to sleep or wakefulness. Various cultures recognize the influence of time on the patterns of life. Throughout history, time has been called the great teacher, the great healer, the great legalizer, and the great leveler. In our experience, time may stand still, slip away, or fly past us. It can be saved or lost, spent or wasted, broken or killed.

Walker and Woods (1976), in a painstakingly detailed study of time uses in households, confirmed a hypothesis that seems relevant. They noted that family composition relates more closely to time use for household work than to any other variables. In relating time use for household work, they identified three significant variables: number of children, age of the youngest child, and employment of wives.

This study would seem to support the major contention of this theory, namely, that the family is the major context for individuals to learn to live in space and in time.

TEMPORAL PERSPECTIVE AND INDIVIDUAL DIFFERENCES

As McGrath (1988) noted:

> There are important cultural, subcultural, and individual differences in temporal orientations and perceptions, in the experience of time, in the tempo and pace of life, and in the allocation and use of time across potential activities. At the interpersonal level, many aspects of social interactions are marked by interpersonal synchronization of rhythms of behavior and recurrent cycles of development and socialization. At more macro-system levels—formal organizations, complex behavior settings, and sociocultural level systems—many critical problems center on key temporal issues such as temporal uncertainty, temporal conflict, and the inherent scarcity of time. (p. 9)

TIME AND PERSONALITY DEVELOPMENT

Without discounting other characteristics, the three major characteristics of time that are especially relevant to the present theory are (a) response latency; (b) time allocation and use; and (c) temporal perspective.

Response Latency

The two extremes of the distribution of control are defined by an immediate response, which implies discharge, as in immediate, reactive verbal rebuttals, oppositional responses, or quick actions, as seen in hyperactivity, impulsivity, and drivenness. The individual tends to respond with a very fast latency between the presence of a stimulus, such as a glance, a word, or a sentence from someone who is assumed to be important or in an authority position. Under these conditions, responding takes place with little if any thinking about the consequences of the response itself. The underlying behavior in immediacy is usually coupled to an attitude of "I know better." In criminal behavior, there is the additional attitude, "I won't be caught." Both attitudes suggest the absence of reflection and thinking, and the presence, instead, of defective controls.

At the other extreme of the dimension of control, there is a significant interval between the introduction of a stimulus, a glance, a word, a sentence, and the subsequent response. In extreme cases, there may not be any response at all. This delay is found when the individual is fearful of responding, being preoccupied by the consequences of the response as well as the meaning and implications of the stimulus itself ("I wonder what he meant by 'hello'?"). Interfering and controlling conditions such as sadness, anxiety, and worry may all be present when the response is late and inappropriate, as in obsessiveness and compulsivity.

Time Allocation and Use

Juster, Stafford, and their co-workers (1985) conducted one of the most extensive and exhaustive studies of time allocation in households, leisure time, and work, as recorded from diaries and other time estimates. It would be impossible to summarize all the rich data gathered by this team. The major implication of this research pertains to the allocation of time according to personal priorities, that is, we spend time with people and in activities that we deem important to us. Time is an indication of how we choose to live and with whom and what we want to live. Commitment to an intimate relationship may be assessed by how one partner spends time with the other partner. How work is perceived in relationship to the importance of the home can be assessed by how much time a person spends in the work setting in comparison to the home. The value of leisure activities can be estimated by how much time the individual spends in such activities.

Most often, individuals think that a particular activity, such as work, controls a great deal of their time. On the other hand, some individuals feel they control their time at work as well as at home or in leisure activities. In other words, people vary in how much control they give or keep in relation to their allocation of time. Some people see themselves as not having any choice, whereas others feel that they can decide how they are going to use their time. Time usage, to a great extent, depends on the individual's priorities (Chapter 12).

Thus, a time analysis of what an individual actually does versus what the individual says can be used as a measure of motivation. Time allocation, then becomes a measure of commitment, involvement, and priorities. For instance, many men report they spend as much time as their wives doing household chores. However, a time analysis of their household chores usually shows that women are still much more involved in household work than their male counterparts.

Temporal Perspective

Temporal perspective pertains to an individual's perception of the past, present, and future including the degree to which he or she feels controlled by these perspectives. Some individuals live for the moment, others live for the hereafter; some are not concerned by temporal restraints, others are so immersed in their past that they cannot live in the present; some only think of the future and tend to postpone any present gratification, whereas yet others want gratification of any kind immediately, as soon as they can get it and no matter how they can get it. Can we make any sense of all these individual differences in temporal perspective? Chapter 6 explores answers to this important question.

TIME AND INTERPERSONAL STYLES

An appropriate interpersonal style of a conductive–creative change-oriented nature means a balance of discharge–delay functions, leading to a positive outcome, such as negotiation and democratic problem solving. Inappropriate interpersonal styles of an abusive–apathetic or reactive repetitive nature (immediacy and impulsivity) are based on either overemphasis on too much discharge at the expense of delay or too much delay with little or no discharge (obsessions and compulsions). Under these conditions we would expect negative outcome in most interpersonal transactions. Thus, positive and constructive negotiation is more likely to take place in relationships characterized by a balance of discharge–delay functions, as in conductive–creative interpersonal styles, whereas no negotiation or unsuccessful negotiations would more likely take place in reactive–repetitive and abusive–apathetic relationships. A balance of discharge–delay functions would lead to interpersonal victories ("I win, you win") and eventually to successful negotiation and problem solving, but extremes in either delay or discharge or alternations between the two extremes would lead to defeats ("I win, you lose"; "You win, I lose"; "We both lose").

TIME AND PRIORITIES

Although the issue of priorities will be reviewed in Chapter 12, we need to consider some of its aspects here. For instance, Seltzer (1986) examined what she called "time-disordered relationships" which arise when an individual's various social spheres and role sets are not temporally synchronized. The three major types of relationships considered by Seltzer are (a) family; (b) work; and (c) age grade categories, such as the individual who marries late, returns to school, changes his major vocation, has children in middle age, or retires young. She employed categories to cover most responses to time-disordered relationships: (a) conformity (sameness), (b) rebellion (oppositeness), (c) innovation (similarity–differentness), (d) ritualism (symbiosis), and (e) retreatism (autism). On the basis of these responses, Seltzer suggested the following hypotheses:

1. The greater the degree of temporal asynchronization among the individual's various social spheres, the greater the number of time-disordered relationships he or she will have, and the greater will be the sense of stress.
2. Temporal asynchronization within a single social sphere produces less stress for an individual than does temporal asynchronization between spheres. The latter, in turn, produces less stress than the two in combination: asynchronization both within and between spheres.
3. The more an individual values a social sphere, the more stress will be produced by events that are temporally off schedule.
4. The more an individual views events that are temporally off schedule as being under his control rather than as being externally enforced, the less stress will be produced by these events.
5. The greater the success experienced in a given social sphere, the more activities that are off schedule in that sphere will be a source of stress.
6. Middle-aged and older people who view the scheduling of events as under their control perceive themselves as younger than do those who view the scheduling as externally imposed.

Bengtson, Olander, and Haddad (1976) formulated a conceptual model of family solidarity that in many ways resembles the present formulation in terms of differentiation and congruence as well as priorities (Chapter 12). Biologically and physiologically self-differentiation is formulated in the following ways:

(a) changes in the relative importance of various needs with advancing maturity; (b) changes in perception, cognition, and sensation with advancing age; and (c) changes in life outlook and responses to social stimuli, brought about by the idiosyncratic ways in which each person experiences life. (p. 241)

Socioculturally, Bengtson, Olander, and Haddad (1976) postulated a second set of factors to account for intergenerational similarities and differences: (a) Each generation is born into a different historical period, shaped by different social events; as a consequence, the personality system of each family member is formed in a different zeitgeist; (b) social institutions change over time, so that the various developmental roles (as student, parent, provider, and other roles) have different meanings for the numbers of successive generations; and (c) status in social institutions tends to increase with the years, and hence, gives the older person both greater rewards in the position and a greater stake in the status quo (p. 241).

Lauer (1981) concluded the following about the relationship between social change and social time in cultures rather than individuals: (a) Timing is crucial in planned change; (b) the success of an attempted change is a function of the sequence of activities that comprise the implementation of that change; and (c) a curvilinear relationship exists between the tempo of change and experienced stress; (d) the greater the tempo of change, the greater the gap between the generations; (e) the stronger the orientation to the future, the greater the willingness to change; (f) the greater the orientation to the future, the greater the value of activism; and (g) the greater the orientation to the future, the greater the tendency to democratization (pp. 143–144). Whether these generalization can apply to individuals remains to be seen.

TIME AND THE DEVELOPMENT OF RATIONALITY

Control functions of discharge–delay are basic to the development of thinking and cognition. Without controls, there cannot be time to reflect and to introspect, to plan and to consider available avenues of action or no action. The hyperactive child and the impulsive individual act out with little or no thinking; whereas the obsessive individual spends a great deal of time and energy reviewing all the various possibilities, pros and cons, without ever reaching a decision or acting. Without controls, thinking cannot develop in the child nor further mature in the adult, especially in developing a temporal perspective, an assessment and establishment of plans and goals and avenues of action to reach those goals. Thinking, reflection, introspection, planning, and considerations of pros and cons for any situation require the ability to stop and to delay action, concentrating instead on processing relevant information or acquiring relevant information. Hyperactivity, impulsivity, and acting out are the outcome of the individual's inability to delay actions and to think through the possible consequences of his or her behavior. (For a summary of all that is required in thinking, see L'Abate, 1986).

Relationships between discharge–delay functions and rationality are complex and difficult to explicate at this time. The model of rationality summarized in Figure 5.1 shows that the most relevant dimension of this model of discharge–delay functions relates to the impulsive–reflective dimension. Among the many dimensions that make up thinking and rationality, the dimension of impulsivity–reflectivity, on the lower left side of the figure, has been subjected to a great deal of research that cannot be summarized here. Briefly, then, impulsivity derives from discharge tendencies perhaps learned since childhood, whereas reflectivity derives from delay tendencies also learned since childhood. These tendencies may become amplified or corrected toward the middle as the person

Cognitive Styles

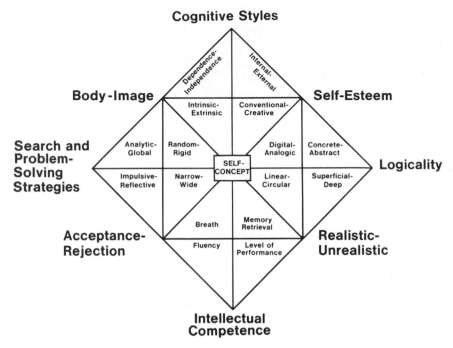

Figure 5.1. A model for rationality (R). From L'Abate (1986).

grows older. They may reach a peak and may become modified as the individual learns to correct them by balancing them more appropriately with age. The ability to think, however, is basic to the ability to negotiate.

TIME AND THE ABILITY TO NEGOTIATE

The ability to bargain, solve problems, make decisions, and negotiate is based on the ability to think through what needs to be done in intimate and interpersonal relationships. Perhaps negotiation with others is usually preceded by internal negotiation: what the individual is planning to do and is willing to consider as personally acceptable or unacceptable. It requires an invariant sequence of steps (L'Abate, 1986; L'Abate, Ganahl, & Hansen, 1986), such as focusing on relevant issues, expressing feelings about those issues, brainstorming on various courses of action, considering pros and cons for each course of action, deciding and agreeing on a preferred course of action, monitoring the success or failure of a course of action, going back to consider whether to keep on the same course of action, modify it if necessary, or switch to another course of action.

Extremes in Discharge–Delay Tendencies and Development

Extremes in discharge tendencies follow an unusually predictable developmental path. Other names in the psychopathology literature for the discharge dimension are externalization and alloplasticity; and for the delay dimension, internalization and autoplasticity. A child may begin to be negativistically oppositional, as shown by temper tantrums on one hand, or fearful, anxious, and phobic behaviors on the other. Aggression may appear either as sibling rivalry or shyness and feelings of inferiority and inadequacy (Rothman & Wetz, 1989). In adolescence, hostility may become out-and-out rebellion as in juvenile delinquency or acting out sexually, or may take the form of depression or anxiety. In adulthood, oppositeness and rebellion may take the form of many interpersonal conflicts at home and work or the opposite extreme of somatization and clinical depression (Table 5.2).

Relationships between Space and Time

Figure 5.2 illustrates and summarizes the relationships between both assumptions of space and time. On the horizontal axis, approach and avoidance are divided into internal and external. On the vertical axis, control is divided into subjective–receptive on the internal side and objective–expressive on the external side. The subjective side can be measured through many self-report measures of temporal perspective available on the market. Time can be measured objectively by rate and speed of response as well as by duration and frequency of time allocation.

TABLE 5.2.   **Extremes in Discharge–Delay Tendencies and Chronological Development***

Discharge Externalization Alloplastic	Age in Years	Delay Internalization Autoplastic
Negativism Temper tantrums Oppositeness	2–6	Phobias and fears Shyness Overconformity (sameness)
Hostile aggression Sibling rivalry	6–13	Feelings of inferiority and inadequacy
Rebellion Juvenile delinquency and/or sexual acting out	13–21	Depression and/or anxiety Early marriage Somatization
Marital, family, and/or occupational conflicts	> 21	Postpartum depressions Fears and phobias Single parenthood?

* Adapted in part from Rothman and Wetz (1989).

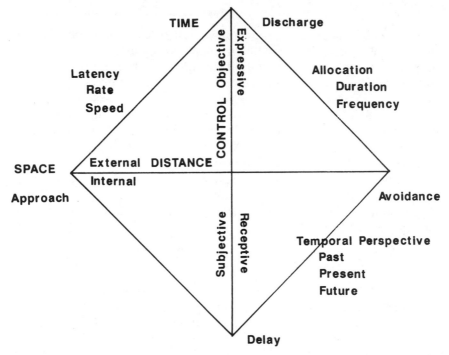

Figure 5.2. Relationships between assumptions of space and time.

Space and Time and Defensive Reactions

At a more complex level, both assumptions can be combined to provide a tentative classification of defensive reactions, as seen in Figure 5.3. The lower left quadrant of that figure, characterized by approach and internalization is the location of most functional defenses, such as admission of personal responsibility and error, the awareness of shame and guilt, and at a less functional level, placating at the intimate and interpersonal level (L'Abate, 1976). The lower right quadrant, characterized by avoidance and delay, represents suppression and repression at a functional level with dissociation, detachment of affect, and intellectualization at a less functional level. In the upper right quadrant, characterized by discharge and avoidance, are drivenness at a semifunctional level, and acting out, hyperactivity, externalization, and impulsivity at a dysfunctional extreme. The upper left quadrant is characterized by approach and discharge and features deception, blaming, and projection. Whether denial should be located in this quadrant is debatable.

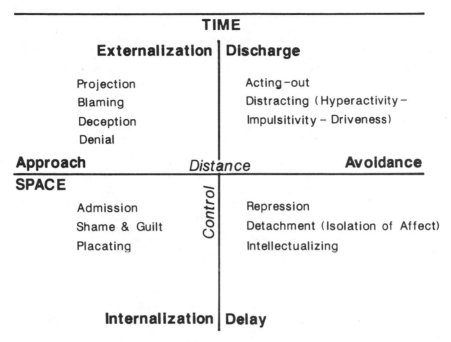

Figure 5.3. Assumptions of space and time and defensive reactions.

Approach–Avoidance, Discharge–Delay Tendencies, Dependency, and Intimate Relationships

The relationships among tendencies for approach–avoidance and discharge–delay with dependency in intimate relationships are summarized in Table 5.3. At the highest level of functioning, interdependence indicates what is a fact of life. If two or more people live under the same roof and are related by emotional, legal, or physical bonds and ties, they will have to depend on each other in a reciprocal fashion. Here is where mutuality, reciprocity, and synergism will be functioning. To obtain such a result, all parties involved in the interaction will have to mediate, modulate, and modify their approach–avoidance and discharge–delay tendencies to pay attention to the same tendencies of the others. Without an agreed-upon balance in both tendencies, there could be no order, continuity, and collaboration. At this level, the conductive–creative style would be present and functioning.

At an intermediate level of dependency, there would be either denial or overdependency producing or being produced by the inability to negotiate and mediate approach–avoidance and discharge–delay tendencies.

TABLE 5.3.   Approach–Avoidance, Discharge–Delay Tendencies, Dependency, and Intimate Relationships

Level of Dependency	Definition	Nature of Intimate Relationships
Interdependence	Balance of approach–avoidance and discharge–delay	Committed, equal, reciprocal, intimate; controls mutually shared; conductive–creative, cooperative–synergistic style
Denial of dependency versus overdependency	Conflicts in approach–avoidance and discharge–delay	Manipulative, competitive; controls imbalanced, conflictful, impulsive and/or delayed; reactive–repetitive style
Symbiosis versus autism	Extremes in approach–avoidance and discharge–delay	Abrupt reversals, from intensely explosive violence to extreme passivity and withdrawals; controls either lacking or extremely rigid, inconsistent, and/or contradictory; abusive–apathetic style

Where one would tend to approach, the other would tend to avoid. Where one would tend to discharge, the other would tend to delay. Hence, neither party to the interaction would be able to achieve satisfaction for her or his dependency. While one may value wanting to be dependent by taking care of the other, the other may not value such a dependency at all, looking at the offered care as a form of control and imposition. The reactive–repetitive style would be more likely to take place at this level of dependency.

At the lowest level of dependency, extreme dependency would result in symbiosis, while extreme denial of dependency would result in autism and alienation. Both conditions are seen in extreme battering and murder by one partner of the partner who wants to leave the relationship. Here is where physical violence, verbal attacks, and sexual abuse would be more common, if not commonplace.

Consequently, the three styles in intimate relationships, reviewed in Chapter 3, achieve further elaboration when both approach–avoidance and discharge–delay tendencies are balanced or unbalanced. Interdependence is seen in functional relationships where these tendencies are balanced with a conductive–creative style. Conflicts in the denial of dependency and overdependency are relevant at an intermediate level of dependency, as seen in the reactive–repetitive style. Extreme dependency is seen in symbiotic relationships while extreme alienation is seen in people who are unable to live with anyone else. At this extreme, the abusive–apathetic style is the norm. Further elaborations of this tripartite classifications will be made in the next chapter.

CONCLUSION

The experience and use of time relates to personality development and to how we choose to solve problems and negotiate issues in our intimate and interpersonal relationships. If we rush and react immediately, we foreclose any possible interpersonal negotiation. At the other extreme, if we delay arriving at a decision and consider the pros and cons of too many possibilities, we cannot determine what alternative to choose, if any. Somewhere in the middle of the discharge–delay continuum is the optimal range, where bargaining, negotiation, and problem solving are possible. To negotiate, we need another person. An internal dialogue may be necessary, however, to prepare for successful negotiation.

PART THREE

Modalities and Competencies

CHAPTER 6

Being Equals Presence

. . . meaning is born of interdependence. . . . Without relationship there is no language with which to conceptualize the emotions, thoughts, or intentions of the self.
(GERGEN, 1991, p. 157)

We appear to stand alone, but we are manifestations of relatedness.
(GERGEN, 1991, p. 170)

Being is a developmental process that needs to be distinguished from Doing (Chapter 7) and Having (Chapter 8). The purposes of this chapter are to (a) add further clarification to a definition of Being as presence, (b) grapple in greater detail with this seemingly difficult and theoretically evanescent concept, and (c) reduce it to concrete, visible, and possibly measurable processes. In Chapter 4, the assumption of space was viewed as basic to the ability to love, and in Chapter 5, the assumption of time was viewed as basic to the ability to negotiate. The latter had already been elaborated in a previous formulation (L'Abate, 1986). The process of showing, expressing, and sharing love—*being* with someone who loves us and whom we love—was also elaborated then as including at least three different sets of behaviors: (a) physical care, being able to care for ourselves and for others responsibly and practically (i.e., economically and physically); (b) seeing the "good" qualities in ourselves and loved ones that overshadow the "bad" ones; and (c) forgiving the "bad" in ourselves and in our loved ones. To forgive, we need to give up expectations of perfection, performance, problem solving, or production in ourselves and intimate others. Among other factors, forgiveness means giving up the perfectionistic fallacy of equating perfection with "goodness" and imperfection with "badness." Without these three basic processes, it would be very difficult to show love for anyone, including ourselves, because we need to share hurts and admit our inherent vulnerability to being hurt by those we love, fallibility in hurting them, and neediness of the very people we have hurt and who have hurt us (L'Abate, 1986). At the outset, to clarify all these notions, including the relationship between Being and Love, we must distinguish Being from non-Being.

BEING, DOING, AND HAVING

Personhood involves competency in Being ourselves, as well as in Doing and in Having. Interactional skills in intimate relationships are involved in Being. Being ourselves involves the ability to be intimate, to share the self with others while not losing or fearing the loss of self or of its unique boundaries. Doing things involves the ability to deal with information or data and to perform skills and services. Is it possible to be oneself without doing things or carrying out activities alone or with or for others? Having money and possessions involves the ability to earn a living and of buying judiciously what we need to survive. Being may involve the individual's whole presence, whereas Doing and Having may involve only parts of the self. Doing and Having are both objective. They can be readily measured. Being may seem more subjective at first blush, but can express itself in many objective ways, directly or indirectly, verbally or nonverbally (physically), consistently or inconsistently.

Non-Being is achieved through Doing and Having. To achieve and maintain meaning in our existence, we need to *be* with ourselves sufficiently enough to balance our Being and our Doing and Having. This balance may fluctuate over the life cycle, but our Being needs to be firmly in place and ahead of the rest. Without it, Doing and Having become empty and futile pursuits. Can we love ourselves without demands for performance, production, perfection, or problem solving? Can we love ourselves unconditionally without having to justify ourselves by either Doing or Having? Can we love ourselves while Doing or Having nothing?

Conflicts in the areas of Doing and Having derive from our inability to Be—to be in touch with ourselves and our feelings, and to share our innermost hurts and fears of being hurt with those who love us and whom we love; that is, we must be emotionally available. Conflicts and dysfunctionality derive from our inability to distinguish and separate sharply issues of Being from issues of non-Being, such as Doing and Having. Issues of Being deal with how close, caring, and compassionate we are with ourselves and with those we love, all of which require the sharing of feelings and of hurtful experiences. Issues of non-Being, such as Doing and Having, deal with power; decision making and problem solving require mostly negotiation.

Being comprises two separate, yet interlocking, processes: importance and intimacy, respectively (status) and (love) in Foá and Foá's 1974 original formulation. Functionally, Being as presence is defined by these attributes, among others: (a) showing commitment to growth for both self and (selected) others by being emotionally available to self and loved ones; (b) appreciating and encouraging self and loved ones; (c) spending time with loved ones; (d) having a sense of common purpose with loved ones; (e) being congruent between values and commitments of time and energy; and (f) showing positivity. None of these processes can take place, however, unless we are able to attribute importance to ourselves and to loved ones and to be intimate with them.

WHAT IS BEING? FEELING IMPORTANT AND GETTING INTIMATE

The first and major attribution that takes place in personality formation, between partners from the outset of their relationship and between parents and child from conception and even before, is the attribution of importance. Singer (1987) arrived at the conclusion that ultimately love consists of the "bestowal of value." This act of bestowal does not seem too different from the attribution of importance. Thus, love, the attribution of importance, is modulated and expressed through approach–avoidance tendencies on the basis of importance and of intimacy, as defined earlier (Chapter 4), as well as by how fast or slowly we do something for someone we say we love, by how much time we spend with the person, and how we perspect the past, present, and future with that person (Chapter 5).

Being Consists of the Attribution of Importance

Being consists of how important we think we are and how we attribute importance to our loved ones (spouse, children, parents, in-laws, siblings, relatives, and friends); it also includes intimacy, how intimate or emotionally available and present we are with ourselves and with loved ones. Being implies the ability to love unconditionally, without demands for performance, production, perfection, or problem solving. Presence, the ability to be emotionally available, is the major sine qua non condition for intimacy, the sharing of past and present hurts and fears of possible future hurts (L'Abate, 1986). This process is not negotiable; it can only be shared. Biringen and Robinson (1991) defined emotional availability as a relational construct, incorporating sensitivity, nonobtrusiveness, responsiveness, and involvement. Even though they applied this construct specifically to the mother–child relationship, there is no reason the same construct could not be expanded to family relationships in general and to the marital relationship in particular. Being, therefore, represents presence, defined as the ability to be emotionally available to self and to loved ones, that is, intimacy. Both modalities of Being, importance and intimacy, are almost completely missing or inadequate and distorted in addictions and in most psychopathological conditions and relationships.

Our sense of self-importance is basic to how we get along in our intimate relationships. How do we show and express this sense of importance? On the job, in our leisure activities, in superficial and short-lived meetings with acquaintances, co-workers, and neighbors. In chance meetings, we all are able to put up a good front, make a good impression, and even fool some people into thinking that we are OK. Are we? All of us can put of a socially acceptable, hail-fellow-well-met facade in brief encounters, but how do we behave in the heat and battle of intimate relationships? Although it is relatively easy to present a nice social facade in short-lived, superficial situations, it is much more difficult to hold onto that facade in prolonged, committed, interdependently private and phenotypical situations in our home (Chapter 1).

Being, therefore, represents the sense of self-importance that is not based on either Doing or Having. It consists of the sense of self-importance that we attribute and give to ourselves either before or after we learn from our caretakers that not to think well of ourselves is very costly. Importance is attributed and exchanged strictly on the basis of our existence: "I am important because I am and not because of what I do or have." This attribution is a decision that becomes part of the process of becoming an individual. If we do not think well of ourselves, who will? If we do not think well of ourselves and love ourselves (warts and all), why should anybody love us, especially our partners and our children?

This decision is based on at least three processes: (a) attribution of importance to self; (b) maintenance of self-importance to match its external manifestations; and (c) self-importance as the basis of personhood, identity, and individuation, partnership in marriage, and parenthood. When self-importance is achieved through either Doing or Having or both (i.e., through external rather than internal affirmation), a downfall is inevitable because these externalities come and go. Even when they last, individuals who achieve self-importance through these external means seem unable to relax and to enjoy themselves but are driven to achieve continuously a sense of importance externally rather than internally. What will happen once they reach the age and stage of being physically unable to carry on?

It is difficult if not impossible to attribute importance to others if we do not attribute it first to ourselves. However, all is not well with the whole concept of self-love and self-interest proposed by Perloff (1987), among others. He placed self-interest and altruism on the opposite ends of a continuum. But as Sevy (1988) indicated, he also invoked self-interest to explain philanthropy, which would fall more in the altruistic extreme. Thus, Perloff, as well as Locke (1988) and Corlett (1988), who were respondents to his article, still is not clear on the dimensions of selfhood defined by self-interest and personal responsibility. Locke took Perloff to task for criticizing Ayn Rand (1964), who emphasized the importance of "rational selfishness" in contrast to "mindless self-indulgence." Locke criticized Perloff for criticizing and misinterpreting the position of Ayn Rand. According to Locke (1988), Rand emphasized the concept of rational selfishness: "A rational person does not sacrifice himself or herself to others or others to himself (e.g., by indicating the use of force or fraud against) . . . contrary to conventional belief, rational selfishness, in practice, makes people more rather than less benevolent toward others" (p. 481). Locke also indicated how in altruism, fear, resentment, and guilt are three of the feelings that control the behavior. Corlett (1988), on the other hand, criticized Perloff for his misunderstanding of utilitarianism, which is to promote the greatest available good or foresee the best available outcome for the world rather than just for the self.

Thus, we have contrasting views about responsibility and selfishness, as emphasized already by Adler and discussed by Steffenhagen and Burns (1987). The whole concept of personal responsibility that Perloff attributed to humanists failed, however, to give relevance to real humanists. Corlett contended that personal responsibility was not as Perloff and other humanists would like us to believe: ". . . responsibility applies to actions freely done, not to choices freely made" (p. 482).

This confusion derives from the conceptual error that no clarity has been or can be achieved by defining various relationships as extremes of altruism, on one hand, and selfishness on the other, or to relate either of these two constructs to normality or to extreme dysfunctionality. We shall see how a model consisting of four polarities from the attribution of importance will allow us to clarify many of the conceptual confusions indicated by previous writers (Figure 6.1).

Being Consists of Intimacy

The ability to be intimate is the second aspect in the ability to love, the other side of the coin of Being as presence. The ability to be intimate is determined by how well or how poorly we attribute importance to ourselves and to loved ones. Being emotionally intimate with people we love and who love us—being close—represents the most difficult but also the most important task of our existence. To be close means to be physically present and emotionally available, without making demands for Doing or Having to ourselves or to loved ones. Being close to someone we love requires that we be in touch with our own vulnerabilities, fallibilities, and neediness. We need to be emotionally available to them when they need us, so that we can have them available to us when we need them. We need others and are needed when we and they hurt because of inevitable losses, failures, errors, and confrontations we all experience in life. We "know" that we love them and that they love us because they hurt when we hurt. Hurting together, and crying together, is the ultimate proof of our love for each other. Under these conditions, no Doing or Having are necessary. Being is paramount! Intimacy is present when equality of importance, commitment, and reciprocity of positive behaviors are present.

To be close to someone we love and who loves us, however, we need to feel separate enough as human beings to be available to them. This

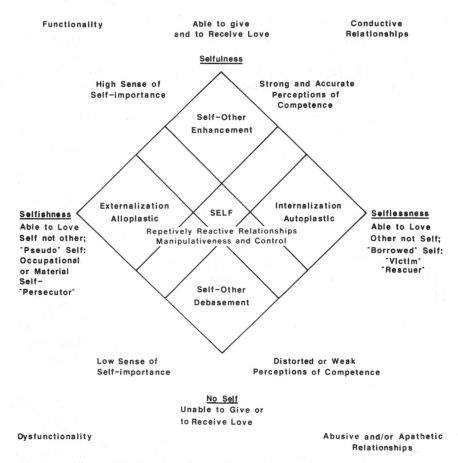

Figure 6.1. The domain of self-definitions and their excesses.

separation is based on our ability to love ourselves and intimate others unconditionally and to feel sufficiently important and in charge of ourselves to be available when they hit rock bottom and hurt. We need to be sufficiently strong to affirm them, reassure them, and console them, because we want the same when we hit rock bottom and hurt. Intimacy is the sharing of hurts. Without the assurance and reassurance of reciprocity in this sharing there cannot be closeness. Loving unconditionally means also forgiving ourselves for our stupidities, a process that allows us to forgive others for their frailties and mistakes (L'Abate, 1986).

Crosby (1985), Clark and Reis (1988), and Balswick and Balswick (1987) do not assume that love will breed intimacy. Intimacy involves crying together in the process of openly sharing fears and hurts. Although the specific aspect of tears may or may not be a valid indicator of intimacy (e.g., actors can turn them on and off for the camera and theoretically under other circumstances, also), most investigators would accept the open sharing of hurts and fears. Balswick and Balswick (1987) encompass communication, self-expression and volitional abnegation of self for the benefit of others in the concept of intimacy. This formulation would disagree with them. A person needs to have a strong sense of self-importance to attend to another's needs without loss of self. In every partnership, there must exist a way for the members to resolve differences of opinion and power struggles (Funt, 1988). Balswick and Balswick (1987) discussed the concept of negotiation within their discussions of intimacy and forgiveness. This formulation would suggest that intimacy and forgiveness cannot be negotiated. They can be shared as experienced feelings. The expression of these feelings—how the person is to be intimate and forgiven—may be subject to negotiation, but negotiation cannot take place unless feelings are shared beforehand.

Self-Importance and Self-Esteem

The concept of self-esteem is an evanescent one in the history of psychology, and defining it has always been difficult (Wylie, 1974). Self-esteem was prominent also in the thinking of Adler (Steffenhagen & Burns, 1987). As discussed in Chapter 2, among the various shortcomings of the self-esteem concept, the major concern is its intrapsychic and non-exchangeable nature. We do not love people on the basis of their self-esteem. We love them on the basis of how important they are to us. We are loved to the extent that we are important to selected others. More recently, Perloff (1987) emphasized the importance of self-interest as a substitute for self-esteem. Both self-esteem and self-interest are aspects, or facets, of the general construct of the attribution of importance to self and others. In this controversy, however, investigators have not differentiated between various types of self-interest or similar self-concepts. Up to the present, no model has allowed the user to differentiate among various manifestations of self-importance. We need a model that will permit a clearer and more useful characterization of the self-concept than the one achieved heretofore. This model will distinguish among self-definitions that acknowledge the importance of the attribution of importance, not only to the self, but also to selected others.

Being, Self-Importance, and Personality Development

The assessment of self-importance may be best discussed in terms of fuctionalities. Self-importance may be seen as a process of maturation, and we may gain understanding of self-importance in the manifestation of a complex of the following relationship skills or abilities: the ability to differentiate ourselves from our family of origin and from significant others (Bowen, 1978; Jung, 1954; May, 1953; Waanders, 1987); the ability to think and decide for ourselves (May, 1953; Taylor, 1986); the ability to recognize the value of self and others and to attribute value through behavior (McGee, 1987; L'Abate, 1986); the ability to accept ourselves (May, 1953) and our limitations (Becker, 1973); the ability to experience and acknowledge our own feelings (Crosby, 1985; Taylor, 1986) and the ability to communicate and share these feelings (L'Abate & Frey, 1981; L'Abate, 1986); the ability to connect and empathize with others (Carkhuff, 1980); the ability to make beneficial decisions for ourselves (Taylor, 1986) and mutually beneficial decisions in relationships (L'Abate & Hewitt, 1988a); the ability to be flexible and to adapt to situations without a loss of the sense of self (Crosby, 1985), and to attach meaning and significance to experience.

Once the positive characteristics of functional individuals are outlined, it becomes relatively easy to identify dysfunctional ones. They either do not show these characteristics or show their opposites: (a) Their intimate and interpersonal relationships are fraught with either overt conflict, or else conflict is denied or hidden from outsiders, covertly, within each individual or between partners, or from the children; (b) communication is unclear, inconsistent, and contradictory because the individual does not say what he or she means and does not mean what he or she says; (c) the individual is unable to engage in either responsive emotional support or responsible, effective problem solving; (d) the individual's outlook is generally pessimistic, dominated by an inherently negative approach toward life; and (e) few or no encouragements or intimacies are present in relation to loved ones, and instead, discounting put-downs, blaming, and insults result in explosions or withdrawals. The individual offers negative rebuttals and defensive counteractions in response to intimate others' behavior. The person who is in charge, or whoever needs or wants to be in charge, is subject to criticisms and discouraging remarks. No one can win with this type of individual, because if anyone wins, it is at someone else's expense. Perceived victories are Phyrric ones, winning while losing.

The most important aspect of this formulation is that basic to the way we all live is our sense of importance. How important do we feel we are? And how important are people who love us and whom we love? The first, basic, functional possibility, once we assert our importance, as well as the importance of others, is *selfulness,* which means "I'm important; you're important," leading to an "I win; you win" interpersonal outcome. *Selflessness* means "You're more important than I am," leading to a "You win; I lose" interpersonal outcome. *Selfishness* means "I'm important; you're not important," leading to an "I win; you lose" interpersonal outcome. The fourth possibility represents essentially *no-self,* whereby we have a no-win situation: "I'm not important; you're not important; neither one of us is important," leading to the double "I lose;

you lose" interpersonal outcome. All four possibilities and their implications will be elaborated in the rest of this chapter.

Consequently, a person's sense of self-importance is the basic internal determinant of most interpersonal situations, especially intimate ones. If we do not feel that we are important, we are going to let others walk over us; we will not be able to draw lines; we will not be able to model for others what it means to love one's self. By the same token, modeling selfishness (making others pay for our importance), or no-self (where no one wins) will lead to conflictful, if not destructive, relationships.

As discussed in Chapter 3, a continuum of likeness seems to be the major variable in attraction, mate selection, and parent–child relationships. The whole issue of likeness, however, may have been couched in limited conceptual terms as well as tested with limited methodologies. This issue includes four possibilities in the attribution of importance previously outlined: selfulness, selfishness, selflessness, and no-self. These attributions can be combined with different degrees of likeness in self-definition, ranging from dysfunctional symbiotic to autistic (the ΛΛ style) at the extreme of no-self, with sameness oppositeness (the RR style) in the selfish–selfless polarity, and similarity–differentness (the CC style) in selfulness, suggesting hypothetical links between the internal genotype, defined according to a continuum of likeness, styles in intimate relationships, and attribution of importance to self and intimate others (Table 6.1).

Selfulness and the Fully Functioning Personality

This section briefly examines the concept of selfulness in the context of the relationship of self and other. This possibility refers to the attribution of importance to self and to "other," who could be our spouse, our children, or our family of origin—whoever cares for us and for whom we care, who is involved with us in an intimate (committed, close, and prolonged) relationship. When this attribution of importance is reciprocal, asserting the equal importance of both parties, the outcome is usually positive, to the extent that behavior is consistent with this implicit or explicit attribution, resulting in shared victories. This outcome can be illustrated briefly by the "I win, you win" proposition, where the importance of self and of other produces equality in the relationship. Equality of importance in a relationship is expressed behaviorally in exchange patterns of mutuality and reciprocity in giving and in getting. Affectively, both equality and reciprocity result in intimacy, or the sharing of hurts and of fears of being hurt, including crying (L'Abate, 1986).

Personal, marital, and parental growth, competence, satisfaction, and contentment are the concomitants of selfulness. Within this possibility, joy, positive feelings, and the attainment of legitimate pleasures will

TABLE 6.1.   Likeness, Self-Definitions, and Styles in Intimate Relationships

Likeness Ranges	Styles in Intimate Relationships	Self-Definitions	Qualities of Relationships (Personal–Marital)	Outcomes
Similarity–differentness	Conductive–creative	Selfulness	Equal–cooperative Reciprocal–fulfilled Competent–contextual Satisfied Stable–growing	Affirmation Intimacy Interdependence Synergism Growth Functionality
Sameness–oppositeness	Reactive–repetitive	Selfish–selfless	Unequal–unhappy Sad–angry Impulsive–passive Unstable–polarized	Conflict Maladjustment in children Divorce Semifunctionality
Symbiotic–autistic	Abusive–apathetic	No-self	Extremely pathological Inconsistent–unstable mood and behavior	Chronic unhappiness Murder and/or suicide Incest Dysfunctionality Homeless dependence on welfare agencies Dysfunctionality

immunize the individual against illegitimate, or unacceptable and ultimately destructive pleasures, such as addictions. At best, this possibility includes only about 25% of the adult population that are immune to addictive behaviors and show limited psychopathology. Emotionally, selful individuals tend to experience, articulate, and express the whole range of feelings and emotions, without relying exclusively on any single emotion. This wide range of emotions is not the case in the following possibilities, where the range of emotions is restricted and limited.

In the selful position, the self is seen as whole, internal, and not in need of external resources. If there is any incompleteness or imperfection, this missing part is seen as the necessary aspect of being human and being, therefore, imperfect. Consequently, imperfections are not allowed to reduce the value of the whole self. Perfection of self is not needed to feel good about the self. Interactions with intimate others are built on the law of reciprocity, otherwise known as the Golden Rule: "Do unto others as you would have them do unto you." Such interactions and decision making manifest full selfulness. Selfulness depends not only on things that benefit the self, but, it is to be hoped, on a transcendence of the self to a larger whole, relationships with others.

A large part of the self remains connected, yet differentiated (Waanders, 1987), uncovering potentials through exploration of self in relationships, and in choice making (Taylor, 1986). Taylor discusses Kierkegaard's view that selfhood is a journey that is not always full of joy, but often full of despairing at the self's immature state. Individuals find themselves in despair when they do not live up to their full potential in life. In this despairing, they may choose to regress, to remain, or to move ahead into discovery. Selfulness may be seen as a process of developing relationship skills that the person learns by being involved in relationships. It is active, chronic, and perhaps extremely subtle at times. In discussing selfulness, functional abilities and competencies have intrinsic value and worth in their relationships with loved ones. It is through the development of relationships that one begins reaching for and achieving these competencies.

Selfishness and the Self-Centered Personality

This polarity refers to the attribution of importance to the self with a concomitant denial of importance of the other, leading to produce "I win, you lose," interpersonal defeats. The selfish individual, by definition, cannot win unless it is at someone else's expense, usually a loved one. Self-indulgence, self-gratification, self-centeredness, and self-aggrandizement are achieved through external means and sources. Self-gratification may take place, in some cases, according to socially acceptable behaviors, such as work addictions or exercise. In most cases, however, self-importance is achieved through illegitimate behaviors, as in most addictions. These behaviors may produce the short-lived euphorias and nirvanic conditions found in various abuses (alcohol, drugs, food, sex, shopping, smoking). Ultimately, someone pays a price for the achievement of such an outcome. Selfish individuals are essentially driven or addicted, going all the way from socially acceptable addictions such as work, to extreme cases of self-indulgence, such as substance abuse. Criminality is one of the most frequent forms of self-indulgence at the expense of someone else.

Selflessness and the Self-Defeating Personality

This polarity implies a denial of self-importance with a concomitant attribution of importance to the other, resulting in the defeating interpersonal pattern of "You win, I lose." What selfless individuals cannot get from themselves and from other human beings, such as love, closeness, and reassurance of importance, are gotten from food or from other substances or material goods. By the same token, love relationships may become as addictive as other substances or activities. This pattern is seen in many addictions involving overuse of prescription drugs or other addictions that are more widespread among women, such as food disturbances (overeating, anorexia, bulimia), love addictions, or overspending.

In the selfless position, the emptiness of self-definition brings about the need to be complete and, therefore, perfect. Since this goal is impossible, this position forces the person to borrow the identity of another, be it the deity, a saint, or someone seen as superior in status and importance, even the person's mate. Although part of this identification is either borrowed or vicarious, another part of the self, the "bad" part, views itself as a victim, especially when the external source is seen as the rescuer from imperfection, emptiness, and incompleteness, which constitute a state worse than death. Both selfish–selfless polarizations can produce extremes in each side as well as mixtures of both polarities; that is, a person can be both selfish and selfless at the same time, which would produce the no-self position, or alternate between the two polarities, going from selflessness to selfishness, as in the manic-depressive condition. Selflessness leads to self-debasing, self-defeating, dependent, depressed personalities, and manic-depressive personalities, including suicide. Suicide can take a variety of different self-defeating forms. Semi-functional individuals in this position are hardworking, perfectionistic, and extremely responsible.

The major characteristic of selflessness lies in the inability to draw lines. The person is unable to put limits on how others will discount him or her, denying self-importance, both verbally and nonverbally (the "condom line"). Individuals who show such characteristics, in various degrees and forms, are unable to put limits on themselves, their parents, their mates, and their children, becoming codependent, and therefore, becoming addicted to those on whom they depend (L'Abate & Harrison, 1992). They cannot draw lines to protect themselves and their bodies; they cannot draw lines to assert themselves; and they cannot draw lines to limit their partners or their children (especially sons, for selfless women, and daughters, for selfless men). For some of these individuals everything is negotiable, including contacting and marrying murderers or convicted felons.

The inability to draw lines derives from a sense of selflessness, a sense of emptiness, and the inability to fill this vacuum inside without any sense of self-importance. This sense in the selfless individual is all external just as the sense of self for the selfish individual is based externally, even though externals may vary. In some women, the sense of importance may come from giving to others, whereas the sense of importance for selfish men is achieved through receiving or taking from others. Either way, these individuals fail to establish an internal sense of self-importance that can only be given by ourselves to ourselves—nobody else is going to give us that sense of importance.

No-Self

This possibility might be reached as the outcome of most severe addictions and psychopathologies, where the individual denies the importance of the self and of the other, leading to a "I lose, you lose" interpersonal outcome. Here is where the most severe psychopathologies are to be found. Some of these psychopathologies may be free of addictions, because the individual is too dysfunctional and too out of touch with reality even to become addicted. Addictions transmit themselves from one generation to another through a process of socialization that repeats abusive behaviors modeled from the previous generation. Therefore, what may be transmitted is not genetic predisposition, as maintained by many researchers, but a defective predisposition in the attribution of importance, which more often than not is taken by the no-self position. Implications for expanding this model of self-importance to psychopathological conditions will be discussed later in this chapter.

Selfishness and Selflessness Equal Repetitive Reactivity

Whereas selfishness tends to produce more character disorders and criminalities, selflessness tends to produce self-defeating, dependent, depressed, and affective personality disorders, each with different kinds of addictions. Usually individuals who have been socialized for selfishness, mostly men, meet, match, and marry women who have been socialized for selflessness. The attraction between selfless women and selfish men is mutual because each needs the other to complement and assumedly fill and complete an incomplete self. Emotionally, most selfish men express themselves by externalizing feelings and relying on feelings of anger or euphoria; they tend to manipulate and control women through anger and ultimately, through addictions. Most selfless women tend to rely on internalizing fear, guilt, anxiety, and worry as expressions of their internal emptiness. Although selfish men may start as rescuers, they tend to become persecutors. Selfless women tend to become victims, rescuers, and martyrs, or, as they often describe themselves, "doormats." This incomplete attribution of importance produces a defective sense of identity that needs to be filled and fulfilled by defective means. Selfless individuals borrow identities, such as victim, deity, or partner; selfish individuals take on pseudoidentities, such as their occupational identity. Many selfish men do not have an identity separate from their occupational role. Selflessness produces a "borrowed self" for those individuals, mostly women, who need to identify and follow the examples, roles, and behaviors of an idealized leader, as if he or she were the person's own self. By the same token, selfishness produces a "pseudoself," for those leaders who want to create and fabricate an idealized public image of themselves for the purposes of attracting faithful followers. The most normative example of a pseudoself lies in the occupational identity of many individuals who assume their work identity as their main, lifelong guiding principle, with the parallel denial and discounting of other primary selves, such as "human being," "person," "husband/wife," and parent (L'Abate, 1986). Selfishness provides, for example, charismatic cult leaders, whereas selflessness provides the "sheep," groupies, camp followers, devotees, and fanatics of those very leaders. Both borrowed and pseudoselves or self-definitions tend to produce the Drama Triangle, consisting of victim, rescuer, and persecutor, which is at the basis of pathological relationships (L'Abate, 1986).

Another qualification could be made about the selfish–selfless polarity, and that is, stereotypically selfish individuals value work more than home, whereas selfless individuals value home more than work. Neither is able to spend a great deal of energy on leisure for the pleasure of leisure, for its own sake. They need to justify their existence by performing and producing either at work or at home. By the same token, the noself position makes it practically impossible to function in any one of these settings except in borderline cases, where at best, the person may be able to function marginally in one setting and poorly in the other two.

The dialogue that takes place between selfless women and selfish men is one where the woman is indecisive, uncertain, unclear, and in many cases so dependent on the man by asking him to make the decisions, acquiescing to his decisions, and essentially assuming all the responsibility, while he assumes most of the authority. He makes decisions; she carries them out. The particular separation of power, the inability to share power together, was demonstrated by a family where the man, a financial tycoon, essentially made all the decisions, and his wife, the daughter of missionaries, executed the orders, demanding that their two children take on all the household responsibilities. He was completely free of responsibilities. However, he wanted his orders, which included making menus for supper, to be carried out to the letter, and he checked out what everybody had done when he came home from work. His wife colluded with him strongly in following his domination blindly, obediently, and uncritically until the two children started acting out in adolescence. Even then, the father rejected any possibility of family treatment. Instead, he made sure that the children would receive individual therapy because neither he nor his wife was going to change. His wife was very supportive, sharing with him part of the authority while she essentially followed his orders.

In selflessness, gullibility is another way of fooling yourself into believing someone's story, no matter how unlikely. For instance, Jane came for help six months after she discovered that her husband Henry was having an affair with his secretary. He was slowly moving out of the house, even though he professed wanting to stay married to her. He suggested that they continue the marriage so that he could have two women available for his insatiable sexual needs, which also included occasional homosexual contacts. Henry was an extremely driven man who exchanged cars every six months, indulging himself in spending more than he could afford in buying clothes and suits, buying himself the latest computer hardware and software, and paying little attention to Jane or their children. He was involved in traveling a great deal. In some of these travels, he took along his mistress, who was willing to go along with this arrangement since he had promised her marriage and was buying her expensive jewelry. The selflessness of Jane was almost suicidal. She would allow him to come in and go out any time he wanted. She would go to bed with him and would have sex even though he either had sex with his secretary before he came home or called her after having sex with Jane, in Jane's presence. No matter what he did, she stood for it, or if she drew lines, the lines were always inconsistently and weakly applied. He, in turn, disregarded anything Jane said or did. She finally went to see a lawyer to serve him with divorce papers. Although the lawyer told her very explicitly not to tell the husband, she did it any way. He then started to manipulate her, even promising to come in for therapy. When he saw that Jane really meant business this time in wanting a divorce, he promised her that he would see the secretary for one last time and then let go of her. He asked Jane if she would mind if he went to the racetrack with his mistress because he had already bought the tickets?

More often than not, selfless individuals are able to give love but have difficulties in receiving it, whereas selfish individuals are able to receive love but not give it. Many clinical marriages illustrate the dialectic of this polarization, the selfish attracting the selfless, usually but not always, a selfish man marrying a selfless woman. Although this polarization may be the product of many sexual stereotypes, it becomes reversed when the woman is the most dominant in the relationship. Otherwise, the man is able to dominate the relationship through the primary importance of his work and his work identity (Doing), using finances and his role as provider (Having) as the raison d'être for his dominance.

At the beginning of the marriage, the selfless woman initially follows blindly and obediently in step with the husband's selfish ideals and plans until pressures (children, finances, husband being away at work, etc.) build up and she is no longer able to go on (L'Abate & L'Abate, 1981). At this point, she may ask the husband for what she wanted all along: emotional availability. By this time, however, the couple is too polarized to hope that the man will be able to become available emotionally to his wife, producing a feeling of letdown and discounting that will affect the relationship adversely. The more unhappy the wife is, the more distant the husband becomes, because he feels burdened by the wife's implicit or explicit accusations of failing her and her needs. She however, cannot state what she wants any more clearly than he does. As a result, both partners end up fighting at one extreme, or avoiding any form of confrontation at the other.

Gullibility, inability to draw lines; being fearful of rejection; being fearful of being independent; being submissive, obedient, conforming; being conventional—these are the characteristics that describe selfless individuals. All that is necessary to describe selfish ones is to use the opposite terms. For instance, what happens between selfish men and selfless women relates to the budgeting of clothes. The man, for instance, may need to dress for his career. His clothing needs take priority over the woman's needs. Consequently, it is more important to use the budget in buying clothes for him so he can look good at his place of business. It will be good for his promotion. Many selfless women may forgo buying clothes for themselves and instead allow the budget to be dedicated to the husband's needs. In that situation, more likely than not, this kind of woman, if a mother, also would allow some of the clothes budget to go to the children rather than to herself. This is part of the self-sacrificing characteristics of the selfless individual who will always put herself last. Sometimes this characteristic is excused on the basis of shyness. Or, it may have a basis in passivity and apathy; the woman expects to be taken care of by the man, cannot take care of herself, and leaves decisions and leadership to the man, who will eventually push the limits. Whereas selfless women as a whole are unable to draw lines in a consistent and firm fashion, selfish men push the limits all the time.

Selfishness develops from childhood. Very likely, the selfless mother was herself inconsistent, contradictory, and weak in setting limits for her son. He was raised and grew up without anybody saying no firmly except for the father, who may have paid little attention or may have been proud to see his son develop like a "man." The selfish individual not only will not accept lines drawn by the partner, but he or she will push them and very likely, in some instances, he or she will not accept limits set up by the job, boss, friends, and co-workers. The inability to draw lines is only matched by the selfish individual's inability to set boundaries for self, always pushing those boundaries, pushing to have more, to do more, and to get more, while giving little in return, especially to the partner.

Many selfish individuals are preoccupied with appearances. Appearance is very important to get promotions and to look good. The emphasis is on the facade of looking good and being "nice" and being "reasonable" to the outside world. These are some of the characteristics these individuals emphasize. They try to sell this bill of goods to the selfless partner, who sometimes buys it as being the reality that is shared with his or her family, rather than questioning the partner's perception of his or her own reality. Selfish individuals tend to interpret reality in terms of their own needs rather than the needs of others. Selfless individuals tend to interpret reality in terms of the needs of others rather than their own.

Selfless mothers produce selfish men (sons), who will grow up to be the opposite of them and like their fathers, and selfless women (daughters), who learn to be very much like their mothers. This is not a hard and fast generalization. Sometimes a son becomes identified with the mother and becomes essentially selfless, whereas a daughter may learn to be the opposite of the mother and very much like the father. The present formulation predicts that a ratio of one out of five exists between selflessness and selfishness. Four out of five selfless individuals are women; four out of five selfish individuals are men. The value of this ratio depends on what criterion is used to define selfishness and selflessness.

The selflessness–selfishness polarizations can be seen in who makes decisions to buy, who takes the leadership to buy what and at what price. The selfish one wants to buy "toys" (implements, cars, mechanical and electronic gadgets, utensils) for himself and considers his purchases to be more important than the purchases of the selfless partner. The selfless partner will not be able to draw a line as to how the money will be spent or may be extremely frugal and rigid in the use of money. One of the many major battlegrounds between partners polarized along the selfish–selfless dimension will be money as well as possessions. What goods shall be bought and who shall buy them and what are the decisions that cannot be made? In many cases, the woman who cannot take a decisive stance allows the selfish man eventually to preempt her.

In addition to decisions about goods and money, other battlegrounds are the division of household responsibilities and the kind of information that should be let into the house, ranging from television to newspapers to reading materials. More often than not, the selfless partner chooses to perform all the services in the house to leave the time free for the selfish partner to do whatever he or she pleases. This pattern is exemplified in the stereotype of the selfish partner guzzling beer in front of the television while the selfless woman sweats over the stove, cooking and cleaning. Many conflicts between partners pertain to power issues that focus around Doing (who shall render services, what kind of information should enter the house) and Having (who shall buy what, and once we have bought it, who shall use it). These major areas of conflict will occur in households of many polarized couples, and their children will learn very fast how to be either selfless or selfish according to gender identity and closeness to either parent.

One of the issues relating to the selfless–selfishness dimension is why do selfless individuals tend to marry selfish ones? The answer lies in how they are both raised and socialized by their parents. If a selfless woman is raised in a family where mother and father are fighting or bickering, or there is always a continuous state of tension, anything less than tension will produce boredom and emptiness. Consequently, this person will seek and find someone who can create the same level of uproar, the same level of conflict, the same level of chaos and abuse that existed in the family of origin. Likewise, a selfish man must find someone who is similar to his mother—who is willing to give and who puts no limits on him. Each gender has a hidden agenda of requirements for a marriage partner. Many selfless individuals, in talking about why they keep marrying the same kind of selfish, self-centered, self-indulgent men, mention that these are the only kind of men who "excite" them. Men who would treat them well, with respect and admiration, would bore them to death. In the same way, selfish men cannot accept a woman who asserts herself, who sets boundaries, who puts limitations on their behavior. Therefore, they will only accept women who lie down and allow them to do whatever they please.

Consequently, the marriage of selfless and selfish individuals is not a free choice to the degree that would be found in the marriages of selful individuals. It is an extremely determined behavior that can be predicted by the personality characteristics of the individuals. Selfish men usually assume a supermacho or conservative stance and values because these attitudes work best for their interests. It is important for the woman to be at home—barefoot, pregnant, and at prayer—so she will remain dependent and conform to their will. In many cases, these men will use brutal, physical, sexual, and verbal confrontations to assert their dominance. They may even use biblical scriptures to justify the obedience they demand from their wives. They see themselves as the ones with authority, making all the decisions, and with few responsibilities. The woman assumes all the responsibilities and none of the authority. In their marriage, therefore, they are repeating the same kind of conflictual marriage that existed in their families of origin.

The idea of changing by getting professional help is completely alien for many selfish men. They cannot see that any change should take place in themselves, although sometimes, begrudgingly, selfish men will allow their wives to get help. Two thirds of the workload of many therapists consists of women seeking help out of the many dilemmas arising from their marriages to driven or selfish men.

SELF-IMPORTANCE AND ACCEPTANCE VERSUS DENIAL OF SELF-IMPORTANCE

The self is an inferred process of development, where the individual is the focus of attention, as shown predominantly by the use of the pronoun "I" (Holland, 1985). The healthy narcissism necessary for selfulness, as an ideal interactive process, is illustrated by the evidence on invulnerable children who grow out of or learn to outgrow rather dismal family environments (Anthony & Cohler, 1987). In either reactive position—selflessness or selfishness—the "I" pronoun is given up or is used to enhance the self at the expense of the partner. Mainly in the constructive and conductive position of selfulness is the "I" pronoun used to affirm the self without putting anyone else down. This focus deals with a variety of attributed dimensions that are relevant and important to the individual, such as lovability, importance, impression, competence, mastery, and self-determination.

The concept of self-importance and parallel acceptance of self, as used in the marital relationship (Crosby, 1985; Marks, 1986), represents the cornerstone for playing various roles, as a person, as a partner, and as a parent (L'Abate, 1986). It has the function of integrating whatever is experienced or attributed to the self, serving as a modulating, moderating, and planning construct on how an individual sees himself or herself and how behavior follows from this definition. Self-importance and acceptance of self mean being able to tolerate ourselves as we are, warts and all, forgiving our errors, stupidities, and weaknesses, at times without criticisms or qualifications. This acceptance could be unconditional, without insights into our destructive behavior or it could be moderated, modified, and modulated by a critical appreciation of self as an ongoing, albeit flawed, process in continuous need of calibration and modification. The latter process is more evident in selfulness, where the self is accepted unconditionally. The individual, however, may also be sensitive to a parallel awareness of possible and potential sources of error. Thus, acceptance of self can be either unconditional but critical or unconditional and uncritical. Accepting the self does not mean being unaware of our shortcomings.

Acceptance of self implies also a certain degree of criticalness that allows us to consider our warts—their size and number—and decide what to do with them (i.e., eradicating them if they hurt too much or leaving them alone if they are irrelevant in intimate relationships). Hence, the process of critical self-acceptance is evident and effective in selfulness but inadequate in selfishness and selflessness, and practically nonexistent in no-self, where criticalness is nonexistent.

Denial of self or other means discounting, devaluing, ignoring, avoiding, and not dealing with one self or the other (meant as the loved one, partner, parent, or very close person). In this denial, the self or the other is considered as unimportant, as flawed and irrelevant to survival, as if that self did not exist. Thus, the individual's denial means the rejection of self or other as significant to existence. The extreme outcome of denial of self is suicide. The extreme outcome of denial of other is homicide.

Self-Importance and Attachment Patterns

How do individuals become socialized into the four types of selfhood? Typically, women who could be described as selfless tend to attract and be attracted by men who could be described as selfish and who, even before and certainly after marriage, tend to ignore them, discount and disparage them, put them down, and abuse them verbally, physically, and sexually. Children from these marriages tend to fall into one of these two patterns, often according to gender lines. Stereotypically, most boys follow the same characteristics of selfishness as their fathers, modeling in opposition (oppositeness) to their mothers and in conformity (sameness) with their fathers, according to the likeness continuum described in Chapter 3. Most girls model after their mothers (sameness), and in opposition to their fathers. Either type of socialization produces a defective, incomplete identification because, at best, the self is manifested and expressed only in reaction to someone and not independently of someone, as in selfulness. Consequently whoever is socialized according to abusive, apathetic, and repeatedly reactive child-rearing practices, will tend to learn to react to most stressful situations using inappropriate, abusive or apathetic, self–other destructive means of expression. These means could be directed against the self and/or against others. The incompleteness in the sense of self-importance will be expressed according to lifelong patterns learned automatically since childhood and internalized without verbal awareness, just as the child learns language. This reservoir of automatically learned habits and reactions, without the individual's awareness of how he or she has learned abusively apathetic and repetitively reactive patterns, is what Freud and others have called the "unconscious." We do not know and are not aware of these patterns any more than we are aware of how we learn to speak.

Support for this view can be found in robust and reliable results of the Stranger Situation developed by Ainsworth and her co-workers (1978), a study that has produced a great many cross-cultural and experimental confirmations (Bretherton & Waters, 1985; Mahoney, 1991; Parkes & Stevenson-Hinde, 1982). In this procedure, an infant (or child) and the mother encounter a stranger; the mother then leaves (abandons) the child and the stranger remains with the child. From this experience, four distinct patterns of attachment in children have emerged: (a) Pattern A is defined as *anxious avoidant*—after reunion with the mother, the child avoids eye contact with mother and does not cling to mother; (b) Pattern B is defined as *securely attached*—once mother comes back, after a short outburst the child becomes quickly reorganized and resumes playing; (c) Pattern C is defined as *anxious resistant*—the child deploys anger and contradictory patterns of alternating between seeking and resisting contact with the mother, very much in an oppositional fashion (e.g., wanting to be picked up when released and wanting to be released when picked up); and (d) Pattern D is defined as *disorganized disoriented*—it is characterized by two different patterns, controlling-punitive and controlling-caregiving.

In these four patterns, the researcher can find the seeds of self-importance. For instance, pattern B may more likely lead toward

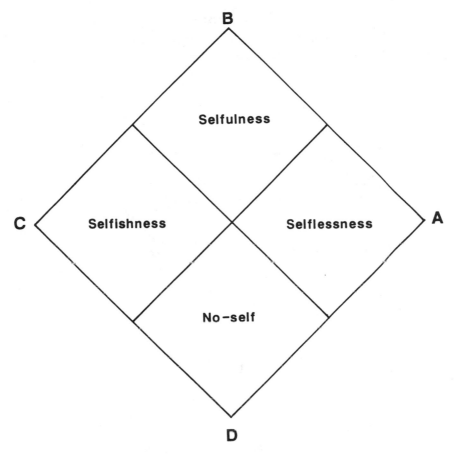

Figure 6.2. Attachment types and selfhood.

selfulness, whereas Pattern A may eventually lead toward selflessness. Pattern C may lead toward selfishness. Pattern D may lead toward no-self. These extrapolations are shown in Figure 6.2.

SELF-IMPORTANCE AND DEPENDENCY

These four patterns of selfhood also may relate to dependency, as shown in Figure 6.3. We would expect that individuals in the selful position would interact in an interdependent fashion with intimate others. Individuals characterized by selfishness would interact by denying their dependence. Individuals characterized by selflessness would interact in a dependent fashion, as shown in so-called codependency (L'Abate &

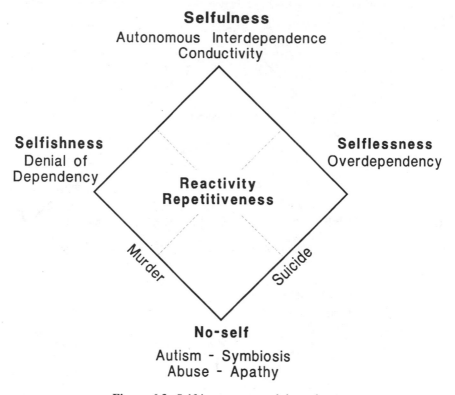

Figure 6.3. Self-importance and dependency.

Harrison, 1992). Individuals characterized by no-self would interact in either a symbiotic fashion or in a alienated fashion, denying their dependency on one hand and being dependent on the other.

SELF-IMPORTANCE AND EMOTIONS

Most theories of emotions shy away from predicting specific patterns of emotionality with specific personality characteristics (Mahoney, 1991). On the basis of the self-importance model presented here, we can begin to hypothesize possible connections between the four selfhood polarities and emotionality, as summarized in Figure 6.4. The feeling that is fundamental and relevant to all human beings is hurt, that is, traumas, stresses, threats, griefs, mournings, mortifications, put-downs, and all the experiences, humiliations, anguishes, sorrows, and sufferings that include psychological or emotional pain (L'Abate, 1986, submitted for publication). We cannot live and not be hurt, no matter how protected we may be by

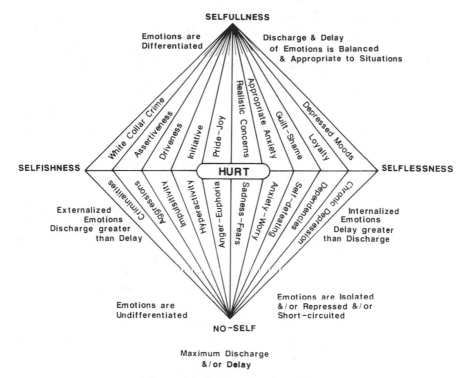

Figure 6.4. Selfhood and emotions.

our caretakers. Furthermore, if we do not learn appropriately to deal with these hurts, we cannot grow to be fully functioning human beings. In selfulness, emotions are differentiated between what the person experiences and feels and what and how that person expresses him- or herself. Furthermore, the selful individual can distinguish between various feeling states appropriate to the situation. In selfulness, the individual experiences and expresses hurt feelings in an appropriate fashion, using intimate others to share whatever hurtful experience or event may have taken place, finding and using being intimate with loved ones to decrease the level of hurt. The individual is able to process feelings using rationality as a bridge between the experience and the expression of hurtful feelings, as illustrated by the ERAAwC model (see Chapter 1).

In less than selful positions, the experience of emotions is not differentiated and distinguished from its expression. When emotions are expressed, they may involve the lowering of self-importance of either self or others. In selflessness, there is an abundance of worry, anxiety, depression, and—in the extremes—suicide, either emotional or physical. In selfishness, the prevalent emotion is anger, displayed as hostility and revengeful infliction of pain to others to make up for pain suffered by the self. The avoidance of painful or even unpleasant feelings brings about impulsive or explosive acting out where an external target needs to be destroyed. Here the concept of being is nonexistent. Feelings are expressed through doing or having.

In the no-self position, emotional experience is either not expressed at all, although it may be felt at the physiological level, or it is expressed through violent, suicidal or murderous outbursts. There is either avoidance of emotional expression, or the expression is destructive. There is very little in between these two extremes. Intimacy, then, can be achieved in selfulness, questionably in selfishness and selflessness, and certainly not in no-self.

The central importance of the experience and expression of hurt is especially relevant to how we "know" we love someone. The best way to find out whether we love someone is to see whether we can share our hurts together. Sharing hurts is, indeed, the ultimate proof of love. Sharing hurts means allowing ourselves to be vulnerable, admitting our frailties and fallibilities, and accepting our inherent neediness as human beings. However, it takes a great deal of strength to admit being vulnerable, fallible, and needy. Hence, only people who can be in charge of themselves, "strong" selful ones, can allow themselves to be and to be seen as "weak." Crying, then, becomes the ultimate expression of this process, when we share our hurts with someone who is willing and able to reciprocate with us at the same level. Crying indicates that we feel "bad" and show congruently, in words and deeds, what we feel. People who perceive themselves as "weak" or are afraid to be perceived as such, cannot let themselves go and admit to their inherent vulnerability. Hence, intimacy can be achieved mainly by individuals who are strong enough to allow themselves to be weak (L'Abate, 1986).

SELF-IMPORTANCE AND THINKING PATTERNS

Chapter 5 presents and summarizes various rational processes that make up what we call rationality. Very few authors, however, have been able or have been courageous (or foolish) enough to hazard possible links between personality patterns and different thinking strategies. The self-importance model allows taking the risk of predicting some possible relationships of this type. Hypothetically, creativity may be found on the side of a certain amount of creative selfishness, between selfishness and selfulness (Figure 6.5). On the other hand, conventionality seems to be the major pattern of thinking for individuals on the selful-selfless side. Criminal thinking, on the other hand, would be found more likely on the selfish–no-self side, whereas confusion would be found more likely on the no-self–selfless side of the selfhood figure. These hypotheses are

Figure 6.5. Self-definition and thinking patterns.

only tentative, however, because a great deal depends on the operational definitions of all the constructs in this prediction. In arriving at these definitions, we need to consider the dialectical nature of these four patterns of thinking; that is, creativity may derive from confusion, and criminality may be the outcome of conventionality.

In commenting on the relationship between creativity and personality functioning, Arieti (1966) noted how similarity has a function in creativity as well as in psychopathology:

> The seriously ill schizophrenic, although living in a state of utter confusion, tries to recapture some understanding and to give organization to his fragmented universe. This organization is to a large extent reached by connected things which have similar parts in common. Many patients force themselves to see similarities everywhere. In their relentless search for similarities they see strange coincidences, that is, similar elements occurring in two or more instances at the same time or at brief intervals. By considering these similarities as identities they attempt to find some clarity in the confusion of the world, a solution for the big jigsaw puzzle. (p. 726)

By the same token, in creativity and scientific pursuits, innovation takes place in making connection or seeing similarities where no such connections had been made heretofore: "The creative leap occurs when observed facts are correlated; that is, when by perceiving a heretofore unsuspected identity, a conjunctive path or a new order is discovered"

(p. 736). The conditions Arieti considered important for creativity were: (a) aloneness, (b) inactivity, (c) daydreaming, and (d) remembrance and inner replaying of past traumatic conflicts. Arieti, therefore, considered the ability to think in terms of similarities a common guiding principle in normality as well as in creativity and psychopathology. The difference between the creative and the psychopathological process lies in finding validity in the former and invalidity in the latter. The creator interfaces similarities from disparate and discordant sources in a way that eventually becomes recognizable to other observers. Such consensus is absent in the similarities of disturbed individuals.

SELF-IMPORTANCE AND TEMPORAL PERSPECTIVE

In taking the risk of predicting further links between the selfhood model proposed here, it is possible to go even further and hazard possible hypothetical links between selfhood, temporal perspective, and speed of response (Figure 6.6). On the vertical axis of temporality, in selfulness there would likely be a healthy concentration on the present and on the future, with little negative influence from the past. In selfishness and selflessness, there is greater stress on the present as still affected by the past; whereas in the no-self position, the individual cannot separate from the negative past and may be completely influenced and dominated by it at the expense of the present and the future.

On the horizontal axis of Figure 6.6, speed of response should be appropriate in selfulness, fast in selfishness, slow in selflessness, and contradictorily either fast or very slow in no-self.

SELF-IMPORTANCE, PERSONALITY DEVELOPMENT, AFFECTIVE DISORDERS, AND PSYCHOPATHOLOGIES

From this model of self-importance, we can derive a classification of the psychopathologies. From a position of selfishness, extremes in narcissism, sadism, and criminality are derivable. From selflessness, we can trace extremes in masochism, depression, and affective disorders (Glickauf-Hughes & Wells, 1991; McGrath, Keita, Strickland, & Russo, 1990; Sobel & Russo, 1981). A no-self position evokes more extreme psychopathologies such as borderline personalities, addictions, dissociations, homelessness, and psychotic conditions. Figure 6.7 expands this model to various psychopathologies as supported by the research of Wolf, Schubert, Patterson, Grande, Brocco, and Peddleton (1988), among others. These investigators performed a factor analysis on items from structured interviews of 205 psychiatric inpatients. They isolated three different groups. Group 1 consisted of individuals

Figure 6.6. Selfhood and temporal perspective.

diagnosed as alcoholics, antisocial personalities, and drug dependent, a group that the selfhood model would describe as selfish. Group 2 included individuals diagnosed as showing symptoms of primary depression, mania, and secondary depressive disorders, a group that this model would describe as selfless. Group 3 was made up of schizophrenics, which the model presented here would describe as no-self, representing extreme forms of apathy from past parental and familial abuses (see Figure 6.7).

Psychometrically, RR and AA patterns (Chapter 3), as measured by the MMPI, show as high peaks on Depression (Scale 4) and/or Anxiety (Scale 8) for the selfless position and as high peaks on either the Psychopathic Deviate (Scale 4) or the Mania (Scale 9) or both for the selfish position. In other words, in clinical marriages, a self-centered, oftentimes narcissistic character disorder or driven ("selfish") individual usually marries a fearful, dependent, and scared ("selfless") individual, as discussed earlier. The selfish position usually implies an exaggerated denial of dependency and proclamations of alleged autonomy, whereas

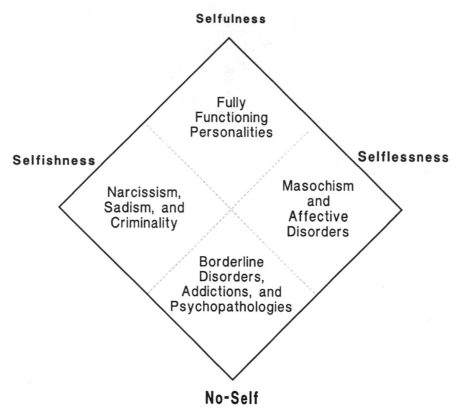

Figure 6.7. Selfhood, personality, affective disorders, and psychopathologies.

the selfless position parallels an exaggerated need for dependency and conformity.

In elaborating on relationships between a continuum of likeness (Chapter 3) and the model of self-importance, the following links can be proposed. The most common polarity of sameness–oppositeness is in contrast to a behavioral explanation of straightforward modeling. Modeling theory would only describe the conforming side of behavior, but would be at a loss to explain oppositeness, including rebellion, noncompliance, and nonconformity. Thus, individuals who use the selfish position (mostly men) would be characterized by an identification of oppositeness, usually to their main caretaker, the mother; whereas individuals using the selfless position would be characterized by blind and unquestioning conformity to their caretaker, or sameness. Once individuals characterized along these extremes attract and marry each other, they develop a reactive marital pattern characterized by rebuttals, revengeful reactions, and essentially a repetition of the same–opposite dialectic developed from their families of origin (L'Abate, 1986). In extreme cases, where behavioral apathy and emotional atrophy are present, physical, verbal, or chemical abuse follow and develop, if not in the couple, in their offspring.

From this continuum of likeness, it is possible to derive that selflessness grows from a family context of blind conformism or sameness, and selfishness grows from a family context of rebelliousness or oppositeness that attacks parental values. In terms of parental practices, no-self would grow from abusive–apathetic parent–child relations, where only physical survival functions, such as food, shelter, and clothing are minimally available. Reactivity in both selflessness and selfishness derives from parental practices where attention and love are contingent and conditional to the child's behavior; that is, the child received the minimal attention required, but this attention is usually reactive to the child's immediate needs rather than determined by the caretaker. Only in selfulness are parental practices noncontingent. Attention to physical as well as psychological needs is given freely, at will, and unconditionally, regardless of the child's behavior.

Therapeutically, this type of marriage produces husbands who deny any need for professional help (Fenton, Robinowitz, & Leaf, 1987; L'Abate, 1987b) unless they become depressed because of business reversals and failures, middle-age crises, and threat of divorce from the wife, or the development of misbehavior in the children. Their wives, who admit the need for help, assume a rather helpless, hopelessly dependent, and oftentimes depressed position in therapy. Once the initial depression is under control, and assuming the husbands refuse to join their wives in treatment, it might be useful to have these women develop a written Bill of Rights for themselves, setting up boundaries and guidelines about what they will accept or will not accept in the relationship (L'Abate & Harrison, 1992). They need to be taught how to deal with their husbands as adults and how to prevent manipulation by abuse, coercive anger and reactive explosiveness.

The classification derived from a model of self-importance is also in line with the classification of depressed individuals by Arieti and Bemporad (1980). They described three different types of depressed individuals. One type, whom they described as being made up mostly by women, would fit into the category of "selflessness." Typically, these women were described as self-sacrificing, self-blaming, diligent in their work and obediently submissive "to obtain praise and support from her husband" (p. 1359). Their self-esteem was derived mostly from their reliance and dependence on the dominant other: "She derived her satisfaction, indeed meaning, from pleasing her husband and being a model housewife and provider. She had little sense of self apart from her relationship with her husband and could not conceive of living without him" (p. 1361). The second type of depressed individuals, made up mostly by men, fits into the selfish polarity. Arieti and Bemporad described this individual as being organized around a:

> . . . dominant goal of success, achievement, and glory, mostly for the sake of the goals and to satisfy their self-esteem, which is inextricably bound with this goal. This type of men [sic] are described as being "seclusive, arrogant, and obsessive" driven to the point that they made it difficult for others to collaborate with them. The marriage of one of these men was described thusly: "His marriage was, at best, a disaster. He expected his wife to plan her life around his work and expected special treatment from her because of the alleged importance of his work. He had no hobbies or interest but was consumed by fantasies of his glorious future, when everyone would respect him and treat him with deference." (p. 1362)

Arieti and Bemporad considered the third type of depressed individual to be much more dysfunctional than the two previous types because of the chronic inhibition of any type of pleasure and almost no involvement in everyday activities with anyone. They were either men and women who lived mostly for and with their work and had no meaningful relationship or tie to anyone. Most individuals in this category would fit into the no-self position. According to Arieti and Bemporad, these individuals never married or their marriages were too short-lived to make any impression. The conclusion that is relevant to the thesis of this chapter, according to Arieti and Bemporad, is:

> Depression is related to sadness but also implies a deviation from the normal way of experiencing sadness. Sadness (the normal responses of the human being when apprehending a situation that he would have preferred had not happened and that he considers adverse to his well-being) has positive values . . . In other words, the normal person is able, to a large extent, to metabolize sorrow and sadness. On the other hand, the person prone to depression in many instances lacks this capacity." (p. 1365)

GENDER DIFFERENCES AND SELF-IMPORTANCE

From the proposed model of self-importance, we can derive some specific predictions that can be verified, at least epidemiologically. This model considers that each of the four quadrants in the self-importance model (Figures 6.2 through 6.7) includes approximately 25% of the population ($\pm$ 5%). As far as sex differences go, the two top and bottom quadrants of selfulness and no-self contain an equal number of men and women, but the two middle quadrants of selfishness and selflessness contain much more disparate sex ratios. Women in the selfless position make up at least 80% or four fifths of the individuals in that quadrant. The reverse is estimated in the selfishness quadrant, where approximately 80% are men. Thus, one out of five individuals in the selfless category are men, and one out of five people in the selfishness category are women.

The reasons for these percentages and reversal between the genders can be found in the following arguments and data. Twenty-five percent of the population is included in either the selfulness or no-self categories; that is, there are no sex differences in either good adjustment (selfulness) or very miserable adjustment (no-self). Sex differences are pronounced in the selfish-selfless categories. A variety of data would support that conclusion: (a) The Manhattan project found that only 20% of the people interviewed were free of neurotic symptoms; and (b) Only 10% of most couples interviewed considered themselves to be "happy," or by external evaluations "well adjusted."

As far as the sex ratios in the selfishness–selflessness categories are concerned, earlier arguments suggested that, as a whole—at least in the past—some women may have been socialized for selflessness, whereas some men may have been socialized for selfishness. The data that need to be considered are as follows: (a) 95% of all battered individuals are women, the rest (5%) are men; this means that 95% of batterers are men; (b) more somatic internalizations occur in women than in men, with a ratio of five to one (Robins, 1986, pp. 236–237); and (c) more instances of anxiety, depression, and related disorders (self-defeating and/or dependent personalities) take place in women than in men (Barrett, Biener, & Baruch, 1987; Cleary, 1987), whereas men have higher ratios of acting out, character disorders, and criminalities. This pattern occurs because (a) women, who are socialized to give more than to receive (Belle, 1987), participate in larger social networks and enjoy confiding relationships more than men, who usually rely on just one supporter, the wife; (b) more women are socialized to care about people and their problems than men and are more likely to provide help to them than men (how many nurses or social workers are men?), so they are affected by interpersonal stressors more than men (Wethington, McLeod, & Kessler, 1987); and (c) there are substance-specific sex differences (Biener, 1987)—women use prescription psychotropic drugs more than men, who use alcohol much more than women.

No wonder women live longer than men. Their self-definition is consistent with their homemaking role, but men must have other tasks that will help them make up for the loss of self-definition through work. However, if the self is not defined in its most human terms ("I am a human being first, husband [wife] second, and parent third"), then retirement can be such a loss that nothing is left to the self. This, tragically, is why many men die shortly after retirement.

EVALUATION OF THE SELF-IMPORTANCE MODEL

To evaluate the validity of this model, some points need to be made beforehand:

1. It is better to make specific, testable predictions and be wrong than to make general and untestable predictions that are always right. Consequently, all the predictions that are made from this model need to be evaluated and tested. They can all be tested on a variety of grounds.

2. This model predicts that only 25% of the total of the total population will reach an acceptable level of selfulness; 50% of the population will reach a reactive-manipulative level of self-importance, either on the selfless side or the selfish side; and 25% will remain essentially in the no-self category. Specifying these percentages will allow an epidemiological evaluation and validation of this model (a) against the rates of so-called healthy and functional couples and families, (b) versus all the depressions on one hand, and (c) acting-out criminal behaviors on the other, and (d) plus the percentages of people who are diagnosed as having some kind of a psychiatric condition above and beyond depression or criminality.

This model then would allow us to evaluate norms according to various cultures and see whether there is a fit with epidemiological data rather than with anything else that has been made up. Again, this is part of the "better to be specific and wrong" than to be "general and right" concept. In this way, the model can be evaluated not only epidemiologically but also in other ways. Evaluation of the model can take place through a paper-and-pencil self-report test, the Problems in Relationships Scale (PIRS), already published (L'Abate, 1992a). Evaluation of the model can take place also through a workbook especially derived from the model. This sort of validation will be discussed at greater length in Chapters 13, 14, and 15.

CONCLUSION

In this chapter, a model of self-importance has been proposed that is linked to individual differences in styles in intimate relationships, gender differences, attachment patterns, dependency, emotionality, thinking, temporal perspective, and psychopathology. The admittedly grandiose nature of this model requires further epistemological and empirical validation.

CHAPTER 7

Doing Equals Performance

. . . Activity may become manifested in mental as well as physical activity and be evidenced in approaching any situation by engaging in some sort of action.
(BURKS & RUBENSTEIN, 1979, p. 55)

Doing is made up by the acquisition or propagation of information and the performing and receiving of services. The ability to process, retain, and apply information from our environment requires activity. We cannot hope to acquire and retain information passively. Acquisition of information is an active, relational, and interactive process, as shown by the caretaker teaching a child to speak. The child must interact with the speaker by paying attention and imitating the speaker's sounds. The acquisition of this information eventually becomes transformed into services, as in education first and in a job later on in life. Thus, in addition to love and status, another major resource exchanged between caretakers and children is information. It may consist of nonverbal and verbal messages first and of written messages later on. This information is received first and given out and exchanged later.

Functionally, Doing as performance is defined by (a) flexibility and adaptability in fulfilling role demands; (b) balance in the use of internal and external resources; (c) ability to communicate; (d) agreed-upon rules, values, and beliefs that demarcate duties and responsibilities; (e) varied repertoire of coping strategies; and (f) ability to engage in problem-solving activities that will result in the resolving of issues and of stresses (Dunst, Trivette, & Deal, 1988, p. 25).

Education is the major example of how information first is acquired and later on exchanged for services. However, before the introduction to formal education, the child receives most information through play and exploratory activities. Thus, activity is basic to the acquisition of information and the performance of services. Figure 7.1 shows a summary model for activity. Activity for activity's sake, without a goal or a context is essentially meaningless. Performance has meaning only when viewed within a context, or a specific setting, be it home, work, or leisure-time activities. Chapters 9, 10, 11, and 12 will consider activity within its relevant contexts.

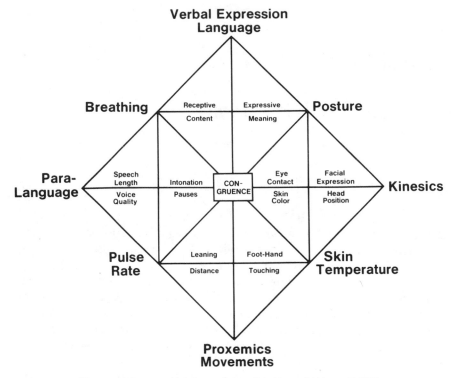

Figure 7.1. A model for activity (A). From L'Abate (1986).

When the child starts to receive information, the family, therefore, becomes the first information-processing system. The child receives information from what family members talk or do not talk about and from what is allowed or not allowed into the home in terms of visitors, newspapers, books, magazines, television programs, music, or just noise.

Thus, by stressing the importance of activity, we cannot underestimate the importance of exploration and play in the development of personality and interpersonal competence. Education does not need to be formal. A great deal of information is acquired in the processing of curiosity, creativity, and confidence—what a child is allowed to approach and avoid. Play, sports, and extracurricular activities are all important in acquiring information and developing the ability to perform services for self and for others.

THE RELATIONSHIP BETWEEN INFORMATION
AND SERVICES

Foà and Foà (1974) found a significantly negative correlation between information and services, indicating that people who are interested in acquiring or producing information may have a different value system from people who are interested in services. This negative relationship is not at all surprising because people interested in services are not usually interested in acquiring or propagating information. Among psychologists, for instance, there is a wide schism between experimental psychologists, interested mainly in acquiring, testing, and propagating "scientific" information, and clinical psychologists, interested in applying that information, even if it is not purely "scientific."

The same kind of cleavage exists in many areas related to information, such as schools and universities. Many faculty members in the arts are quite contemptuous of colleagues in applied departments. Physical theorists look down on engineers, inorganic chemists look down on organic chemists, and so on. Were it not for continuing education requirements, many service-oriented professionals would not keep up with advances in their fields of expertise. The temporal perspective of these two value systems may be different. Those interested in information may have more transcendental goals than those interested in performing services where the immediacy of giving and receiving may be greater. Even among applied psychologists, there may be differences between those who perform psychotherapeutic services for a private practice versus those who are interested in prevention, according to a public health model. The dimension of discharge–delay (Chapter 5) may be relevant here.

THE NATURE OF DOING

Doing is characterized by at least three relevant processes: (a) performance, (b) problem solving, and (c) perfection.

The Meaning of Performance

Many of us, under stress or as a way of life, feel that we need to perform and to be active to justify our existence. If we work hard and work well, somehow we shall be rewarded, either here or in a hereafter. Doing, under these conditions, is equated with the self as a "doer" to the point, sometimes extreme, that performing becomes the ultimate and only goal in life. This pattern is shown by the lives of workaholics, driven obsessively to work for the sake of work, forgetting anything else in life but the

compulsion to work. It could be housework, as in the lives of perfectionistic homemakers, or it could be work in the marketplace. Either way,
when these individuals are asked whether they could stop working, the
answer is an amazed look, followed by a reply to the effect that only two
major states of being are possible to them: work and sleep, with nothing
in between. When asked whether they could enjoy doing nothing, their
reaction is one of not having ever thought about a possibility that seems
completely alien to their way of thinking and of living. Stopping any activity is equated to going crazy, dying, or losing all meaning in life: "Life
is work," and no other alternative is contemplated.

Performance as Problem Solving

One aspect of this compulsively driven activity is the tendency to see
life as a continuous sequence of functional problem solving—putting on
Band-Aids and putting fingers in the dike—as the way to deal with
life's problems. In this stance, reason and reasonability are paramount.
Whatever the problem may be, there must be a reasonable way to solve
it, since there is a reason or reasons why the problem developed. Facts,
logic, and reasoning are the royal roads to solve all the human problems
that beset us.

   This stance cannot deal with emotional problems because they do not
fit logical schemes or reasonable solutions. The person, instead, looks for
causes, reasons, and logical explanations for whatever problem that may
have arisen and suggests reasonable solutions, usually based on cold logic
and functional processes. He or she seeks more information (i.e., reasons) as a way of implementing solutions or improving performance. Being compulsively all reasonable and knowledgeable means to be perfect,
or pretty close to it. An individual who knows all the facts, all that is to
be known, will be able to be perfect and to solve problems through appropriate activities. Under this condition, there is little room for Being.

Doing as Perfection

Flaws, errors, frailties, failures in performance are indications of imperfection, therefore, they need to be banished from the face of the
earth. To be correct, to solve problems, and to perform means to be (and
to be perfect). To be incorrect, flawed, means to be "bad" and, therefore, to be imperfect, a quality unworthy of human beings. Successful
performance and functional problem solving prove our perfection, our
"goodness." To be perfect means to be accepted. To be imperfect means
to be rejected. This imbalance results from conditional rather than unconditional love.

CONFLICTS IN PERFORMANCE

Most conflicts in the area of performing focus on who should do *what* in the home, taking responsibility for routine chores and tasks that need to be done for survival purposes and to keep the household running smoothly. They take place when those involved cannot express their feelings in a nonjudgmental, helpful fashion. In the workplace, there may be conflicts of performance relative to turf issues, responsibilities, and power issues.

CONCLUSION

This chapter, in comparison with other ones, is relatively short because activity—doing or performance—has little if any meaning outside the setting in which that activity is taking place.

CHAPTER 8

Having Equals Production

. . . money is imbued with enormous power. In fact, except for a few idealists, money is power.

(YABLONSKY, 1991, p. 6)

One of the most important kinds of social power is money.

(LINDGREN, 1991, p. 67)

Having comprises money and goods or possessions. Functionally, Having is defined by a relative appreciation (a) for the functionality of goods and money, with an awareness that most intimate relationships are based on more than Doing and Having; (b) that money is a means to an end—the more consensual that goal is with loved ones the better (appropriate, useful, creative) its use will be; (c) that "What I have is who I am" is an ultimately limited and limiting definition ("Who I am" does not need justification if identity is based on selfulness); and (d) that money can be a source of power to be negotiated or to be given and taken away as blackmail and bribery.

Money is the most concrete way to keep score and to establish success or failure. A person may use money to reward, manipulate, control, and achieve goals, including achieving "self-esteem" and status, or self-importance. Having means a way of life where products, payments, and possessions may give the most meaning. Not having either of these resources means Non-being and might be equated with a failure to achieve life's goals. Conflicts about these two resources of achieving meaning are too common to even mention. In this stance, only the bottom line of production is what counts. In our culture of consumerism, this *is* the bottom line: No product = no meaning. Life must produce tangible, palpable goods or else it is not worth living. In this stance, quantity rather than quality is the goal to be measured and assessed, whether it is the number of cars, houses, or windows washed, the product is the best way to keep score and to assign meaning. Success is measured by how many products or numbers of the same product have been built, fabricated, delivered, and sold. Payments, therefore, represent a way of keeping score on these products.

THE MEANING OF MONEY

For some people, making and using money is the major road to survival. If a person lives in poverty, money permits few if any extras. Money means different things to different people. For some, money is reality. For others, money is security, and for others, control. For many, money and "happiness" are used as substitutes for being close and intimate to someone. Often, money becomes an emotional issue, especially when emotions and feelings are not otherwise expressed and shared (Yablonsky, 1991). The many distortions and deviations in the use of money show us how even this medium of exchange represents how a person develops or fails to develop.

THE FUNCTIONS OF MONEY

Money possesses at least seven symbolic functions, not always separate or separable from each other. These functions as well as their relative ranking may vary from one individual to another and yet be quite overlapping. To one degree or another, however, they are present in all of us.

- **Money as Survival.** For some people, money means immediacy, that is, taking care of immediate human needs, such as food, shelter, and warmth. Some people are not able to go beyond this function. When a person is poor, money means avoiding starvation, getting a roof overnight, and a warm place to stay when it is cold outside.
- **Money as Reality.** If and when survival needs have been satisfied, money still remains part of our everyday confrontation with taxes, bills from various sources, making and meeting a budget, and so on. Here we are going from the most concrete to the most abstract and from the most immediate to the least immediate need. Reality is one aspect of survival. Reality, in part, is based on the ability to make money and to have the money that our needs require. Money, under these conditions, allows us not only to live and to survive but, in some cases, to have the pleasures and the comforts of life that would otherwise be missing. In some ways, this is an objective function, since physical survival and reality are interconnected. Both functions are part of our objective perception of the world.

    Without money, we fall into extreme dependency. With money, instead, we attain a certain degree of freedom and independence. This reality is the ability to use money as we see fit, in some cases responsibly, and in some cases irresponsibly. Thus, we could separate two major reality functions for money. One is born out of responsible functions, where survival and enhancement of self and other are paramount. The other is an irresponsible and inappropriate way to make and to use money, to gain wealth at another's expense. There is a critical difference between somebody who works 40 or 50 hours a week to earn a salary versus a drug dealer who wants to make big money quickly without working for it.

- **Money as Self-Importance.**   For some people, money is a way to keep score on how important they are, (the more money they have, the more important they are). Money, consequently, is equated with status. All the trappings and appearances of having money and showing it ostentatiously are exaggerated when a person drives a flashy car and lives in a shack. Here, money is used as an attempt to make a good impression and stress the facade function of money, perhaps at the expense of its substance. Under this function, the use of money becomes an extension of self: "I am how much money I make." Thus, the sense of self-importance, instead of being based on an internal construct of importance, is based on an external one. Regardless of how much money a person makes, the money is used to bolster self-esteem and a sense of self-importance. It essentially becomes an external representation to indicate how important the person feels. Money may be used lavishly to buy objects and things that would enhance self-image not only to the self but to enrich the appearance or facade level of one individual.

- **Money as Security.**   For some people money means security, that is, not having to worry about where the next dollar will come from; relying on money achieves personal security. When people equate personal security with money, then they never have enough money to feel reassured. It will take more and more money for the person to achieve the ever-receding assurance of self-worth. Thus, money does allay anxieties about our physical existence. It is not substitute, however, for internal security based on knowing the self and valuing personal intimate relationships more than money. Money cannot buy love, closeness, and intimacy. Decreasing anxiety about self, others, life, and reality through money results in security with an external focus that fluctuates with the marketplace. Money, then, refers to something that is predictable, tangible, and concrete; it performs the function of reassuring us not only about the present but also about the future.

- **Money as Control and Manipulation.**   Money also can be used as a form of control. In this function, money means manipulating the self or others, as in the case of penny-pinchers, who die ostensibly poor. After their deaths, they often are found to have extensive holdings either in cash or in stocks and bonds. This function also is evidenced by tycoons who accumulate millions of dollars to achieve a sense of self-importance or control over the environment. For others, money brings authority and the ability to manipulate those who rely and depend on the one who controls the money.

- **Money as Instant Gratification.**   A function that cuts across all the previous functions is experiencing money as a form of gratification. Through money, a person can gratify legitimate as well as illegitimate desires and wishes. Here lies the ability to discharge or to delay. On one extreme are people who demand what they want when they want it. They cannot wait to get what they want. On the other extreme, there are people who defer any gratification not only in this world but in another.

- **Money as Independence.**   Money is related to the independence and dependence dimension. Money, then, becomes a means to an end. The teenager wants to make money to buy a car. This car, then, becomes the symbol of independence. Moving out of the parental home also means independence. As long as money is used either to achieve independence or to keep a person dependent, no growth can really take place. Selfulness, interdependence, and mutual emotional availability are not a matter of money.

THE MEANING OF POSSESSIONS

Products need to be moved and sold to produce money that can be exchanged or kept to facilitate living. Money, then, becomes the means to obtain possessions, a static hoarding of goods that may represent a person's worth and importance. Goods are not limited to inanimate things. Sometimes, people driven by possessions see other human beings as objects to be possessed, not as separate individuals in their own rights. Possessions also may represent sameness and security, the refuge from the world and escape from everyday pressures. Goods may be a distraction as well as a unique form of enjoyment.

The major work about the meaning of possession has been performed by Csikszentmihalyi and Rochberg-Halton (1981). They asked people about the meaning of special things in their homes. From their answers, these investigators were able to find two major meanings about possessions. One related to cherished possessions that give continuity to a person's life and across generational lines, such as family heirlooms, special gifts, and mementos. The second related to the functional and enjoyment functions of objects, such as the TV or radio.

Prentice (1987) followed up this research by identifying two kinds of people in relationship to the value ascribed to their possessions. One group valued the symbolic, sentimental aspects of their possessions.

The other group, instead, valued the functional, instrumental aspects of things:

> People who favored symbolic possessions endorsed symbolic appeals and values, and their favorability toward symbolic appeals was enhanced by controlling for values. Individuals who favored instrumental possessions showed no differences in their evaluations of the two types of appeals and values and no relation between attitudes and values, perhaps because the measures were insensitive to their instrumental orientation. These results suggest that people who favor symbolic and instrumental possessions differ systematically in their attitudes and values, with strong evidence for the self-expressive orientation of the symbolic group. (p. 1001)

It would be interesting to see how these two groups position themselves in relationship to Being versus Doing and Having. At the very least, I would predict that people who stress a symbolic orientation would value emotionality more than rationality, whereas the reverse would be relevant for people who stress instrumental values at the expense of symbolic ones.

NEGOTIATING DOING AND HAVING

The ability to negotiate Doing and Having is based first on differentiating the *structure* of negotiation from the *process* of negotiation. If the structure is out of focus, the process will be also. The structure of negotiation needs to be concerned with how authority (making decisions) is balanced with the responsibility to carry out those decisions. Decisions in and by themselves could be once in a lifetime, orchestrational ones, like moving to another town or selling the home; or they could be instrumental everyday routine decisions, such as "What shall we eat tonight?" Most conflictual decisions are concerned with the content of what is being negotiated (L'Abate 1986), that is, what *information* will be allowed in the house ("What TV channel shall we watch?"), *services* ("Who will wash the dishes?"), *money* ("How much money are we going to earn this year?"), and *possessions* ("What shall we buy with this money?"). When presence (Being) is not shared, or is used, fused, confused, and diffused with power (Doing and Having), polarizations and conflicts in relationships surely will ensue.

The process of negotiation is somewhat more complex. It is made up of three different components or strands—Ill, Skill, and Will. To separate various strands of this process, it is useful to look at the *level of functionality* (Ill) of the system (individual, dyadic, familial, etc.). This level is described by the three different styles already presented (Chapter 3), going from dysfunctional *A*busive–*A*pathetic relationships (AA), to intermediate *R*eactive–*R*epetitive relationships (RR), to the more functional *C*onductive–*C*reative (CC) interpersonal relationships (the ARC model).

Second, we need to look at the quality of *competence to negotiate* (Skill). This quality is described by the ERAAwC model (Chapter 1), consisting of five different components: (a) *E*motionality, the use or misuse of affect (Chapter 4); (b) *R*ationality, the use or misuse of thinking (Chapter 5); (c) *A*ctivity, the use or misuse of energy to behave (Chapter 7); (d) *Aw*areness, the use or misuse of what is conceived as a self-corrective, change-oriented mechanism (L'Abate, 1986); and (e) *C*ontext, the realization that most behavior is relationally contextual and that we need to pay attention and use both internal and external cues to make sense of it. No successful negotiation can take place unless all five of these components are used, somewhat sequentially, in the process. If feelings and emotions are short-circuited or blunted and remain unexpressed, as in many conflictual situations, then how can we expect that anybody will be able to negotiate anything? Most people confuse blowing steam, getting mad, and expressing feelings with negotiation. We want to negotiate, an extremely rational process, when we are controlled mainly by emotions. How is successful negotiation possible under those conditions?

Third, we need to look at the level of *motivation to negotiate* (Will), because without it, no negotiation can take place, no matter how functional and competent the individual may be. This level of motivation needs to take into account two different sets of priorities, as discussed in Chapter 12.

CONCLUSION

The ability to negotiate Doing and Having, therefore, is derived from the structure of negotiation. It is concerned with (a) who has authority versus the responsibility; (b) orchestrational versus instrumental decisions about the content of the decisions to be made; and (c) content consisting of services and information (Doing), and goods and money (Having).

The process of negotiation is a multiplicative function of three basic structural characteristics: Ill × Skill × Will. We pick up most of these qualities, either positively or negatively, from our family of origin and we transmit them to our family of procreation. We may be able to negotiate in work and leisure settings, but the basic issue is whether we can negotiate with intimate others at home.

PART FOUR
Settings

CHAPTER 9

Home

Parenting is an emotional experience.

(DIX, 1991, p. 3)

As argued here and elsewhere (L'Abate, 1976, 1983a, 1985a, 1986), although the home is where most of us spend two thirds to three fourths of our time, it has remained terra incognita for mainstream personality theorists (Dunne & L'Abate, 1978). This neglect can produce as ultimate outcome only a limited and flawed understanding of personality development, hampering seriously the predictive validity of any past or current theory. Personality, as here defined, would encompass not only how the individual behaves within intimate family relationships in the home, but also how he or she behaves outside the home, on the job, and in leisure time (Marks, 1977).

The inadequacy of traditional personality and developmental theories that consider the family as the major source of growth and correction in personality development is beginning to improve (very slowly).

THE THREE MAJOR SETTINGS

The ordering of the three settings of this theory, home, work, and leisure (Chapters 10 and 11, respectively) is based, in part, on the average amount of time we spend in each setting even though there are exceptions. Some individuals spend more time at work than at home, and others spend most of their time in discretionary activities. Nonetheless, normatively speaking, most of us spend two thirds to three fourths of our sleeping and waking time in our homes. Out of the 168 hours a week available to us, on the average 40 are devoted to work. Of the remaining 128 hours, approximately 50 to 60 may be devoted to sleep and personal grooming and caretaking. The rest of the time (approximately 70 hours) is spent on discretionary activities.

In terms of time, therefore, work should rank third rather than second. However, its importance for survival, as well as its intrinsic importance and its intensity of commitment, especially in the puritan work ethic of North America, puts it in second place. In some cultures, work may indeed be third. Its placement however, is still a subjective decision that depends a large extent on the personal priorities of each individual (and of each theorist). Hence, the need emerged for an additional construct of priorities (Chapter 12) as an important component of this proposal.

A Resource Exchange Classification of Settings

Barker (1968) as well as others (Moos, 1973, 1974, 1976; Schoggen, 1989) have attempted classifications of major settings, with different degrees of fit or validity. In addition to the structural classification used in this venture, based on the average amount of time spent in each setting, another classification of settings can be achieved functionally, according to what resource or resources are exchanged in a particular setting. Although there may be an overlap in resources exchanged in any particular setting, this additional classification stresses where one of the six resource classes postulated by Foà and Foà (1974) is mainly exchanged, as shown in Table 9.1.

TABLE 9.1.   A Classification of Settings According to Resource Exchange Theory

Modalities	Resource Class	Settings	Survival Functions	Criterion for Evaluation
Being	Status	Home	Emotional, interpersonal, moral, and intellectual	Ability to love (presence) and to negotiate (power)
	Love	Home		
Doing	Services	Hospitals, professional services, offices, hotels, public institutions	Physical, legal, psychological(?)	Performance (quality)
	Information	Schools, scientific research centers, libraries, media, bookstores, publishing houses	Educational, intellectual, moral(?)	
Having	Goods	Industry, agriculture, restaurants, shops, malls, livestock, animal husbandry, mines, construction, and repairs	Physical	Production (quantity)
	Money	Banks, savings and loan associations	Economic	

Why would this classification or any other classification of settings be useful? Because, if we want to understand personality–environment interactions, as many personality theorists tell us (Peterson, 1992), then we need to understand the specific functional, survival characteristics of each setting, each with its own peculiar task-demands, requirements, rules, and rituals that decrease variability. Each setting produces its own peculiar and specific norms.

Primary settings consist of transactions involving a primary resource whereas secondary and derived settings feature the exchange of more than one resource. Both classifications—the one suggested here (Table 9.1) and the one used in this volume (Part Four)—are complementary because each is based on a different criterion: Part Four uses a structural one based on the average amount of time spent in one setting, whereas the setting shown in Table 9.1 uses the survival function.

DIFFERENTIATION IN THE FAMILIAL CONTEXT

As noted in Chapter 2, home and the family have not been considered either in personality assessment, or by most personality theorists. The process of personality differentiation takes place isomorphically within the individual and familial level. Indeed, the home directly influences context in which the individual seeks to achieve a self-definition, selfhood, or an identity. A family, however, is more than the combination of its members. Rather, it is a unique, finely tuned system, composed of subgroups. In today's society, the family often functions to meet basic survival needs. The family also serves to foster socialization skills, to provide psychosocial protection for its members, and to act as an intermediary between the individual members and the culture. The family's subgroups (parents, parent–child, siblings) carry out the necessary tasks that allow the family to function (Minuchin, 1974). The family strives for a certain degree of homeostasis, or sameness, in which both groups and individuals operate to maintain continuity and meet the demands of its developing members. Clear boundaries among subgroups allow each subgroup to carry out its functions as well as to maintain contact with the other subgroups. Finally, the individuals' needs for a sense of belonging are fulfilled by boundaries between who belongs to what groups within and outside the family.

In every partnership, members must have ways to resolve differences of opinion and power struggles (Funt, 1988). Scanzoni and Polonko (1980) found that the ability to negotiate in marriage rests on the previous experience in negotiation and in the parity or disparity of power of each partner. Balswick and Balswick (1987) discussed the concept of negotiation within their discussions of intimacy and forgiveness.

TASKS REQUIREMENTS OF HOME AND FAMILY SETTING

Most of the responsibilities in the home can be broken down into four specific (and often overlapping roles), each with its own demand characteristics: (a) caretaker, (b) provider, (c) partner, and (d) parent. This theory does not have much to contribute as far as these roles are concerned. A great deal has been written about them outside of most psychological literature. However, the unique contribution of this theory consists in stressing the significant influence of the home and of the family setting to personality development as well as the ordering of this setting in relation to other settings.

- **Caretaker.**   Responsibilities in this role are of two kinds. One refers to what could be classified as nurturant qualities, very difficult to define, usually belonging to partner and parent roles. The other refers to those instrumental qualities that deal with the physical and material well-being of the home, such as cooking, purchasing, repairing, fixing, and cleaning. They are directed either to the inside or the outside of the home (e.g., mowing the lawn, cleaning cars).
- **Provider or Breadwinner.**   This role deals with the fiscal, monetary, economic aspects of family living (salary, income, credit rating, mortgages, debts, etc.). How much money comes into the home and how is it spent? Often, what really matters is not how much money comes into a home, but how it is spent. Allocations of money and taking care of the checkbook are very important activities for the physical survival and well-being of the family (Bernard, 1981).
- **Partner.**   How well a person functions as marital partner depends on a variety of personality competencies that have been elaborated at length elsewhere (L'Abate, 1976, 1983a, 1985a, 1986). In either partner or parent roles, two major sets of skills are necessary: the ability to love (Chapter 6) and the ability to negotiate (Chapters 7 and 8). However, how can a person be a parent without a partner?
- **Parent.**   We assume that partnership and parenting skills are God-given and are automatically learned through our roles as children, watching our parents. Consequently, since we learned from mortal, fallible human beings, most of us are bound to perpetuate the errors of our parents. In fact, most of us, even psychologists, make this assumption implicitly and forget that none of us received much training for partnership and parenting—probably the two most difficult and fundamental roles of our lives. Being a parent is a lifelong task, because we not only need to be parents to our children, but also to our parents, progressing also to grandparenthood. Selfhood is basic to all these roles.
  Parenting is a tough, but rewarding task that, once assumed, lasts a minimum of 18 to 21 years (Jensen & Kingston, 1986). Taking on

the role involves more than supplying money or changing diapers. A realignment of priorities within each of the parents must occur, leading to the attribution of such importance to the child that all needed sacrifices seem reasonable. The relationship of the husband and wife will never be the same again, even when the children leave home or die, because parents never stop being parents. To parent effectively, a couple must have an adequately intimate relationship and be willing to set priorities and make sacrifices called for by the parenting experience. To assist children to become selful individuals, the parents need to be close to the selful pole themselves.

PERSONALITY DEVELOPMENT AND THE FAMILY LIFE CYCLE

Personality development and change in an individual is influenced and, in turn, influences the family of which the individual is a part. The task of the family is to allow for change in its members while still maintaining a sense of continuity (Melito, 1985). The task is not easy because change often is not a smooth process (Hoffman, 1979). Sometimes, it appears that every step a family member takes developmentally can disrupt the family structure. The family needs to adapt to the member's physical, cognitive, and psychosocial changes (Combrink-Graham, 1985). The family is momentarily disrupted as old solutions no longer work and thus need to be altered. New solutions may not be satisfactory to all members at first.

The key to successful change in the family and in its individual members is flexibility. Flexible exchange (give and take) is necessary between its subgroups to alter their compositions and definitions. The biggest changes in the family occur over the entrance or exit of a family member (Terkelson, 1980). The period in which adolescents begin to explore alternatives and work to solidify their identities apart from their families is the beginning of many exits from the family. They include the adolescent's departure, and the grandparents' retiring, aging, and death. For both the adolescent who is leaving home and for the family which the adolescent leaves, it is necessary to mourn the change and loss before reestablishing a new family structure. At this time, family members often regress to an earlier pattern of interacting that may be evidenced in subtle ways, such as a mother doing her son's laundry. Eventually, a successful completion of this stage will depend on the family's ability to establish new generational boundaries by redefining membership and definition of the subgroups, and the amount and type of contact between the groups.

At this stage of the family life cycle, it is important to work toward a change in the system that would allow for a successful disengagement of the adolescent (Haley, 1973). This process, examples of which are graduating from school, working and becoming self-supporting, eventually moving out of the family home, and becoming romantically involved, varies with the individual and the family.

DIFFERENTIATED FAMILIES AND PERSONALITY CHANGE

A family context that promotes the growth of its members has been described as one in which the structure and hierarchy of the family subgroups are clear and flexible, allowing for adequate communication between subgroups (Lewis, Beavers, Gossett, & Phillips, 1976). Differences between members, negotiations, and changes are accepted. No one is seriously threatened by changes in other members because they have other supports and ties on which to fall back. For example, after the child leaves the family, the parents still have a strong marital coalition. Furthermore, this type of family expresses variety in emotions, instead of being characterized by one predominant emotion (e.g., anger). Finally, they react to people in the present, rather than focusing on past or future circumstances.

In the functional family, both family cohesion and adaptability accommodate the maturing members without threat to the family as a whole. This environment fosters the individual's ability to differentiate from his or her family. There is a positive, linear relation between the degree of the family's ability to balance separateness and connectedness among its members and the individual's ability to achieve a psychological separation (Sabatelli & Mazor, 1985).

Adolescence

A study by Grotevant and Cooper (1986) confirms that individuation is a function of the group context and is also dependent on the ability to be separate and connected at the same time. They assessed the interactions between high school seniors and their parents and the psychological competence of those teenagers. Individual questionnaires and family group tasks were used. They found individuation in the adolescents to be reflected by the adolescent's degree of self-assertion, separateness, ability to express differences between self and others, mutuality and respect for others' beliefs, and permeability to those beliefs. Mutuality and permeability were two factors that included the ability to connect. An analysis of the family context suggested that adolescent identity development occurs when the adolescent's personal growth was encouraged in the basic context of connectedness.

Adolescents who most easily made the transition between high school and going away to college and displayed the greatest degree of autonomy had parents who were confident, displayed congruence between beliefs and actions, and were able to differentiate between their own needs and those of their child. Furthermore, these parents tended to provide situations where the developing adolescent could begin to develop autonomy within a safe context (e.g., through extracurricular activities, summer jobs). Thus, these parents encouraged the personal growth and explorations of their children.

Parenthood

Being a parent is a lifelong commitment that does not cease when our children have grown up and are gone from the home. Oftentimes, in middle age we become parents for our parents in their old age. We need to make decisions for their physical welfare and well-being that involve a great deal of parenting care. When we become grandparents, we need to know how to keep distance "with care" from our children who are now embarking on their careers as parents. We need to give up the role of parenting and assume other less arduous roles (grandparents, retirees, widows, etc.).

In all these trials, errors, and tribulations, the main points to remember and reiterate are (a) children are visitors and, therefore, rank third after self and marriage; (b) the marriage partnership is the major avenue and vehicle for parenting; and (c) children are to be enjoyed not endured. The last point is a difficult one to grasp. How can we enjoy what is painful, irritating, unfamiliar, and downright burdensome? How can parenthood be, or become, enjoyable?

Transition to Parenthood

Becoming a Mother.   Becoming a birth mother involves numerous physical adjustments that have been studied in detail (Hytten & Leitch, 1971). The psychological adaptations to pregnancy have been examined by several researchers, who agree there are certain psychological stages through which the woman must pass successfully to mother the new baby adequately (Mercer, 1986; Rubin, 1984; pp. 54–56).

Early and extended contact with the baby influences the mother's relationship to her baby for years after the birth (Klaus & Kennell, 1982). Touch (Rubin, 1984), gazing into the baby's eyes, performing caretaking activities for the baby and getting responses from the baby from these activities (the baby gazes into the mother's eyes, snuggles into the mother's body when held, responds to touch with facial expressions of contentment, and moves rhythmically to the inflections and rhythms of the mother's voice) (Klaus & Kennell, 1982), are all involved in the initial attachment of the mother to the baby and the enduring bond between them that must develop for mothering to take place.

In these ways, the mother begins to love (attribute importance to) the baby, and the baby begins to love (attribute importance to) the mother. The very helplessness of the baby implies physical intimacy of the mother with the baby, which has the opportunity to develop into psychological intimacy and a mutually rewarding relationship (Klaus & Kennell, 1982).

Becoming a Father.   May (1980) and Mercer (1986) suggest that the attitudes of fathers affect parental behavior more strongly than previously suspected. Mercer (1986) surmised that this outcome may be related to the need of the woman to receive during pregnancy in order to give to the infant after delivery. The expectant father's style of relating to his wife's pregnancy (May, 1980) is one of the influences on general parental behavior. Two of the styles identified by May (1980) (expressive and instrumental) seem to be closely related to distinctions between Being and Doing.

Similarities and Differences.   Early studies emphasized the mother's transition to parenthood. The father's transition was assumed to differ significantly. It appears now that major differences center on the man's lack of the physiological experience of pregnancy. Early attachment and bonding behaviors of both parents are almost identical, although among fathers they may take place over a longer period of time (Klaus & Kennell, 1982).

Early Parenthood

Early Motherhood.   In the first few weeks of parenthood, the mother must adapt to the all-encompassing needs of the totally dependent and helpless infant (Friedman, 1986, pp. 61–63). Mercer (1986, pp. 119–162) described the first month as one of "pervasive fatigue and frustration" for the mother. After the birth of the first baby, so-called traditional mother–wife and father–husband roles tend to be assumed even in previously egalitarian families (Cronenwett, 1982; Friedman, 1986, p. 62). The mother, especially if she is breastfeeding, tends to assume the majority of infant care activities. The necessary recovery period following childbirth accentuates maternal role assumption by the woman (Mercer, 1986, pp. 119–162).

Early Fatherhood.   Men often experience similar changes in the transition to parenthood. Cronenwett (1982) found that differences in the research method yielded different results when father involvement in child care was studied, but that the overall transition to fatherhood experience seemed to be similar to the overall transition to motherhood experience.

When the father takes on household maintenance activities during the "fourth trimester," he usually relinquishes them rapidly after his wife's recovery. His focus becomes much more that of breadwinner, as the reality of caring for his wife while she cares for the baby becomes an issue (Friedman, 1986, pp. 62–63).

Similarities and Differences.   Men tend to take on a more serious attitude concerning work and the support of the family after the birth of the first child (Lidz, 1983, pp. 476–477; Friedman, 1986, pp. 62–63). Much more information is needed to delineate the effects fatherhood has on men and how this experience differs or is similar to the effects mother-hood has on women.

THE IMPORTANCE OF THE FATHER IN PERSONALITY DEVELOPMENT

In a study that is relevant to the assumption of the theory concerning selfhood definition as well as the ability to love and to negotiate, Morris et al. (1988) rated videotaped problem-solving discussions between fathers and sons for father–son interactions and problem-solving efficiency. These fathers then observed taped playback and expressed their thoughts according to a standardized procedure. Their recorded thoughts were then classified according to their positivity–negativity, and self-, family-, child-, or nonspecific references. Results of this analysis indicated that fathers of well-behaved boys, compared with fathers of aggressive boys, as nominated by their classroom teacher, were more efficient problem solvers, modeled more frequently behavior designed to reach agreeable problem solutions, were better educated and held more prestigious jobs, rated their families as more cohesive, more expressive, and less conflictual, engaged in significantly more positive solution behavior, and facilitated problem solving by engaging in more constructive, problem-oriented behaviors, which led to solution agreements. Fathers of aggressive boys listed more thoughts about their sons, but the majority expressed negative attitudes toward them. They also listed more negative and fewer positive thoughts about their families.

CONCLUSION

We are least prepared for the most responsible and most lasting tasks of our lives. Preparation for fulfillment of these task requirements is minimal if not nonexistent. Who we are as persons determines who we are going to be as partners and parents.

CHAPTER 10

Work

The key factor here is that work is an activity; it is not rest.

(*HALL, 1986, p. 13*)

In addition to the foregoing intrafamilial competencies, we need to evaluate extrafamilial competencies—work and leisure (Lee & Kanungo, 1984a, 1984c). Thus, the purpose of this chapter is to consider work-related skills that imply the ability to negotiate, and certainly not the ability to love. Work requires two separate but intertwined sets of skills: (a) specific occupational skills properly relevant to the job itself (filing, drawing, writing, problem solving, ditchdigging), and (b) extra-job skills that may be just as important as the first ones. The latter refer to how the person is able to get along and play political (power) games within a specific work setting. This set of skills requires interpersonal sensitivity, contextual acumen, and savoir faire. It may have little to do with the substantive job skills necessary for success. Yet, these skills may make the difference between promotion and stagnation on the job.

In Western culture, many people, especially men, identify themselves according to their occupational roles (Crandall, 1984; L'Abate, 1986). In fact, this role oftentimes represents the major source of gratification and identification at the expense of other roles that seem secondary to the person's occupation. Stereotypically, we seem to identify ourselves by what we do or what we have as possessions, instead of who we are as human beings. What happens when we lose our jobs because of being laid off or retired? Do we have any self left? How does this major identification aid or interfere with our roles at home? There is no question that the literature on work and personality development is copious and certainly much more explicit than can be presented in a few pages.

WORK AND PERSONALITY DEVELOPMENT

Like the influence of the home on personality development, work has been relatively neglected in personality theories. It is either not mentioned at all, or if and when mentioned, it is not related to personality.

When personality development is related to work, the links are still tenuous and unclear. It is necessary to refer to a number of references about work to discern possible connections (Greenberg & Steinberg, 1986; Hackman, Hoffman, Moos, Osipow, & Tornatzky, 1986; Hall, 1986; Karasek & Theorell, 1990; LaBier, 1986; Landy, 1989; Matteson & Ivancevich, 1987; Plas & Hoover-Dempsey, 1988; Quick, Hess, Hermalin, & Quick, 1990; Sundstrom, 1986). Again, a review of the literature would be inappropriate here for the purposes of expanding on this theory. However, investigators should not underestimate the importance of work on personality development.

WORK AND SELF-IMPORTANCE

What kind of person is nice at home and at work? What kind of person is nasty at work and nice at home? What kind of person is nice at work and nasty at home? What kind of person is nasty in both settings? Work requires two sets of skills from all of us. On one hand, there are the substantive skills that are required to work: knowing how to draw for the draftsperson, knowledge and application of the law for the lawyer. In addition to these skills, however, interpersonal skills are needed to deal with fellow employees, employer, clients, and the public. Sometimes, these extra-job abilities may be even more important than the substantive job-related skills, as in the case of managers and other leaders who are picked and promoted for their political and interpersonal skills rather than just for job skills. In fact, many promotions may be made on the basis of these skills rather than on the basis of substantive job-specific ones (Schuler, 1984).

In dealing with these four possibilities across home and work (nice–nice, nasty–nice, nice–nasty, and nasty–nasty), we need to consider the level of presentation of the individual and how he or she wants to impress others at home or in the workplace. Additionally, specific personality characteristics may go with specific jobs. For instance, individuals who value numbers (engineers, statisticians, accountants) may be impaired in working in intimate situations. People who like to work with people may be uncomfortable working by themselves or on strictly rational tasks without emotional exchanges. Individuals with strong approach tendencies toward others may choose different career paths from those with strong avoidance tendencies. The tendency to wait and delay may produce thoughtful thinkers and intellectualizers, whereas direct discharge and expression is appropriate for good sales representatives. Thus, in studying the relationship between personality development and job choice, the researcher needs to look at the level of presentation as well as at how the individual functions in space and time.

PERSONALITY COMPETENCIES AT WORK

One of the major issues in identity formation and personality development relates to equating occupational skills, status, title, or competencies
with competencies needed in the home. It does not follow that being a
competent psychologist will make a person ipso facto a competent human
being, partner, and parent. We generally expect that occupational competencies will automatically transfer from the work setting to the home.
Nothing could be further from what actually happens. Being a competent
marriage partner and parent may have little or nothing to do with occupational competence. Newspaper articles are full of anecdotes about people
who achieve success in the marketplace or the limelight of politics or en-
tertainment at the cost of failures on the home front (L'Abate, 1975).

Indeed, occupational competencies are completely different from
family competencies, and probably little or no transfer can take place
from one setting to the other. The demand characteristics of the two settings are too different to expect generalizations. Generalizations can be
made only in a few instances and only on a few dimensions. At home, we
are expected to love and to be loved and to negotiate emotionally intimate issues. At work, ability to love and to negotiate emotional issues
may be a handicap. Coolness, control, and cognitive logic and rationality
may be what is primarily required, in addition to specific occupational
competence.

LaBier (1986) argued that situational effects of the workplace and occupation on the individual are greater and oftentimes more stressful than
any historical, developmental, or intrinsic personality factors. He argued
that the individual careerist in today's work setting experiences an increased amount of stress and anxiety because of the pressing emphasis on
success. The lack of knowledge about the corporate culture and value
systems operating in large organizations and corporations has made it
difficult for many therapists to treat individuals experiencing job stress
and situational emotional crises.

The values of the workplace often have little similarity to those of the
individual employee and often cause internal and familial conflicts. A
young careerist must solve and resolve conflicts between personal values of self-importance and career ambitions. The two possible outcomes of this conflict are either betrayal of self-integrity or feelings of
inadequacy. The careerist who chooses upward movement and struggles
for promotions feels that personal values need to be given up for the
good of the company and the career. This denial leaves the individual
feeling self-betrayed. The careerist who instead chooses to preserve
personal values and give up career ambitions may remain stationary on
the hierarchical scale eventually ending up depressed and out of place in
the corporate ladder. These feelings of personal inadequacy may be

generated by the inability to fit into the ethos of the company's implicit and explicit demands for loyalty to work before anything else. This inability to reach a sense of self-importance through the work setting manifests itself through symptoms such as anxiety, depression, and underlying rage.

HOME, FAMILY, AND WORK

Since Masserman's (1970) and Veroff and Feld's (1970) early works, the literature addressing the interface between home and work has increased rapidly in the past few years (Bohen & Viveros-Long, 1981; Cramer, 1984; Geerken & Gove, 1983; Gerstel & Gross, 1987; Goldsmith, 1989; Pleck, 1985; Repetti, 1987; Staines & Pleck, 1983; Swanson-Kauffman, 1987; Ulrich & Dunne, 1986) to the point that a review would go above and beyond the purposes of this chapter. In their introduction to this topic, Lee and Kanungo (1984b) commented:

> Work and family have generally been viewed as unrelated topics, and it has generally been assumed that events, activities, and relationships in one area did not have much to do with those in the other (p. 13). . . . As new forms of family and new forms of work emerge, we need models for helping us understand what family is and what work is and what relationships might exist between the two. (p. 14)

In reviewing the empirical evidence relating to relationships between these two settings, Nieva (1984) concluded:

> Research leaves much to be known about work–family linkages. Data are limited and often the questions differ, depending on the sex of the population of interest. . . . The positive effects of each sphere on the other also need examination. Much of the research on work and family has tended to overlook the possibilities of positive spillover (p. 28) . . . the opportunities for shifting gears between work and family, for example, may alleviate rather than create stress. Role may reinforce rather than disrupt each other (p. 29) . . . in-depth understanding of the work–family interface will come about by dealing with specific work situations (for example, professional versus blue-collar workers) and specific family situations (for example, single parents and dual-career couples) because insights about the interdependence of work and family are unlikely to be generalizable across all work situations and all family situations. (p. 31)

In reviewing job satisfaction and domestic life, Crosby (1984) suggested, "The best predictor of a positive approach to work is a full life outside of work" (p. 41). In fact, a replicated finding from the various studies was family status as the best predictor of work satisfaction: "To our question: What creates a happy work life? came the surprising answer: A full home life" (p. 46). In going over the studies on this linkage, Crosby concluded: "There exist some positive types of people who like their jobs and who also arrange to have a full and happy home life" (p. 51). Apparently, such individuals can be identified and their characteristics measured. Lee (1984) suggested an important methodology to study what she called "life space structure effectiveness" in a way that is consistent with the present notion of competence × setting transactions. She suggested three states (personality characteristics?) that may lead to positive mental health status: equilibrium, social integration, and self-efficacy.

CONCLUSION

How much time, energy, and involvement a person commits to work may or may not detract from how one functions at home. Either setting, however, is insufficient to satisfy what we do with extra time left over from either setting. This extra time may be used for discretionary activities, as discussed in the next chapter.

CHAPTER 11

Leisure Time

Relative leisureliness . . . is more nearly in accord with our subjective experience than the split between leisure and its opposite. . . . Leisureliness is a question of degrees of freedom.

(ELLIS, 1985, p. viii)

Leisure is a voluntary enterprise, whether expressed strictly through observable behavior or in a more experiential or abstract terms.

(WADE, 1985, p. ix)

Competencies in leisure-time activities are important for enjoyment of life and personality development (Franken & van Raaij, 1982; Gentry & Doering, 1979; Hirschman, 1984; Holman & Epperson, 1984; Iso-Ahola & Buttimer, 1981; Rapoport & Rapoport, 1975; Stamps & Stamps, 1985). Leisure-time activities or discretionary nonwork pursuits, as they have been called, are an integral part of how we function as individuals. Under the rubric of leisure are included all the leftover skills for discretionary activities that are neither home, family, or work related. There are no demands or requirements here (Harvey, 1984). In fact, although the previous two settings, home and work, demand obligatory skills, in this case, the only requirements are those imposed by the individual on him- or herself (Crandall, 1984; Kanungo & Misra, 1984; Robinson, 1984). Hence, the term *discretionary* means that the behavior is internally initiated and maintained, in contrast to the previous two settings where activities are, to some extent, externally determined.

Play is an important part of leisure and it is also a very important component of personality development throughout the individual's life cycle (Caldwell-Brown & Gottfried, 1985; Caplan & Caplan, 1973; Cohen, 1987; Herron & Sutton-Smith, 1982; Levy, 1978; Lieberman, 1977; Piers, 1972; Schwartzman, 1978; Slovenko & Knight, 1967; Sutton-Smith, 1986). Through play, the child learns to initiate activities free from parental or environmental constraints as realistically determined by economical and physical limitations of space and time. Play allows the child to explore and engage in self-determined, pleasurable activities that increase the sense of mastery over the immediate environment. It increases the child's sense of self-importance by allowing the experience and expression of fantasies that could not be allowed otherwise. How and how much the child plays increases the process of exchange with the immediate environment with a minimum of social constraints and an enlargement of the child's sense of self and of self-importance. Play allows adults to let go of serious family and work matters and concentrate on pleasurable activities that are different from everyday routine drudgery. Play becomes a break from painful reality and a medium for relaxation and renewal. Through play activities, individuals avoid burnout, despair, and dullness. Play, like any other human activity, may become an addiction, as considered in Chapter 15 in greater detail, especially if it is used to distance or distract from dealing with hurt feelings (see Chapter 6).

In coping with stress, leisure is just as useful as any other stress-reducing strategy. Without leisure-time activities, individual development becomes stale and dull. Burnout may well be due to the inability of many individuals to enjoy life and value leisure just as highly, if not more highly, than work. Outings, vacations, and hobbies that reduce stress are just as important as many of the other skills required at home and at work. To undervalue leisure-time activities is to invite stress, boredom, and eventual burnout. Many of us learn stress-reducing leisure-time activities from our families, but some of us learn to value leisure because there was so little of it in our families of origin.

It is just as crucial to work as to do nothing, and it is also just as crucial to acquire, learn, and have leisure skills as work skills. We need to realize that just Being is as significant as Doing and Having. Unfortunately, many of us have grown up with the equation that Doing or Having are equivalent to Being. Hence, we stress performance or production at the expense of presence and existence. We are as good as our work. Consequently we find it hard to do nothing, to accept ourselves as we are on the basis of our Being rather than on the basis of our performance or production. Performance or production then are equated not only with goodness but also to personality. Consequently, we are unable to separate the two aspects, with especially dire consequences in the raising of children, where what they do equates with what they are. As a result, we cannot be idle, we cannot reflect, we cannot take time to do nothing. We need to justify our existence through our work and find self-definition in our occupational role rather than in our roles as human beings and their derivatives (married, single, parent, grandparent, etc.).

In the past, we have polarized ourselves between the sexes in defining ourselves either through our work outside the home or inside the house (men define themselves according to their jobs and women according to their roles as housewives). These pursuits leave little time to develop leisure-time skills, except driving somewhere (Doing), shopping, or visiting somewhere. Developing leisure-time skills (including doing nothing) is especially relevant in old age and retirement. Once our work is finished and we can no longer define ourselves according to our job, what is left? Nothing.

LEISURE AND PERSONALITY DEVELOPMENT

As with the two previous settings, home and work, leisure has been relatively neglected by most personality theorists. A search of the literature on how leisure may interact with personality characteristics yielded even smaller pickings than that on home and work. If there are no task requirements for discretionary activities, how can they be linked to personality development? If leisure is a matter of personal choice and preference, how can these choices be linked to personality development? For instance, religion, as a discretionary activity, may or may not play an extremely important role in personality development. Indeed, religion may be used to define the self at the expense of other areas of interest. Likewise, a sport may define an individual even more than home or work. It is not rare to find people who define themselves according to their favorite time activity ("I am a spelunker," "I am a sailor"). Thus, self-definition may take place according to leisure activities rather than any other setting (Bammel & Burrus-Bammel, 1982). Orthner (1975), as well as Orthner and Mancini (1989) have found that leisure patterns are extremely important for marital satisfaction over the life cycle.

TOWARD A CLASSIFICATION OF DISCRETIONARY ACTIVITIES

There are many ways to classify discretionary activities. One way consists of using locations only (church, lodge, malls). Another way consists of distinguishing between *transit* and *transitory* settings. For instance, going from one setting to another may take a great deal of time. For some people, going from home to work (transit), may take all their spare time except on weekends. Thus, transit settings may become roads, cars, airplanes, airports, busses and bus depots, trains and train stations. Other individuals may spend no time on transit because their work setting is the same as their home.

Transitory settings, on the other hand, represent those settings that may be necessary for survival but that take a relatively short portion of time, such as grocery stores, shopping malls, doctors' offices, bars, beauty salons, barber shops, and churches. In some cases, the church setting, although seemingly transitory, may have tremendous influence over all other activities, including home and work. In fact, it may become an important source of self-definitions ("I am a Christian," "I am a Buddhist").

Another set of transitory settings refers to vacation settings, such as hotels, resorts, and sightseeing and sports-related settings (tennis clubs, tennis courts, golf courses, skiing runs, etc.). Each of these transitory settings requires specific behaviors with their own demand characteristics, rituals, rules, and regulations.

Another way to help distinguish between these nonwork, leisure activities, relies on the specific nature of the activity itself. A tentative classification based on five different dimensions with their defining polarities is presented here. For other classifications, the reader is referred to Harvey (1984), who concluded his survey by generalizing that "discretionary time is spent primarily at home, primarily in the company of other people, primarily in the evening, and primarily on activities of over an hour's duration" (p. 119). For an analysis of conceptual and definitional issues, the reader is referred to Kanungo and Misra (1984), among others already cited.

Active versus Sedentary

This dimension covers activities according to the sheer degree of movement and action required, going from running a marathon at an active extreme to watching television on the opposite side.

Solitary versus Social

Working in a basement workshop could be considered a solitary activity, while meeting with the Elks' Club twice a week would represent the other extreme of sociability.

Inside versus Outside the Home

Working in a basement workshop would require working inside the house with occasional forays either to buy materials or to sell finished products, whereas joining the Elks' Club would require being away from home.

Indoors versus Outdoors

A person could exercise in his or her home gym, whereas others would rather run outdoors, come hell or high water.

People versus Things Oriented

Working in a workshop would obviously require dealing with objects and things, whereas working in the Elks' Club would require dealing with other people. This dimension considers specifically how much family and friends are valued in a person's life (Duck, 1983). Each of these alternatives has its own rewards and costs, mostly determined by the individual.

WORK AND DISCRETIONARY ACTIVITIES

As Lee and Kanungo (1984b) commented in their introduction to this linkage, "Effective management or work and personal life requires an adequate understanding of the nature of work and nonwork interaction and a proper integration of work and nonwork spheres of life" (p. 63). In this regard, they lamented "the lack of integrative theories and research paradigms in this area" (p. 65).

In reviewing the evidence relating to this linkage, Near (1984) concluded, ". . . quality of work life contributes little to the overall experiences quality of life (p. 70). . . . work and nonwork domains really have little influence on one another" (p. 75). Near presented three models to explain possible relationships between both domains: an aspiration/attainment model, a self-esteem model, and an integrated model, concluding, "The development of a theoretical framework for describing the process by which work becomes associated with nonwork is crucial to an understanding of individuals' attitudes and behaviors in both domains" (p. 70).

In pursuing the same linkage, Crandall (1984) concluded:

> There are few if any systematic lines of research on work and leisure interaction (p. 86). . . . In the light of the quality-of-life research discussed later, it becomes clear that work is not the engine that drives all the rest of life. . . . Leisure is an important component of many lives and may become more so in the future. . . . In the future the role of all components of life should be considered in a broad framework. (p. 88)

Crandall (1984, p. 102) suggested a two-by-two model that could be helpful in identifying types of individuals according to their work (high versus low) and leisure (high versus low) ethic, producing: (a) self-actualizers (high on both), (b) hedonists (low in work and high on leisure), (c) workaholics (high on work and low on leisure), and (d) unfulfilled/dissatisfied (low in both). It would be important to identify so-called personality correlates of these four types to find better linkages between personality characteristics and work–leisure activities.

HOME AND DISCRETIONARY ACTIVITIES

Fridgen (1984), in considering interrelationships in this linkage, stated: "The home is the center for personal development" (p. 244). If he is correct, as the present formulation would like to believe, then past personality theories (see Chapter 2) are either invalid or irrelevant, because they, as commented repeatedly, ignore outright the home and family in their texts.

Phillips (1968) developed a complete and well-researched interview schedule to measure social competence at home, which included a typology of occupational types and levels of attainment at work, and a complete list to evaluate nonwork and discretionary leisure-time activities. This schedule could be easily adapted into a structured questionnaire to relate social competence, as defined by Phillips, with competence as defined here and by others (Marlowe & Weinberg, 1985; Wine & Smye, 1980). What kind of personality, as defined traditionally in vacuum, will make a competent partner and a parent? Will competence in one setting transfer to another setting? Will we find a *g* factor here as in the case of intelligence or will we find that competencies in one setting will not transfer to another?

These questions deal with what personality theorists have called "cross-situational consistency" (Mischel & Peake, 1983). As long as they ignored home, work, and leisure as the very settings where personality manifests itself, how could they find it except factitiously? Will success at work be predicated and predicted on how the person uses the family as a refuge, as a support and refueling system (Fehr & Perlman, 1985)? What happens to people whose major personal identification is equated with occupational status and success—"I am what I do"? What happens to them when they retire, are laid off, or worst are fired? What personal emptiness does this occupational primacy cover and protect?

Snyder (1974) found that there are low- and high-self-monitoring individuals, who indicate great individual differences in their attunement to external interpersonal cues. Years later, Reiss's work with families (1981) supported this view. He found that certain families are environment-sensitive, whereas other families seek consensus among their members rather than external approval. This consistency between interpersonal and family orientation would go a long way toward understanding how a great many of us learned internal or external orientations from our families of origin, a much more important consistency than the cross-situational one sought by personality theorists. Cross-setting consistency can be defined only by a continuum with functional settings as well as dysfunctional extremes in all three settings—home, work and leisure. Hence, minimal functioning in all three settings could fall in the middle of the continuum. LaBier (1986) took a much stronger position in stating that the dysfunction produced by the work situation leaves the individual impaired in all areas of functioning, including home and leisure.

INTERRELATIONSHIPS AMONG SETTINGS

In dealing with the inevitable overlap among these three settings, home, work, and leisure, the contributions edited by Lee and Kanungo (1984b) are extremely important. In this regard, Lee and Kanungo (1984c) noted: ". . . it is clear that there are new problems and opportunities in coordinating work and personal life and achieving personal well-being. There is also a need for theory and research that might offer insights or guidelines that would be helpful to those most affected by these (social and economic) changes" (p. 6). As Crandall (1984) concluded in his review, most relationships among these three domains are "reciprocal and interactive" (p. 94).

However, the issue of cross-situational consistency, dear to the hearts of personality theorists, may need to be reframed in terms of priorities (L'Abate, 1976; 1986). How does a person juggle and balance demands and expectations from one setting to the other (Marks, 1977)? The relevant literature is beginning to study the conflicts and role strains that derive from the great balancing act we all play every day of our lives (Cramer, 1984; Kelly & Voydanoff, 1985; Kingston & Nock, 1985; Lee & Kanungo, 1984b; Nock & Kingston, 1984; Staines & Pleck, 1984).

CONCLUSION

Leisure and discretionary activities are just as important for personality development as home and work skills. The ability to play, to relax, and to enjoy doing nothing is just as important as doing something. Furthermore, leisure should allow a person time to take time for him- or herself, to use that time to introspect, reflect, and think retroactively, about the past, as well as proactively, about the present and future. Without time to think, the individual may find that even leisure-time activities become another of the many areas of driven competitiveness present at work or at home.

CHAPTER 12

Priorities

. . . the key dependent variable in motivation became choice behavior.
(WEINER, 1991, p. 925)

Choosing priorities requires the ability to order, rank, and organize competencies according to (a) personal needs and values, (self and selfhood); (b) contextual demands, marriage, children, relatives, work, friends, and leisure; and (c) life stage demands, at any specific stage of the person's life cycle. Originally, priorities were divided into intra- and extrafamilial ones. The juggling of these areas involves the construct of priorities that motivate people to negotiate, with themselves and intimate others, important issues in their lives (L'Abate, 1976, 1986). Implicit in the concept of priority is the concept of importance. We order our priorities according to the importance we attribute to them. Priorities describe the relative importance given to: (a) self, (b) marriage, (c) children, (d) relatives, (e) work, (f) friends, and (g) leisure-time activities.

In addition to the intra- and extrafamilial division, priorities can be considered in two other ways. Vertical priorities relate to how we deal with issues of Being, Doing, and Having, which is a developmental process. Horizontal priorities, on the other hand, are strictly structural and contextual. Although determined by past historical or developmental factors, they consist of the ordering of the three major settings, work, home, and leisure time. If home is not where the individual feels loved and important, he or she may go to another setting where acceptance, importance, and recognition are given for a price, as in a bar or on the gambling table. Work may become an overwhelming priority to the point of becoming an addiction. When a person does not feel wanted, needed, or important in either home or work or both, importance may need to be bootlegged from somewhere else.

Functionality takes place when this sequence is followed flexibly along the individual, marital, and family life cycles. Dysfunctionality occurs when the self is displaced and made less important than other priorities (White, 1991). Dysfunctionality takes place when one or more priorities are used at the expense of other priorities.

The ability to set priorities is an important factor in relationships. There is a relationship between priorities and the definition of self. Traditionally, men have tended to define themselves in terms of jobs and careers and have prioritized time and energy in that manner. Women, traditionally, have set priorities and defined themselves in terms of motherhood. This gender difference has made for an imbalance in power and roles, which damages intimacy and the ongoing family atmosphere. There are various views of defining self in terms of transcendence and in terms of existence. It is important that selfulness be developed as a priority in terms of the person's separation from his or her family of origin and Being from Doing or Having (L'Abate & Talmadge, 1987), and within the context of committed relationships. Children and work must be assigned a subordinate priority because partnership is a prerequisite to parenthood and that children are only visitors to the relationship. Once an effective partnership exists, the atmosphere is healthy for the advent and raising of children (White, 1991).

The salience and satisfaction derived from each setting remains an individual prerogative that then determines how each setting is ranked in respect to the other two (L'Abate, 1986). What is relevant here is Lee and Kanungo's (1984a) conclusion:

> . . . it is possible to distinguish different domains of life, like work, family, and leisure (p. 259) . . . Each domain can also be reduced in importance by increasing the importance of the other domains. Activities in the leisure area can be direct antidotes to the negative effects of stress . . . Work, family, and leisure represent three areas in which people can juggle and counterbalance demands and difficulties to maintain equilibrium. (p. 262)

Priorities involve the process of differentiating among modalities, resources, skills, and settings. In addition, we need to differentiate disclosure (expression and sharing of painful events), which requires presence, from skill acquisition, which requires practicing new behaviors. Perhaps a better way to make this distinction would be to stress that skills required for presence are mostly receptive and relatively passive, whereas skills for negotiation require acquisition and active practice of new skills usually not available in the individual's repertoire. Women may stress the importance of receptive skills, whereas men may stress the importance of expressive skills, especially motor ones.

The ordering of the three settings (home, work, and leisure) is based on the amount of time we spend in each setting. Of course, there are exceptions. Placement of resources, modalities, and settings, however, still remains a subjective decision that depends on the personal priorities of each individual (and of each theorist). Hence, the need emerged for an additional construct of priorities as an important component of this theory.

A person cannot predict how competence in one setting will transfer to competence to another setting. For instance, someone may be a devoted husband and parent, but be a mediocre employee. Or, a person may be a tiger at work and be a better than average provider, but be incompetent as a spouse and as a parent. Hence, the concept of priorities has a motivational function (L'Abate, 1986). How we allocate our time and energies to one setting is determined by definite choices we make about the way we want to live our lives. This is a concrete and measurable approach for dealing with the difficult problems that have beset motivation as a theoretical concept (Brody, 1980). To achieve and maintain meaning in our existence, we need to be in touch with our selves sufficiently enough to balance our Being with our Doing and our Having. This balance may fluctuate over the life cycle, but our Being needs to be firmly ahead of the rest. Without it, Doing and Having become empty and futile pursuits.

How successful a person is in either of the three settings depends on the priorities of that particular individual. If he or she defines primarily in occupational terms ("I am an engineer," "I am a nurse)" rather than domestically ("I am a husband, "I am a father"), it will follow that the person may be successful at work and a failure at home. In the same way, avocational pursuits sometimes overshadow both domestic and occupational roles ("I am a runner"). Balancing all three settings to avoid shortchanging any of them is one of life's great balancing acts. Hence, to predict how a person will behave in each of the three settings, we will need to have information about how home, work, and leisure-time activities are valued in relationship to each other.

VERTICAL (DEVELOPMENTAL) PRIORITIES

This topic has been discussed in previous publications (L'Abate, 1976, 1986). The following is a further elaboration of the same topic.

Self and Marriage

The arguments of Peele and Brosky (1975) concerning addictive love relationships are relevant to the issue of priorities. Essentially, these authors considered symbiotic dyads, couples who give up their selves for the sake of the relationship and marriage. The priority of self is given up for supremacy of the relationship or of the children. They illustrated their argument with case histories. What happens when the self is given up for marriage? It restricts the life of the couple, it lowers the level of enjoyment, it limits their links with other individuals. It is usually based on low self-esteem (their term) and a great deal of insecurity. In other words, the choice of priorities in marriage and the family stems from the nature of the genotype, how differentiated or undifferentiated an individual is.

Marriage and Children

The functional sequence of family roles can only be personhood before partnership and partnership before parenting (White, 1991). Each role cannot survive well without the preceding ones. If and when the self is given up either for the marriage ("I want to make you happy!") or for the job, there is hell to pay later on. Someone in the family is going to become symptomatic in one way or another. After the birth of the first child, the couple must begin to relate to each other as the parents of their child as well as spouses (Lidz, 1983). The woman becomes to the man not only his wife, but the mother of their child. The obverse is true for the man. These changes in their relationship may be at the least disconcerting, and at the worst a major difficulty. The transition to parenthood, rather than providing glue for their relationship, may provide a wedge between them and precipitate dissolution of their marriage (Lidz, 1983). For these reasons, parenthood needs to be a reasoned choice made by a couple who have a full and intimate partnership with each other.

An addictive marital relationship may produce children who themselves may develop weak self-images and eventually enter into symbiotic, restrictive relationships with peers and members of the opposite sex. Even though the addictive marriage may not show outside strain or may appear functional, the addictive aspects to the marriage may be sufficient to influence the type of relationships engaged in by children of this marriage. Naturally, during the course of the family life cycle, depending on their degree of dependency, children will occupy an important position. However, if the partners sacrifice either the self or the marriage for them, dysfunctionality will take place. Children are third (visitors) in the functional family, as mentioned earlier.

Hence, the issue of interfamilial priorities is directly related to the balance of extramarital priorities and self-differentation. If a person's self is based on an occupational definition, it leaves little room for that individual to define him- or herself solely in human terms. The occupational definition takes priority over the definition of the self as an independent human being ("I am a person first and foremost") in the marriage and with progeny. The woman who defines herself in terms of occupational role as a "housewife" or "mother" may be missing the completeness of herself as an independent human being, first as a self, second as a wife, and third as a mother. Thus, either in men or women, if the self is classified according to occupational or instrumental roles, it may leave a vacuum in, or be the by-product of, a defective self-definition that relies on external props.

Having a baby is not a short-term experience. Rather, it means taking on a minimum 18- to 21-year commitment to the baby (Jensen & Kingston, 1986). Within that commitment are socialization tasks such as gender role modeling, religious and secular socialization, and education (Jensen & Kingston, 1986; Rollins & Thomas, 1979).

Parents, Siblings, In-Laws

Much has been written about sibling bonds and rivalries. There is also quite a bit of material about parent–child relationships and their effects on each other. But there is little material available on in-laws and their interactions and influences on their married children. However, in-law problems generally constitute a major area of conflict between spouses, which should provide impetus to correct this lack of research in the near future.

Parents, in-laws, and siblings are part of the natural, extended support system that allows us to survive emotionally. We all need blood ties and a common historical background to help us in times of need. If we cannot find support among the extended family, where shall we look for it? The new parents must adjust to being parents as well as being husband and wife. If there are other children, they must adjust to being siblings to the new baby, a process likened to that of a wife adjusting to her husband bringing home a concubine and telling her that she must love this new resident of their home. Schvaneveldt and Ihinger (1979) described methodological problems of studying sibling relationships. Despite these limitations, they concluded that older siblings are in a pivotal position to influence the younger children in the socialization process.

The parents of the couple now become grandparents and must relate in new ways to the new parents (Friedman, 1986). Mercer (1986) emphasized the changes that occur in the relationship between the new mother and her own mother after the first child is born. The relationship becomes more that of peers than of mother and daughter. These changes may extend to the relationship of the new mother with her mother-in-law, and the new father with his own father and his father-in-law.

HORIZONTAL (STRUCTURAL) PRIORITIES

Work

The coming of a child may lead to extensive modifications in the work habits of the partners. The woman who planned to return to work after birth, may change her mind when faced with the reality of the baby and the intensity of her feelings for him or her (Friedman, 1986). The father, as mentioned earlier, may feel deeper responsibility to be the major breadwinner in order to permit his wife to be the principal caregiver of their baby. In a society that values success and achievement at the cost of personal comfort and satisfaction, work assumes greater significance than just a job. To some individuals, the job signifies the core of identity and a major reason for living. There are individuals and families who literally cannot do "nothing." They need to perform and produce.

Friends

Some friends are substitute family members; some are even better than family members. A sure way of discriminating between friends, neighbors, and acquaintances lies in seeing who is available to us emotionally when we need someone to comfort and support. Some friends travel well, some do not (like wine). Finding which one is which is a continuous process that takes a lifetime and that ultimately contracts itself into, at most, a handful of tried and true friends. They furnish the bulk of the support system that is available to us when the family may not be for logistical or other reasons. Friends, therefore, need careful and caring cultivation as valued individuals, next to family members.

Leisure

Consciously or unconsciously, new parents make choices about their leisure activities. The reality of the time required to care for the helpless infant, the need of the wife to recover physically from the birth experience, and the energy required for the psychological and social adjustments combine to cause the couple to realign their priorities.

CONFLICTFUL POLARIZATIONS IN INTIMATE RELATIONSHIPS

There are dimensions of relationships, especially marital relationships, that as yet defy either immediate recognition, rational description, and/ or quantifiable conceptualization and empirical quantification (L'Abate & Bagarozzi, 1993). The major implication from the viewpoint of priorities is their effect on conflict in intimate relationships. For instance, emphasis on emotionality (E) in one partner might clash with rationality (R) in the other partner. Or, one partner may view or use emotions more than reason, whereas the reverse is true for the other. However, these dimensions become easily recognizable and visible when couples become polarized at each extreme. Polarizations in couples, therefore, represent differences in personal priorities (Being versus Doing or Having). In addition to the fantasy–reality polarization considered elsewhere (L'Abate & L'Abate, 1981), at least three other dimensions seem to be interrelated with each other, or may be different manifestations of the same underlying polarization along the main dimensions: (a) power versus presence, (b) acceptance versus denial of self-importance, and (c) emotionality (E) versus rationality (R).

Each of these dimensions is discussed separately. Approach versus avoidance of emotionality with its concomitant polarization in the confrontation of unpleasant affect, when unattended to, may eventually blossom in its extremes into a full-fledged depression. Typically, but not always, women express their feelings of dissatisfaction and unhappiness by blaming their husbands, whereas men will avoid dealing with both their feelings and consequently their wives by stressing a rational ("reasonable") approach to the marriage and marital difference. Short-circuiting of E leads to extremes in either compulsivity and obsessiveness or impulsivity. Most couples who marry on the basis of complementarity, that is, on the basis of deficits in the self-structure that supposedly will be fulfilled and satisfied by the partner, eventually become polarized along a major dimension of self-definition, where the selflessness of one partner ("You are important; I am not") is counterbalanced by the selfishness of the other ("I am important; you are not").

Power versus Presence

The first dimension deals with the major polarization in marriage: power versus presence. By presence is meant the ability to be and being emotionally available to self and other without demands for perfection, performance, problem solving, or production. Presence means the individual loves both self and partner unconditionally as important human beings regardless of what they Do and Have, but mainly on the basis of their existence: "I am important because I am. You are important because you are." In functional marriages, both aspects are clearly defined and fairly differentiated. They are used additively or synergistically to increase marital growth. In dysfunctional marriages, both aspects are ill defined and poorly marked, fused, confused, and diffused to the point of a subtractive division in the marriage. By power is meant the ability to negotiate Doing (information and services, or performance) and Having (money and possessions, or production).

Most conflicts in committed, prolonged, and close relationships derive from two sources: (a) our inability to separate sharply issues of power from issues of love, and (b) to become intimate, because we find it difficult, if not impossible, to share our hurts and fears of being hurt. Love and hurt are inextricably interwoven because loving someone means giving them the freedom, license, and power to hurt. We are not hurt by strangers. We are most vulnerable to the hurts of our loved ones. L'Abate and L'Abate (1979) considered that difficulties in becoming intimate derive from three paradoxical (contradictory) positions: (a) We need to be two separate human beings in our own rights in order to be together as a unit when we need each other—when one of us hurts; (b) we hurt and are hurt mostly by those we love and who love us—we hurt when they hurt and vice versa; and, consequently (c) we need to console and to seek consolation from those very individuals who have either created or received the greatest hurts from us, making the whole process of intimacy very difficult to reach. No wonder intimacy is a difficult condition to achieve, even in so-called functional marriages.

There are at least three different levels of intimacy so defined: (a) Level 1 when neither sex expresses and shares sad feelings helpfully, as in the AA style (Chapter 3); (b) Level 2 when either one of the two sexes may express sad feelings properly, but the other one cannot or does not hear them or share them reciprocally ("dumping"), as in the RR style (Chapter 3; eventually this level may regress to Level 1); and (c) Level 3 when both sexes express and share sad feelings reciprocally and helpfully, as in the CC style (Chapter 3).

Emotionality versus Rationality

In the complementary marriage described initially, women who rely on emotionality over rationality as the major avenue of self-expression tend to marry men who use rationality (reasonableness, logic, factuality, etc.) and activity rather than emotionality as their major avenues of self-expression. This is a complementary arrangement. If and when the couple can combine emotionality and rationality to enhance each other, the road to intimacy becomes wide open. However, if no exchange is possible, this complementarity tends to become polarization because the relationship is based on perceived self-deficits rather than on perceived self-strengths: the partners marry each other to fill in areas where they feel they are lacking. The emotional woman marries the rational man because of her attributed (and unfortunately sometimes uncritically accepted) emotionality, whereas the rational or overly rational man needs the emotional or overly emotional woman to make up for perceived inadequacies in emotionally expressive areas.

Presence, as emotional availability, means being close and empathic on a reciprocal basis when one of the two partners hurts. However, if one of them, usually the man, is unable to deal with and to come close to the woman when she is hurting, even minimally, then a negatively spiraling feedback loop starts to build up that increases the distance between the two. That loop may start at the outset as simple unpleasantness and discomfort. When one is unattended and not responded to appropriately by the other, the loop may escalate into an ever-increasing feud. In this case, unpleasant feelings tend to escalate to sad feelings that may eventually escalate to veritable hurts. The man may become increasingly irritated and eventually angered because of his inability to deal with the wife's feelings and her increasing blaming of him for how she feels.

Most of the struggles and polarizations between men and women in relationships derive from an inability to handle sad and hurt feelings (L'Abate, 1986, manuscript submitted for publication). Some men, especially those who are driven and seem to be action-oriented superachievers, are unable to deal with sad and hurt feelings within themselves. Consequently, they usually are unable to deal with similar feelings in their wives. These men (perhaps Type A or something akin to it) tend to attract and marry women who are just as unable to deal with feelings of vulnerability (L'Abate & L'Abate, 1981). Although such husbands tend to avoid feelings, their wives do approach and experience them. Women are biologically predetermined to deal with pain from the very onset of the menstrual cycle. However, some wives may tend to express pain through externalization onto or against their husbands, making them feel responsible, guilty, and therefore inadequate, because it is their "fault" that these women feel the way they feel (L'Abate, 1980). In such cases, the husband is the "culprit" for whatever is going on in marriage. The wife tends to blame him for not paying attention to her feelings, avoiding her when she needs him, being too interested and involved in his work, and not paying attention to her and to the family. The husband cannot get close to her because of the index finger pointed at him. She cannot get close to him because she tends to perceive him as the "enemy," creating an adversary process where blame, fault, and acrimony increase in a spiral of charges and countercharges. Neither sex wins. Both feel defeated.

The inability to approach emotionality brings about another possible dimension of complementarity that in extreme cases becomes polarized. It lies in the admission or denial of depression (L'Abate, 1987b), where typically the woman will admit to her vulnerability, sadness, and frustration while the man maintains a stoic facade of the strong, silent type stereotyped in thousands of movies. He is not (that is, he does not feel) depressed, therefore, he does not need any help. That admission however, often is as resistant to change as is denial. The partner who admits and who blames her- or himself, by the very act of admission, feels relieved of the responsibility to change, since the one who denies the need is at fault and needs to change.

Priorities and the Life Cycle

Priorities change as a function of each stage in the life cycle of the individual, couple, and family (Chapter 3). A derivation of the present formulation would hypothesize that what happens in old age depends a great deal on the intra- and extrafamilial priorities and resources the person has adhered to during his or her lifetime. If these priorities and resources have been balanced and held in their relative positions of importance within the perspective of self, marriage, and children, then the aging individual or couple should be able to adjust to old age in a relatively peaceful fashion. If these priorities and resources, however, have been mixed up, unbalanced, and emphasized at the expense of others, then it would be expected that aging would not follow a peaceful course.

In old age, not only is there a necessary reordering of priorities because such priorities are no longer as relevant as they once were, but there is also an affirmation of the importance of the family. In fact, many old people move from wherever they are to be closer to either siblings and or their children. The importance of the family is affirmed both at the beginning as well as at the end of the life cycle.

CONCLUSION

According to the view presented here, personality becomes the composite of three different sets of competencies: (a) how the individual behaves at home, at work, and at leisure-time activities; (b) how the individual balances and ranks these three settings horizontally in order of importance and energy expenditure; and (c) how modalities and resources are ordered vertically.

PART FIVE

Applications and
Theory Testing

CHAPTER 13

Testing through Evaluation

Objectivity, then, is achieved through a coalition of subjectivities. . . . In the face of continuous point and counterpoint—both in the public and private spheres—one slowly approaches the awareness that perhaps the monument to objectivity is hollow.
(GERGEN, 1991, pp. 84–85)

The purpose of this chapter is to show how various instruments were designed from this theory's inception to parallel theory construction with theory testing. In addition to tests, however, this chapter suggests more dynamic ways to test the theory through primary and secondary interventions that will be elaborated in Chapter 14. Hence, this chapter will focus on how this theory can be evaluated empirically through test instruments. Chapter 14 will discuss how to test the theory dynamically, through interventions. Chapter 15 will look critically at the adequacy of the theory according to past and present formulations that seem epistemologically related to it, even though they were constructed independently.

This theory needs evaluation regarding its adequacy to describe and explain personality development and competence in intimate relationships. If parts of a theory are found to be inadequate, they can be changed at the level of (a) assumptions; (b) postulates; (c) the models derived from the postulates; or (d) instruments or methods of intervention derived from the theory. For instance, a theory could be valid in the assumptions but not in its postulates. A theory could be invalid in its assumptions; in that case, the whole theory needs to be changed, and it could be essentially invalid. However, as a whole, a theory cannot be tested at the level of assumptions or postulates; researchers usually evaluate and test a theory at the level of its models. A theory could be valid in its postulates, but not its models. Furthermore, a theory could be valid in its models, but not in the instruments designed and derived to evaluate it. Verification, testing, and evaluation are used here as synonymous terms for the same process, to see how valid a theory is and whether it is approximately isomorphic with reality. No theory can be fully isomorphic with reality. It can only be a tentative approximation to that reality as perceived by us.

A theory can be tested or evaluated in three ways. First, a theory can be verified *inferentially,* by relating assumptions, postulates, and models of a theory to similar constructs or concepts of other theories that have been constructed *independently* of the theory itself. For instance, the abilities to love and to negotiate could be measured with instruments that have been created completely independently from the present theory. Many instruments that can measure either one of those abilities are available on the test market (Thompson, 1990). The epistemological leap from this theory to these tests would be a much wider one than from the next two ways to test the theory.

Second, a theory can be verified *indirectly,* through instruments that may be related to the theory but were not derived from it. The measures developed by Foà and Foà (1974) to test resource exchange theory could be used as a way of verifying this theory at the level of personality definition. Those measures were derived originally to evaluate resource exchange theory, but because the present theory is in part based on that theory, these instruments, conceivably, may show some relationship with measures derived directly from the theory. For instance, we could add scores on Status and Love in the original scales developed by Foà and Foà to evaluate the ability to love in terms of Being or Presence. Scores on Information and Services could be added to measure Doing or Performance, and scores on Money and Goods to measure Having or Production. The addition of scores on Doing and Having would indicate the ability to negotiate or the extent of negotiable power. The epistemological leap here, although still inferential, would not be as wide as in the preceding way to test the theory. However, since the present theory is a substantially different version of and expansion from resource exchange theory, it would not be surprising if few if any relationship were found.

Third, a theory can be verified *directly* through instruments specifically derived from the theory itself. Early versions of this theory (L'Abate, 1976) led to two different ways of testing it—through evaluation of process and through evaluation of outcome derived from interventions (supposedly derived from the theory). Process is related to the *verifiability* of the theory, whereas outcome is related to *accountability* of results obtained by the application in practice of the theory. A theory could be eminently verifiable but produce few results. By the same token, a theory could be nonverifiable but nevertheless produce a positive outcome (L'Abate, 1986). Process can be evaluated through content analyses of therapy transcripts and videotapes and through content-free analysis of family interactions. Outcome can be evaluated through paper-and-pencil self-report (verbal) tests and through visual tests for families based on drawings of people and animals administered on a pre-post intervention basis (L'Abate & Wagner, 1985, 1988), as well as other external criteria of improvement, such as decreased medical visits and increased income. Since the early developments and revisions of this theory with paper-and-pencil tests, recent improvements have provided new and different measures of evaluation and methods of intervention (L'Abate, 1990, 1992b).

This chapter reports illustratively but not exhaustively on theory-derived instruments based on paper-and-pencil self-report. For more detailed reviews, the reader is referred to other sources (L'Abate, 1990, 1992b; L'Abate & Wagner, 1985, 1988). Epistemological relationships between this theory and other theories will be reviewed in the final chapter (Chapter 15). A summary of the relationship between theory and theory testing is shown in Table 13.1.

The evaluation strategy developed originally (L'Abate & Wagner, 1988) consisted of constructing two instruments for each of the major postulates of the theory. For instance, the original concept of self-differentiation was measured with a Likeness Scale and the Likeness Grid. In the present version of the theory, this concept was given as much importance as in previous versions (L'Abate, 1976). Greater attention was given here to the self-importance model, as assessed by the Problems in Relationships Scale (PIRS) (L'Abate, 1992b). Priorities were measured with a Priorities Scale and a Priorities Inventory. Congruence–incongruence in communication, was measured through four scales—Blaming, Placating, Computing, and Distracting. These dimensions, even though relevant to Reactivity, were no longer relevant to the present version of this theory. They were measured through a test of 20 true–false items for each of the four dimensions and a multiple-choice "What Would You Do?" test that measured the same four dimensions (L'Abate & Wagner, 1985, 1988). The same strategy has not been followed in the development of more recent instruments, with the exception of distinguishing between nomothetic and idiographic versus *direct* and *indirect* measures of the same dimensions, as elaborated in the following section.

TOWARD A CLASSIFICATION OF EVALUATIVE INSTRUMENTS

The subjective inferences and conclusions derived from a test instrument furnish what is called the *idiographic* (derived from and directed toward the individual) aspects of evaluation. The objective inferences and conclusions from a test or battery of tests furnish what is called the *nomothetic* (derived from and directed toward group norms) aspects of the evaluation. To evaluate people in trouble, we need both. We need to reconcile this controversial distinction and ask whether we can create instruments that will fulfill *both* aspects of evaluation, assessing both idiographic and nomothetic aspects of an individual or of a relationship.

TABLE 13.1. Summary of an Approach to Test a Theory of Personality Development

Tests	Evaluation		Interventions		
	Outcome	Process	Primary	Secondary	Tertiary
	Paper-and-pencil tests	Analyses of interactions	Structured enrichment	Programmed therapy	Therapy
Theory-derived	Verbal battery		L'Abate and Weinstein, 1987	L'Abate, 1986; L'Abate, 1992b	Face-to-face contact and written homework assignments
	Visual battery		L'Abate and Young, 1987		
Theory-related	Foà and Foà, 1974				
Theory-independent	Tests measuring same constructs				

Writing in general and programmed writing in particular, as discussed in the next chapter, allow us to extend this distinction not only to tests but also to programmed self-administered interventions (L'Abate, 1992b).

In addition to the idiographic–nomothetic distinction, which has a long history of controversy in clinical psychology (Howard & Meyers, 1990), another distinction has influenced the creation of most tests in clinical psychology: psychometric requirements that tests relate validly to their *descriptive* nature. Among the many psychometric criteria used to assess the descriptive validity of a test, there was also an additional criterion about their *predictive* validity. The question to be answered referred not only to how validly a test evaluated what it was supposed to evaluate but also to how well an instrument predicted what it claimed to predict. If we cannot predict, we cannot understand. If we cannot understand, we cannot control. If we cannot control, we cannot help!

The additional criterion that came into being once programmed writing became a method of intervention was *prescriptive* validity (L'Abate, 1992b), as explained in greater detail in Chapter 14. How well can a test prescribe treatment, in addition to fulfilling traditional descriptive and prescriptive functions? The answer to this question is as follows: *A test becomes prescriptive and, therefore, linked to treatment, provided the treatment is specifically defined in writing.* As long as treatment is based on the spoken word, the linkage between evaluation and treatment is bound to remain what it has been all along, a wished-for chimera, the Holy Grail, that cannot or will be very difficult or expensive to achieve.

As a recent survey has amply demonstrated (L'Abate & Bagarozzi, 1993), most instruments for personality assessment as well as marriage and family evaluation, including traditional, individually oriented instruments, are mainly descriptive, that is, they stress the importance of understanding in describing individual, marital, and family patterns. However, none of these instruments leads directly into linking theory or evaluation with treatment. The linkage between both enterprises, up to now, has taken place on a catch-as-catch-can basis, without any clear or direct links between theory or evaluation and interventions, because such a link cannot be obtained as long as interventions are based solely on the spoken word.

Through the written medium, it is now possible to design instruments that can provide these links, once we design new ways of intervening with people through programmed writing. After new ways of intervening in writing with individuals, couples, and families are developed, it becomes possible to design new evaluative instruments with that purpose in mind, *provided we use both the written and the spoken medium in therapy* (L'Abate, 1986, 1987c, 1990, 1992b). When the spoken word is the main or the only medium of dialogue between two or more individuals, it becomes virtually impossible to control what is going on between them; even if some control is achieved through structuring, myriad variables that we cannot control still intervene.

Examples of *prescriptive* instruments, still experimental and still in the course of validation, will suffice to illustrate what can be done when writing rather than speaking becomes one of the three media—nonverbal, verbal, and writing—available to use in the (or para) therapeutic exchange (Chapter 14).

A third distinction relevant to the creation of new prescriptive tests is their *direct–indirect* nature. For instance, to assess conflicts in dyadic relationships a Problems in Relationships Scale (PIRS) was created to evaluate couples *indirectly* along 20 dimensions of functioning–dysfunctioning. The same 20 dimensions also can be evaluated *directly* through a Semantic Differential Test. Again, we need both measures to evaluate the concurrent validity of these instruments. When using different measures of the same behavior, what is the extent of agreement and congruence between the two instruments? Programmed writing, in its explicit specificity allows us to link treatment with evaluation in a nomothetic as well as idiographic fashion. For instance, the 20 dimensions of the PIRS are isomorphic with 20 lessons covering the very same dimensions measured by the test. The test evaluates which dimensions, out of the 20 measured, are specifically conflictual for a particular couple, ranking these dimensions from most to least conflictual. On the basis of this idiographic ranking, it is now possible to administer to a couple just those treatment lessons on which they are most conflictual (L'Abate & Kunkel, research in progress).

By the same token, with the MMPI-2, it is now possible to administer a program that is specifically written to deal with each of the 15 Content Scales (L'Abate, Boyce, Fraizer, & Russ, 1992). Consequently, it is also possible for the clinician to prescribe treatment idiographically outside the professional office provided he or she uses nomothetic, programmed, self-administered, written materials. Both instruments also assess extent of selfulness, selfishness, selflessness, and no-self.

THEORY-DERIVED INSTRUMENTS

The tests described here already have been published together with other theory-free instruments (L'Abate, 1991). Here we shall consider only those instruments that are relevant to theory testing.

Testing the Likeness Model

The Likeness model described in Chapter 3 relates to how we see ourselves in comparison with important persons in our lives according to a continuum of symbiosis, sameness, similarity–differentness, opposite-ness, and autism. To evaluate this model, a Likeness Scale, consisting of 20 true–false items and a Likeness Grid, patterned after Kelly's Reper-tory Grid, were constructed (L'Abate, 1976). Hutton (1984) performed one of the first validation studies for the Likeness Scale, derived to evaluate the likeness continuum described in Chapter 3. She found self-esteem scores of men positively correlated to their own Likeness Scale scores, whereas the self-esteem scores of women were positively corre-lated to the Likeness Scale scores of their husbands. Del Monte (1976) found a significant ($r = +.32$) correlation between Likeness scores and conceptual systems of personality functioning. The results of other studies support the validity of the Likeness Scale as a measure of self-differentiation. Reviews of the relevant literature and results can be found in L'Abate and Wagner (1985, 1988) and L'Abate and Bagarozzi (1993).

After establishing satisfactory reliability for all these measures and correlating the Likeness Scale and Grid with the Priorities Scale and In-ventory with 136 undergraduates, L'Abate and Wagner (1988) found a slight ($r = .27$, $p < .05$) but positive correlation between these two mea-sures of differentiation.

The Evaluation of Self-Importance

The *Self-Profile Chart* was developed to measure indirectly the sense of importance the individual attributes to the self (Chapter 6). In this chart, the individual is asked to rate himself or herself along dimen-sions of personal quality, such as intelligence, health, physical attrac-tiveness, morality, and spiritual status, and to fill in a blank dimension of the respondent's choosing. Further ratings deal with success areas as an individual, as a friend, as a spouse, as a parent, as a sibling, as child to one's parents, to one's in-laws, as a worker, and as self in leisure ac-tivities. Ratings from $+5$ to -5 are to be given for the present, the past, and the future. A total score gives a measure of the respondent's view of his or her sense of importance (L'Abate, 1992b). Data concerning the validity and reliability of this test have been collected and are being analyzed.

The Evaluation of Polarizations and Importance in Couples

To test the self-importance model presented in Chapter 6, a prescriptive instrument and a workbook for couples were created—*The Problems in Relationships Scale (PIRS)*. As commented earlier, we summarized most marital problems and polarizations in 20 conflictual and polarized di-mensions (dominant–submissive, weak–strong) and the four dimensions (or extremes) derived from the self-importance model (Chapter 6): selful, selfish, selfless, and no-self. The PIRS consists of 240 items on a 5-point Likert scale, and the development of a parallel workbook, whose lessons correspond to the 20 dimensions measured by the test. This descriptive as well as prescriptive instrument allows us to match evaluation with intervention because the same 20 dimensions of polarization are matched by equivalent lessons to be administered to partners according to how conflictual each dimension is. This is the first example of a test that is *prescriptive* in addition to being *descriptive*. Scores are used to prescribe specific lessons from a workbook isomorphic with the dimensions of the test. It is now possible to identify idiographically which of the 20 dimensions are the most conflictual in a couple and to rank them from the most to the least conflictual. The couple can then be administered just those lessons that correspond to their most conflictual dimensions. In this fashion, we have a nomothetic method in the test and in the workbook. However, the administration of the specific lessons to each couple is idiographic to fit the specific problem areas of each couple (L'Abate, 1992b).

Using the same rationale, we created a simpler instrument to parallel the one just presented, with one form for individuals and another form for couples, *The Semantic Differential for Problems in Relationships.* This instrument consists of simple 7-point ratings for each of the 20 dimensions of polarization; the respondent rates self and partner. The Problems in Relationship Test is an indirect (supposedly subtle) way to assess couples and assign specific lessons from the workbook. The Semantic Differential is a more direct way to measure the validity of these rankings and their more indirect counterparts. In addition, it gives a more direct view of how each partner perceives the other, which is not provided in the other test. Research about the psychometric properties of these instruments is still in progress. Both tests can be found in L'Abate (1992b).

The Evaluation of Intimacy

Originally, L'Abate and Wildman (1973) developed a scale to measure the construct "Sharing of Hurts." This scale (SOH), however, did not show sufficient validity to warrant further use (Sloan & L'Abate, 1985). To correct some of its shortcomings, Stevens (Stevens & L'Abate, 1989) developed a more sophisticated scale that yielded five factors: private values, vulnerability, social desirability, imperfection, and sharing of hurts. From these results Cusinato and L'Abate (1994) derived a positively upward spiral model of intimacy (with an accompanying paper-and-pencil, self-report) instrument to measure seven dimensions: social desirability, communication of personal values, respect for the partner's feelings, acceptance of personal and partner's limitations, sharing of hurts, forgiveness of errors, and valuing of the partner's potentials. This instrument presupposes that three prerequisites are operating to produce intimacy in couples: commitment to the relationship, reciprocal acknowledgment and affirmation of personal importance and equality, and mutuality of behaviors. A parallel program for primary interventions with couples was also developed.

The Evaluation of Priorities

Most of the efforts at test evaluation were directed toward evaluating the validity and reliability of two instruments to measure *vertical* priorities, a scale and an inventory (Chapter 12). Frey (1980) measured differentiation, intimacy, and vertical priorities with the Likeness Scale, the original Sharing of Hurts Scale, and the Emotionality-Rationality-Activity (ERA) Scale, using 74 male and 86 female undergraduates. The ERA scale consisted of nine possible permutations of words emotions/feelings, reasoning/thinking, and action/behavior, which were rated on a three-point scale on the basis of importance to the subject. On the basis of administering other measures developed by Witkin (1965) and based on perceptual field dependence/independence, Frey found that individuals who favor reasoning/cognition tend to be field-dependent. As a result of this and many other findings that cannot be summarized here, Frey concluded: "The emotional system is activated at the moment of perception, and is thus not secondary to the cognitive and/or behavioral systems" (p. 132), supporting the importance of emotionality as being developmentally and clinically even more relevant than rationality, as discussed in Chapters 1, 4, and 5.

Goodrich (1984) validated the Marital Evaluation Questionnaire (MEQ) comprising six scales measuring Likeness, Priorities, Blaming, Placating, Computing, and Distracting. The first two scales were derived directly from the theory, whereas the other four scales were derived from Satir's (1972) model of incongruent relationships in families. Each scale was measured by 20 true–false items. Goodrich administered this questionnaire to 100 couples together with Spanier's Dyadic Adjustment Scale (DAS) and Moos's Family Environment Scale (FES-R). Her results supported the hypothesis that ordering of priorities was related to marital quality. The wife's perception of marital quality was significantly and positively related to the husband's priorities score on the MEQ. The husband's perception of marital quality was significantly related to the similarity between his and his wife's score on the Priorities Scale. The level of differentiation (as measured by the Likeness Scale) was significantly associated with communication congruence for both husbands and wives in Blaming and not the other three scales. Couples were found to be significantly similar in the level of differentiation (as measured by the Likeness Scale) and in terms of Priorities, as well as in the other four communication congruence scales (Blaming, Placating, Distracting, and Computing). Further validation of this Questionnaire was performed by L'Abate and Wagner (1985, 1988), who also reviewed unpublished research relating to tests derived from the theory and designed to evaluate it. L'Abate and Wagner (1985) reported a test–retest reliability coefficient of $+.88$ and an internal consistency reliability coefficient of $+.85$. The correlation between the Priorities Scale and the Priorities Inventory was also positive and significant at the .01 level ($r = +.33$).

Owen-Smith (1985) used both the Likeness and Priorities Scales as well as the Priorities Inventory, which consists of all possible 21 triadic permutations of the categories of self, spouse, children, parents and/or in-laws, siblings, work, leisure, and friends. Each respondent is asked to rank each triad in terms of its importance. Scores can range from 21, theoretically indicating the most appropriate allocation of priorities, to 63, which would represent the least appropriate and therefore, least functional allocation of priorities, according to this theory.

Owen-Smith administered these instruments twice with a 9-week interval to the parents of 53 preschool children (ages 48 to 60 months), who were administered the Thomas Self-Concept Value Test for children. Although no relationship was found between the children's self-concept and their parents' differentiation and priorities, reliability coefficients for the Priorities Scale were high and significant, .86 for fathers and .87 for mothers. Reliability coefficients for Likeness were .81 for fathers and .69 for mothers. Since the fathers' Priorities Scale scores correlated highly with mothers' Priorities ($r = .59$, $p < .001$) and mothers' Likeness ($r = .38$, $p < .002$) scores and mothers' Priorities with mothers' Likeness ($r = .39$, $p < .002$), she combined both scales, yielding reliability alphas of .85 for fathers and .86 for mothers. The reliability for the Priorities Inventory yielded alphas of .97 for fathers and .39 for mothers. An exploratory factor analysis using an orthogonal rotation (Verimax) yielded five factors with eigen values of 1 or greater. The first factor seemed to represent the father's social identity and was loaded on father's work, leisure, siblings, parents, and mother's parents. The second factor seemed to include those variables that represented the interpersonal relationships of the parents with their nuclear family—father's child, mate, self, mother's child, father's and mother's likeness/priorities. The third factor loaded with mother's child, work, self, and likeness/priorities, reflecting the mother's sense of identity. The fourth included father's mate, mother's friends, mother's mate, mother's parents, and the child's age, suggesting an interaction of the mother's and father's interpersonal identities. The fifth was loaded on mother's work, leisure, siblings, and parents, indicating the mother's social identity.

From the mothers' written comments, Owen-Smith concluded that many mothers interpreted the work dimension as "caring for their children and husbands." Univariate F tests yielded a significant difference between mothers and fathers in respect to how they rated mate and work. Mothers tended to rank children first whereas fathers ranked mate as first, suggesting a difference in priorities. These differences may tend to be derived from sex differences produced by different socialization practices (see Chapter 6).

L'Abate and Wagner (1988) found that both the Priorities Scale and Inventory produced significant ($p < .01$) correlations with scale scores of self, children, parents, and siblings, and small but nearly significant ($p < .05$) correlations with friends and leisure. Hence, the concept of Priorities finds convergent validation on the basis of two different ways to measure it. The two exceptions to this conclusion relate to the lack of significant correlations between these measures with mate and work, replicating the same results found by Owen-Smith (1985).

Evaluation of horizontal priorities is strictly measurement of how much time is spent in a particular setting. For instance, normatively speaking, most of us spend two thirds of our time in a lodging that we call home, where we receive our mail and friends, and transact with relatives, friends, and neighbors. We spend approximately 40 hours a week in a place where we work, transact business, and receive a paycheck, usually away from home. We spend leftover time in leisure activities, ranging from shopping, passively watching TV, to active outdoor activities or indoor hobbies. Once this measurement is done, we can evaluate how it compares with subjective perceptions or reports of the person's perceived time and energy expenditures (Juster & Stafford, 1985).

Extent of Functionality and Match with Help-Giving Approaches

In addition to composition (individual, couple, family, group), a continuum of preventive approaches (primary, secondary, and tertiary), and modalities of intervention (verbal, nonverbal, and written), to be elaborated in the next chapter, we need to consider the extent of functionality–dysfunctionality of our clients. Furthermore, we need to take into consideration socioeconomic, educational, and intellectual levels. We cannot prescribe pell-mell psychotherapy to everybody who wants or needs help. It would be a very undifferentiated way to help people. If we were to consider the three levels of functionality according to the self-importance model discussed in Chapter 6, we would obtain at least three degrees of functionality—high, medium, and low to very low. The high level of functionality would be defined and described by creative-conductive selfulness and it correlates according to three sublevels. For instance, the highest sublevel of creative functionality would be defined by superior functioning in all three settings—home, work, and leisure. An intermediate sublevel of functionality would be defined by superior functioning in one of the three settings, with average or below average functioning in the other two settings. Adequate functioning would be defined by average or below-average functioning in all three settings. At this level, primary and secondary prevention approaches would be most appropriate, in any of the four compositions (Table 13.2).

At the medium level of functionality (dysfunctionality, reactive-repetitive characteristics of selfishness–selflessness manipulations), personal and interpersonal conflicts in home, work, and leisure settings may be the norm. Again, the settings would allow us to see how circumscribed or how encompassing conflicts would be. We could then define the degree of dysfunctionality by the number of settings affected by personal or interpersonal conflicts. Three sublevels of medium dysfunctionality could be thus defined. One sublevel would be affecting just one setting, the next sublevel would affect at least two out of three settings, and the lowest sublevel would affect all three settings. Here is where crisis intervention and face-to-face psychotherapy (tertiary prevention) are especially relevant and useful, especially at the outset to reduce extent and intensity of conflict. However, after the initial crisis is diminished, further interventions could consist of combinations of primary, secondary, and tertiary prevention approaches. For instance, immediately after the crisis, face-to-face psychotherapy with a professional could be combined with programmed writing or with enrichment programs administered by middle- to lower-level paraprofessionals (L'Abate, 1990, 1992b).

TABLE 13.2.   Extent of Functionality, Settings, and Continuum of Preventive Approaches

Extent (Levels of Functionality)	Sublevels within Each Level	Settings			Possible Intervention Strategies
		Home	Work	Leisure	
High	Creative		High		Primary and/or secondary prevention
	Intermediate		High to medium		
	Adequate		Medium to low		
Medium	Occasional conflict		Low to high		Tertiary + secondary + primary prevention
	Chronic conflict		Low to medium		
	Intense conflict		Consistently low		
Low	Borderline		Very low		Medication and/or homebuilders + skill training + behavior modification
	Serious		Very low		
	Extreme		Extremely low		

At the lowest level of dysfunctionality, characterized by abusive-apathetic relationships and no-self, all three settings would be affected and influenced by the dysfunctionality. The major criterion of definition here would be the extent and intensity of abuse–apathy. Again, three sublevels would be possible. The first sublevel may imply a borderline level of survival with occasional but repeated bouts of conflictual relations within all three settings. The next relatively lower, second sublevel would be defined by extreme dependence on the welfare system, or its equivalents, such as homelessness, psychiatric hospitalization, or incarceration. The lowest, third sublevel, characterized by murder/suicide, and custodial psychiatric hospitalization or life incarceration would be the easiest one to define. At this level, help giving becomes problematic; because of the very definition of no-self, no one can win under these conditions, not even the most effective psychotherapist. In addition to medication, hospitalization, and incarceration, different models of help giving and intervention may be introduced. For instance, for families, skill training program may be more appropriate than any psychotherapeutic approach. For other couples, individuals, and groups, concrete behavior modification and skill training and psychoeducational approaches relying on specific, tangible incentives and rewards may be more successful than approaches based on verbal or written modalities.

THE LABORATORY METHOD IN PERSONALITY ASSESSMENT

The evaluation of individuals, let alone couples and families, can be a time-consuming and, therefore, expensive endeavor, because of the professional time involved. However, if we were to separate technical from professional skills, some cost savings can result (L'Abate, 1973, 1994). As shown in Figure 13.1, a great deal of evaluation is time consuming, requiring mostly technical skills in administering and scoring tests. On the other hand, the professional skills needed to interpret and report test results require a great deal of knowledge and experience. It takes much less time to acquire technical skills than professional skills. Thus, the relationship between technical skills and knowledge is inversely related. If professionals were to relegate technical skills to technical personnel and retain supervisory, supportive, and leadership skills of interpretation and written reports, the whole enterprise of evaluation would become more efficient and, therefore, more cost-effective.

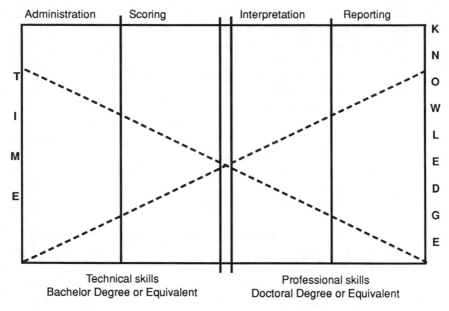

Figure 13.1. Differentiation of technical from professional skills in evaluation.

CONCLUSION

Theory building has developed in parallel fashion with the creation of paper-and-pencil and self-report instruments that were derived directly from various versions of the theory. Supposedly, these tests would help verify the validity of the theory. Unfortunately, most of these instruments were validated by my own students, a bias that needs to be corrected if the theory is to be validated further. To streamline costs and efficiency in psychodiagnostic evaluation, the laboratory method, which distinguishes between technical and professional skills, is recommended.

CHAPTER 14

Testing through Interventions

Verba Volant. Scripta Manent.

If language is a major source of thought, then written language is also a powerful source of thought.

(*Brand, 1989, pp. 2–4*)

How is it possible to test any theoretical framework as long as the modality of testing is verbal? The thesis of this chapter is that as long as modalities of intervention and theory testing rely on the spoken word, it will be practically difficult if not impossible to test any theory, including the present one. The development of personality is understood more clearly when we try to effect change through psychological intervention. Can a theory be used to change relationships? Can a theory be evaluated through interventions? The answer to both questions is affirmative, with the following qualification that—*provided the modality of intervention is written down rather than verbal or nonverbal.* By definition, psychological interventions to help people include the psychotherapies as well as other structured helping approaches—the paratherapies. Both interventions are based on personal, face-to-face contacts and relationships between a professional and dysfunctional people in need of psychological or psychiatric help. Consequently, we will need to find ways and means to test this theory other than just the spoken word. To achieve this goal, we will need to review the field of psychological interventions to make sense of them and relate them, if possible, to the present theory. Before this review, however, we need to ask ourselves, why do we need to classify these interventions? In addition to traditional classifications, this chapter considers other dimensions that are relevant to an understanding of both therapeutic and preventive enterprises in the mental health field as they relate to personality development.

WHY DO WE NEED A CLASSIFICATION FOR PSYCHOLOGICAL INTERVENTIONS?

Humans, in one way or another, have attempted to codify most of their endeavors, whether such classifications are physical, scientific, artistic, or religious. Psychotherapy and the paratherapies have attempted to do so in the past. Previous attempts, however, have been limited and, in the main, unsuccessful in achieving some degree or semblance of satisfactory systematic order (Saltzman & Norcross, 1990; Zeig & Munion, 1990). There are few, if any, references (Garfield & Bergin, 1986) devoted to issues of classification for the psychotherapies and the paratherapies, with the notable exception of Karasu (1986) who will be reviewed here.

Classifications are one way of organizing knowledge and making sense of reality. Little has been written on attempts to classify psychotherapies and paratherapies and to link them to any particular theory. This classification adds dimensions of (a) institutional approaches to helping, (b) a continuum of preventive approaches, (c) knowledge base for helping, (d) skills required for helping, (e) modalities of intervention, and (f) therapeutic emphases. An emerging new and more relevant dimension, the *prescriptive* one, can be juxtaposed to the exploratory or relationship aspect. No other dimensions are usually considered except perhaps the "specific versus common factors" controversy, which will be also considered here in a new light (Karasu, 1986; Lynn & Garske, 1985; Omer, 1989).

We can rationalize this attempt at classification on four grounds, as ways of (a) making sense of reality and, in this case, of the whole enterprise of helping people; (b) categorizing ways of helping in a manner that would allow better understanding of the whole process; (c) finding a more specific link between evaluation and interventions; and (d) linking this theory to practice. The first point represents the rationale for most, if not all, classification systems: to allow for a more or less rational categorization of a plethora of psychotherapies and paratherapies that is now practically and conceptually unmanageable (Saltzman & Norcross, 1990; Zeig & Munion, 1990). A rationale for classification would allow us to compare and contrast various therapeutic and paratherapeutic methods and would represent the baseline for commonalities and differences. This baseline would allow us to comprehend a field that, even to the experienced eye, has reached practically incomprehensible proportions. Hence, classification would allow us to consider the basic dimensions that characterize various psychotherapeutic and paratherapeutic approaches. The identification of these dimensions may eventually allow us to map out their limits and their specific functions. Once this identification is achieved even partially, we may be able to use different or similar approaches synergistically.

As Andrews, Bonta, and Hoge (1990) argued in regard to a classification system for offenders:

> Principles of classification for rehabilitation describe how particular classes of offenders may be linked with particular classes of discretionary

service so that *effectiveness* of service is enhanced. "Effectiveness" has to do with achieving reductions in recidivism, "classes of offenders" refers to preservice differentiations based on the circumstances of offenders, and "discretionary service" refers to direct correctional service such as supervision, counseling, training, and treatment. (p. 19)

These authors advocated four principles for effective psychological rehabilitation: risk, need, responsivity, and professional override. The first three principles are covered in the present classification by the three types of interventions from a preventive viewpoint presented later in this chapter, whereas professional override means making specific professional decisions that take into consideration the first three principles as well as the wider context in which such decisions are made. Whether we deal with offenders, addicts, or patients with psychological or psychiatric disturbances, we are dealing with human beings who tend to relapse into their past behavior patterns and do not know how to employ more rewarding ways for themselves and for others.

We cannot build skyscrapers with our hands alone. We need blueprints and we need a variety of tools, instruments, and specialized personnel to perform the task of building them. Present and future mental health problems facing us cannot and will not be solved with our bare hands, especially when we use just one approach (Lesse, 1987). We will need to know which therapy and paratherapy works for what problem at what cost and with which therapist or facilitator. This vexing question has bothered us since the various psychotherapies and paratherapies came into being; to answer it, we will need to know what we are doing and how we are doing it. A more or less rational classification of the psychotherapies and the paratherapies may be one step in the direction of answering such a question.

A classification of the psychotherapies and of the paratherapies may facilitate us to understand what we are doing in a more specific manner than we would if we did not have such a classification. Such understanding would give us greater certainty in our enterprise. As a result, we may become more flexible and specific in our use of both psychotherapeutic and paratherapeutic methods, because we would at least know which methods make up our armamentarium. Once we do have a catalog, so to speak, of such methods, we will be able to pick and choose the method that fits our interests and sensitivities, allowing for greater specialization and efficiency.

Ultimately, a classification will allow us to match specific forms of interventions with specific problems, including the issue of dual diagnoses. For instance, we may want to use a humanistic, present-oriented, feeling-focused approach with an individual who needs it, but become contextual and even paradoxical in dealing with that individual's family. How can we pick and choose if we do not know what we can pick and choose from? Ultimately, we want to link the present theory to the practice of psychological interventions, as another way of testing the theory.

PSYCHOLOGICAL INTERVENTIONS: A CONTINUUM OF HELPING APPROACHES

These interventions are embedded and are by now institutionalized within the context of societal and institutional methods to "help" control and change troubled people. The fields of psychotherapy and paratherapy are both characterized by a bewildering and mystifying array of different approaches, methods, and forms of intervention with varying degrees of respectability, replicability, and varying claims of effectiveness (Abt & Stuart, 1982; Corsini, 1984; Harper, 1975; L'Abate, 1990; L'Abate & Milan, 1985; Lynn & Garske, 1985; Prochanska, 1984). How are we to make sense out of such a confused and confusing state of affairs? Classification is one way to attempt clarification for such a state. Perhaps out of this classification effort may emerge a more discriminating ability to evaluate major therapeutic and paratherapeutic dimensions, their cultural context, and their limitations. Facing the future with a house somewhat in order rather than in disarray may allow us to obtain greater professional credibility because we will be able to make sense of ourselves and of our endeavors (Cummings, 1987; Lesse, 1987). Before becoming more particularistic, however, it may be important to embed both psychotherapies and paratherapies within the larger cultural context of how the American society deals with two of the basic dimensions of our humanity: pain–pleasure and reward–punishment.

PAST CLASSIFICATIONS OF PSYCHOLOGICAL INTERVENTIONS

Past classifications of the psychotherapies concerned themselves practically, concretely, and structurally with *frequency* of sessions (more than once a week, once a week, once every two weeks, once a month), *composition* (individuals, couples, families, or groups), *duration* (short versus long), *intensity* (supportive versus confrontational), *temporal focus* (past, present, and future), and *therapeutic schools* (humanistic, psychodynamic, behavioral, contextual). A classification of these schools will follow. Another classification pertained to straightforward (linear versus circular) or paradoxical interventions (Weeks & L'Abate, 1982). Differing rationales were found to justify one practice versus another with differing degrees of success in outcome. An underlying quality of the preceding dimensions is *cost,* probably another way to classify psychotherapies and paratherapies.

The major systematic classification derived from past dichotomies has been the one devised by Howard, Nance, and Myers (1987). By using the two dimensions of high–low directiveness and high–low support, they were able to classify most methods of therapy into a fourfold matrix. For example, behaviorism would tend to be high in directiveness and support, whereas rational–emotive therapy would be high in directiveness and low in support. Rogerian nondirectivism would be low in directiveness and high in support, whereas psychoanalysis would be low in both directiveness and support. As ingenious as this classification can be, it needs to be bolstered by evidence to support its validity. This evidence will be difficult to obtain as long as the main or only medium of exchange between therapist and client remains the spoken word.

CLASSIFICATIONS OF INSTITUTIONAL APPROACHES TO HELPING

There have been quite a few classifications of institutionalized approaches to helping. Some of these (Gibbs, 1989; Horwitz, 1990) consider helping people as a form of control or power. Among these classifications, the most influential one was proposed by Brickman et al. (1982). It consists of a fourfold model: (a) morality, (b) medical care, (c) enlightenment, and (d) compensatory interventions (Table 14.1). According to Dunst, Trivette, and Deal (1988), each of these models predicts a different outcome, negative for the first three models and positive for the fourth—the compensatory one. When the locus of responsibility for past behavior and for improvement is added, only the compensatory model, equated with psychotherapy wins out, because it avoids blaming the individual for past behavior but puts responsibility on the individual for improvement.

Horwitz (1990), instead, categorizes styles of social control according to four dimensions: harm, liability, goal, and solution. Using these dimensions, he obtains four different styles: (a) *penal,* where the solution is punishment; (b) *compensatory,* where the solution is payment (as in the welfare system); (c) *conciliatory,* where the solution lies in negotiation; and (d) *therapeutic,* where the solution is "treatment" of "personality" (p. 22). Thus, these two classifications differ on what they call "compensatory." Although Brickman et al. (1982) equate the compensatory model with the psychotherapies, Horwitz considers them otherwise. Nonetheless, both classifications do include the psychotherapies as one form of control or help, indicating, therefore, their already institutionalized nature. Once we see how the psychotherapies and paratherapies are

TABLE 14.1.   A Classification for Models of Intervention*

| Models | Responsibility | | Possible Outcomes |
	For Past Causes	For Future Outcomes	
Morality (church, advice columns)	High	High	Loneliness, exhaustion
Medical care (hospital care)	Low	Low	Passivity, dependency
Enlightenment (AA)	High	Low	Lowered self-esteem, submissiveness
Compensatory interventions (psychotherapies)	Low	High	Empowerment, enablement

* Adapted from Brickman et al., (1982) and Dunst, Trivette, and Deal (1988).

embedded into cultural and societal frameworks, we can begin to make sense of them according to past and present modes of classification.

Perhaps both models could be reconciled if we were to see pleasure–pain and punishment–reward as orthogonal dimensions yielding a four-fold classification (Figure 14.1). The moral model is represented by the religion and the penal systems, using *punishment* or its avoidance as a motivating force. The medical model essentially deals with *pain* and

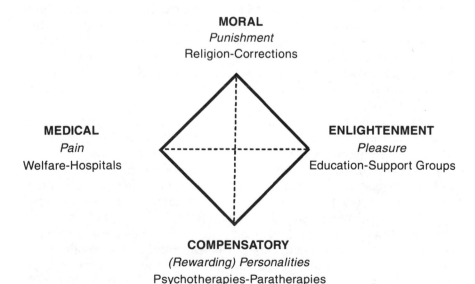

Figure 14.1. A paradigm for institutional interventions.

suffering and tries to alleviate it, just like the welfare system. The enlightenment model, exemplified by the self-help movement, tries to help people find more legitimate and socially acceptable ways of dealing with *pleasure,* such as education and support groups. The compensatory model is exemplified by the psychotherapies and paratherapies. They attempt to make up for what the other three models cannot do; that is, help people find *rewarding* ways to deal with themselves and with each other.

CLASSIFICATION FROM A PREVENTIVE VIEWPOINT

Psychotherapies and paratherapies are differentiated from each other on the dimension of structure: The former are open to what people bring into the therapy session, and the latter consisting of psychoeducational, social skills training programs, do not give this choice. The former are usually open to the number of sessions needed, with the exception of the brief therapy movement; whereas the latter states beforehand the specific number of sessions necessary to complete a program. People who want paratherapeutic help know in advance what the topic of a program is, how long it is going to last, and how much it will cost. Each lesson or session will have a definite theme, topic, or goal, a characteristic that is not present in therapy sessions. Hence, some classifications of psychotherapies may not apply to the paratherapies.

One way of differentiating and classifying psychotherapies and paratherapies would be to view them from the point of view of prevention. The psychotherapies would represent tertiary prevention approaches; whereas primary prevention, which consists of psychoeducational programs, could be conceived as being *pretherapeutic.* These programs range from structured enrichment programs to various social skills training programs for individuals, premarital couples, marriage, and family issues (L'Abate & Milan, 1985; Levant, 1986). Tertiary prevention (the psychotherapies) helps people *in crisis;* primary prevention (the paratherapies) helps people *at risk* for possible future trouble. Secondary prevention, on the other hand, consists of approaches that deal with people *in need* of help, but who may not be in crisis. An example of secondary prevention which will be considered here is writing. Writing can be viewed as being either *paratherapeutic* or *parapreventive* because it is administered *in addition* or as an *alternative* to both primary and to tertiary prevention. It can be used as preliminary, preparatory, or in parallel to either primary or to tertiary prevention, thus becoming one type of secondary prevention (Johnson, Levis, & L'Abate, 1986; L'Abate, 1990, 1992c). Fourteen criteria including risk, reversibility, probability of breakdown, ability to learn, and goals can be used to differentiate among these three types of prevention (L'Abate, 1990). Paratherapies could strengthen the process of psychotherapy if therapists and preventers were able to talk with each other and started using their approaches synergistically rather than separately (Figure 14.2).

Paratherapies can be classified according to the degree of structure and specificity of content. For instance, instructions for trainers of structured enrichment programs (L'Abate & Weinstein, 1987) are given *verbatim,* but instructions for other well-known psychoeducational programs, such as Parent Effectiveness Training (Gordon, 1970), are given in general terms or in training manuals. The result of this decreasing structure defines the role of the facilitator. The less the structure of the program, the greater is the responsibility of the facilitator, to the point that, for instance, the facilitators of the Association for Couples Enrichment differ little from other group therapists as far as structure goes (L'Abate, 1990). In composition, paratherapeutic skill-training programs differ as to their focus and content, as in groups of individuals, premarital couples, couples as partners, and couples as parents, children present or children absent (L'Abate & Milan, 1985; L'Abate, 1990) (Table 14.2).

DETERMINISM AND INDETERMINISM IN PSYCHOLOGICAL INTERVENTIONS

Helping people is the outcome of different belief and value systems among therapists and preventers. As Giacomo and Weismark (1987) indicated, two major value systems (contexts), indeterminism and determinism, are available to theorists as well as therapists. Both contexts can be seen as either two sides of the same coin or as two separate, mutually exclusive dimensions of value systems. To help people, however, both value systems are necessary. The purpose is to show how both systems are necessary once we distinguish between contexts of knowledge and of professional skills.

Therapists whose interventions consistently are at one extreme or the other of the determinism–indeterminism continuum are apt to encounter difficulties. Extremes of strict indeterminism may lead to complete capriciousness with ultimate randomness and variability (chaos). On the other hand, extremes of strict determinism may lead to rigidity, narrowness, and closedness (compartmentalization). This is not to say that an occasional use of either extreme may not be therapeutic (Table 14.3).

Knowledge

From the distinction of determinism–indeterminism derives a major distinction to be made consistently and repeatedly about knowledge. The

TABLE 14.2.   Criteria to Differentiate and Discriminate among Preventive Approaches*

| Criteria | Levels of Prevention | | |
	Primary	Secondary	Tertiary
	Proactive Pretherapeutic Posttherapeutic	Paraactive Paratherapeutic, also on a pre- and post-therapy basis	Reactive Therapeutic
1. Risk	Low to minimal	High: in need but not critical	Very high: critical
2. Reversibility	High: 67%–100%	Medium: 34%–66%	Low to very low: 0%–33%
3. Probability of breakdown	Low but potential	Medium but probable	High and real (actual)
4. Population	Nonclinical: labeled but not diagnosable	Preclinical and diagnosable	Clinical: critical and diagnosed
5. Ability to learn	High	Medium	Low
6. Goals	Increase competence and resistance to breakdown	Decrease stress and chance of crisis	Restore to minimum functioning
7. Type of involvement	Voluntary: Many choices	Obligatory: Decrease in choices	Mandatory: No other choices
8. Recommendations	"Could benefit by it." "It would be nice."	"You need it before it's too late." "Recommended strongly."	"It is necessary." "Nothing else will do." "Other choices would be more expensive (i.e., hospitalization, incarceration)."
9. Costs	Low	Medium	High
10. Effectiveness	High ?	Questionable	Low ?
11. Personnel	Lay-volunteers Pre-paraprofessionals	Middle-level professionals	Professionals
12. Types of intervention	General strengthening	More specific	Specific and specialized
Examples	Social skills training Enrichment	Workbooks	Therapy
13. Degree of structure	High	Medium	Low
14. Degree of specificity	General/low	Individualized/ medium	Specific/high

* From L'Abate (1990).

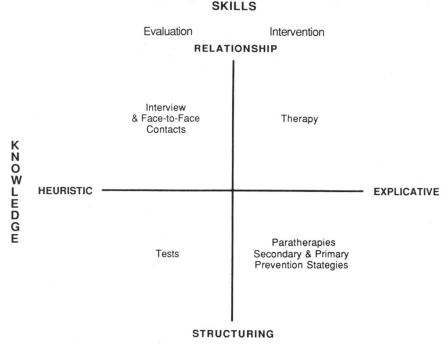

SKILLS

Evaluation   Intervention
RELATIONSHIP

Interview
& Face-to-Face   Therapy
Contacts

KNOWLEDGE

HEURISTIC ———————————————— EXPLICATIVE

Tests   Paratherapies
Secondary & Primary
Prevention Stategies

STRUCTURING

Figure 14.2. Toward a classification of evaluation and intervention approaches.

most interesting and important aspect of knowledge is its dualistic nature. Most sources agree there are two kinds of knowledge (L'Abate, 1986; Rychlack, 1968). One is *dialectic* and based on directly personal, subjectively aesthetic grounds. The other is *demonstrative* and is based on pragmatic, objective grounds. Nystrand (1977) based both kinds on linguistic usage, equating the dialectic with the *heuristic* use of language and the right hemisphere, oriented toward discovery, and the demonstrative with the *explicative* use of language and the left hemisphere, oriented toward justification. The former belongs to the realm of indeterminism. The latter belongs to the realm of determinism (Table 14.3). The heuristic belongs to the personally subjective and phenomenologically receptive side of experiencing, whereas the explicative belongs to the intersubjectively objective, visibly expressive side, discussed in Chapter 1. Whether we see these two as extreme polarities of one dimension of knowledge or two sides of the same coin, there is no doubt that one kind cannot operate without the other and that both are necessary to the whole human enterprise, including also and especially psychotherapy (L'Abate, 1986).

Once this duality of knowledge acquisition and dispersion is accepted, we need to concern ourselves with the skills necessary to "do"

TABLE 14.3.   The Contexts of Theory and Therapy

Characteristics of a Profession		Characteristics of a Science
Indeterminism	(Giacomo and Weismark, 1987)	Determinism
Discovery	(Reichenbach, 1936)	Justification
Dialectic	(Rychlack, 1968)	Demonstrative
Heuristic	(Nystrand, 1977)	Explicative
Aesthetic	(Keeney and Sprenckle, 1982)	Pragmatic
Plausibility		Accountability (results)
Seductiveness (appealingness)		Verifiability (components)
Style	(Technique)	Method
Impressionistic		Reductionistic
Relationship skills		Structuring skills
Extreme variability		Narrowed variability
Unplanned		Planned
Nonprogrammable		Programmable
Nonrepeatable from one therapist to another		Repeatable from one therapist to another
Immediate (mainly for office use)		Delayed (mainly for home use)
Specific to the person and style of the therapist		Specific to the symptomatic behavior to be improved
Idiographic		Nomethetic

psychotherapy. Here, again, we meet another duality, which can be considered either as a continuous dimension with two extremes or as a dichotomy—two sides of the same coin. In dealing with ways of helping people, we need to stress the differences between style and method in both the psychotherapies and the paratherapies.

The model resulting from combining the two types of knowledge (heuristic–explicative) and professional skills (relationship–structuring) as shown in Figure 14.2. When the three media of psychological intervention are added, we obtain the model in Figure 14.3.

Professional Skills

Psychotherapeutic and paratherapeutic processes are the outcome of two sets of therapeutic skills. The first set, relationship skills, represent what the therapist does and says in the office in front of and in contact with clients. The second set, structuring skills, represent what the therapist does and says to help clients change where it matters the most—in the kitchen, in the bedroom, and in the living room, or the office. Relationship skills include warmth, unconditional regard, and empathy. Structuring skills relates to structuring interventions outside the therapy office, such as task assignments, paradoxical injunctions, ordeal work,

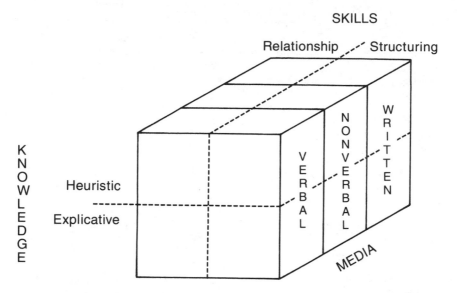

Figure 14.3. Domains of knowledge, skills in intervention, and media of intervention.

and prescriptions, such as marital and family conferences. These two sets of skills represent the omnipresent distinction between the softhearted, aesthetically dialectical *style* of the therapist and hardheaded, pragmatically demonstrative *methods* to deal with symptomatic behaviors. Style is specific to the therapist's person and personality. Method, as a series of repeatable and reproducible steps, is general and applies to the treatment of symptomatic behavior. Both sets of skills, style and method, are necessary for a positive therapeutic outcome (L'Abate, 1986). Relationship skills, by definition, focus on the person and personalities of clients. They are important to establish rapport and maintenance of the therapeutic relationship. Structuring skills, on the other hand, focus on dealing with problematic or symptomatic behavior (Table 14.4).

The first set of relationship skills is dear to the hearts of individually oriented humanistic therapists and preventers (Hart & Tomlison, 1970; Maddi, 1985; Mahrer, 1978; May & Yalom, 1984; Meader & Rogers, 1984; Miller, 1989; Raskin, 1985; Rogers, 1957; Tageson, 1982). The second set of structuring skills is basic to a more systematic approach to symptoms and problems through repeatable methods of stepwise interventions found in more expressively active, even intrusively directive modes of intervention based on written prescriptions, task assignments, and homework assignments away from the therapist's office. This approach is favored by behaviorally oriented therapists (Meichenbaum, 1985; Rimm & Cunningham, 1985; Wilson, 1984) as well as by marital

TABLE 14.4.   Differences between Relationship and Structuring Skills in Psychotherapy*

Style	Method
Relationship skills	Structuring skills
One-shot deal	Sequence of repeatable steps
Dependent and specific to each therapist	Independent of therapist
Nonreplicable or difficult to replicate	Replicable
Asserting clients' inherent worth and importance	Assessing objectively the nature of referral problem and symptom
Dealing with clients as persons and not as objects	Dealing specifically with the symptom
Global, holistic, and subjective	Detailed, particularistic, and objective
Necessary to start and to maintain relationship but insufficient to help produce changes in clients	Insufficient to start and maintain relationship but necessary to help produce changes in clients
Being available emotionally to self and to client(s) verbally and nonverbally	Systematic and planned homework assignments in writing

Relationship Skills	Structuring Skills (writing)
1. Unconditional positive regard	1. Open ("Write whatever comes into your mind.")
2. Warmth	2. Focused ("Write about your depression.")
3. Empathy (Rogers, 1957)	3. Guided ("Expand on the following questions about depression.")
4. Positive reframing	4. Programmed ("Answer the first in a series of eight lessons on depression.")

* From L'Abate (1990) and L'Abate and Platzman (1991).

and family therapists (Foley, 1984; Foster & Gurman, 1985) and preventers (L'Abate & McHenry, 1983).

MEDIA OF PSYCHOLOGICAL INTERVENTION

There are three different media of intervention: (a) nonverbal, (b) verbal, and (c) written. Development, as described in Chapter 3, progresses along the same lines, starting with the nonverbal, then progressing to verbal, and ending with the written. Each medium has characteristics and functions of its own that may or may not be shared by the other two media (Table 14.5).

Nonverbal Medium

Recent studies of Davis and Hadiks (1990) and of Hill and Stephany (1990), among many others not citable here, suggest that the nonverbal

TABLE 14.5. Comparisons among Media of Intervention

Nonverbal	Spoken*	Written*
Earliest to be learned	Learned early in life at home	Learned later in life in school
Easiest form of information	Easier than written language	Harder than spoken language
Automatic/effortless	Takes less effort	Takes more effort
Extremely informative on few cues	More productive per unit of time	Less productive per unit of time
Learned automatically	Learned automatically	Has to be taught
Spontaneous	Spontaneous	Deliberate
Dependent on immediate social context	Dependent on immediate social context	More autonomous of context
Restricted and limited to few channels	More ideas per unit of time	More ideas per number of words
No permanent record	No permanent record	Permanent record
Relatively simple	Less syntactically complex	More syntactically complex
Fairly concrete	Less abstract	More abstract
Immediate	Less time needed for planning and encoding	More time needed for planning and encoding

* Adapted from Weintraub (1981). Published with permission.

medium needs to be acknowledged as a way to access people who may not be otherwise or verbally accessible. Art, dance, and play therapy, among others can be conceived as nonverbal avenues of interventions that could be used synergistically with the verbal and the written. Again, for reasons of space and relevance, the reader is referred to external sources to evaluate this medium as a potentially powerful way to intervene with people in trouble (Table 14.6).

Verbal Medium

The verbal medium has been traditionally equated with psychological treatment to the point that we tend to forget that there are at least two other media of interventions that cannot longer be ignored or avoided, the nonverbal and the written. Since the literature on forms of psychotherapy that use the verbal medium is quite extensive, to the point that the two—psychotherapy and talk—are synonymous, there is no sense in belaboring it here. The major issue with psychotherapeutic interventions is their cost. The cost of individual face-to-face therapy can be prohibitive for many people. Hourly fees may range from $10 or $15 for therapy with a student intern to 10 times as much for an experienced therapist. How might costs be reduced without reducing effectiveness? How can a therapist's

TABLE 14.6. Classification of Media of Intervention and
Functions of Intervention Settings

Channels of Intervention:	Settings	
Media	Inside Therapist's Office	Outside Therapist's Office
Verbal	Evaluation* Direction of treatment Confrontation of issues Motivation for change Generalization to outside Emotional support	Talking with self Dialogue with partner Relatives and family of origin Friends Children Co-workers
Nonverbal	Awareness exercises Nonverbal communications Body movements Dance, art, play Biofeedback Kinesiology	Sports and exercise Nutrition and diet Vitamins Meditation
Written	Therapist's feedback	Open Focused Guided Programmed

* Most verbal functions can also take place without face-to-face contact between
therapists and clients. For instance, they can take place long distance, through the
written medium, depending on the client and the situation.

effectiveness be improved without reducing workload? How can the
present number of clinicians and organizations offer therapeutic services
to the millions of individuals, families, and couples who need help?

Writing Medium

Often, when we use the oral medium for structuring directions or directives, it is necessary to repeat instructions to the same client or from one
client to another when the same problem is presented. To avoid misunder-
standings, selective forgetting, and blatant distortions, as well as save the
therapist's or preventer's time and energy, it has been found useful by
professionals of various persuasions to write down various instructions
to clients (Lange & van der Hart, 1983; Norcross, 1986; Shelton & Levy,
1981). Most of these instructions, however, consist of ad hoc, one-time-
only interventions.

To save time and energy as well as to avoid inevitable distortions
from clients, it is much more efficient to put instructions in writing for
clients to follow step by step, matching one hour of homework for each
hour of therapy. Progress in many fields of human endeavor is based on

a written record rather than the spoken word. No business or human enterprise can flourish and advance without a written record of its transactions. Furthermore, the written medium has the advantage over the spoken medium of being *explicit* and *specific,* qualities that become confused in speaking, no matter how clearly the person may speak. Psychotherapy is one of the few enterprises in which the process (and assumed progress) has been based mainly on the spoken word. L'Abate (1986, 1987c, 1990, 1991, 1992c; L'Abate & Platzman, 1991), among others, have suggested the use of the written medium as the sole form of treatment or complementary or supplementary to the verbal and to the nonverbal media. The combination of either two or even all three media should provide synergistic outcomes that would increase the efficiency and efficacy of most therapeutic approaches, regardless of theoretical predilection.

Writing encompasses a wide range of possibilities on a continuum of structure, varying from (a) *open-ended* such as a daily diary or journal ("Write anything that comes into your head"), to (b) *focused* ("Write about your depression"), to (c) *guided* ("Answer the following questions about what you have already written about depression"), and to (d) even more structured, using *programmed* materials and workbooks ("Answer the following lessons about depression"). Programmed writing consists of a systematic series or a program of various lessons to be completed at home over a period of time, from a minimum of three weeks to as many weeks as necessary to deal with whatever troublesome problem or symptom is presented to the therapist (L'Abate, 1987c, 1990, 1992c).

The process that de Vries, Birren, and Deutchman (1990) called *guided* writing would be located between the focused and the programmed in degree of structure, yielding, therefore, four degrees of structure in the possibly paratherapeutic use of writing. Topics may range from symptomatic behaviors, such as anxiety or depression, to issues of identity and of intimacy. Virtually any topic that is already dealt with in speaking can also be dealt with in writing. In fact, some people with certain character disorders tend to reveal in writing more than they can disclose orally.

Writing is a method for increasing therapeutic efficiency and effectiveness. As an additional structuring skill, it can be used as an alternative to traditionally verbal psychotherapy. Writing has been found thus far to be clinically useful as a separate paratherapeutic approach (Pennebaker, 1990). The use of writing in psychotherapy is relatively new and may have meager empirical support. A rationale for the use of writing in psychotherapy is the splitting of therapeutic skills into relationship and structuring skills. Writing is an application of structuring skills that increases the therapist's influence outside the office and within the home or workplace. Its impact on therapeutic outcome has yet to be fully realized beyond the experience of few clinicians (Bastien & Jacobs, 1974; Phillips & Wiener, 1966). Pennebaker's (1990) research contribution in the use of writing has highlighted its use in psychotherapy. He found that students who wrote on *traumatic* topics for 20 minutes a day for four days showed improved physiological reactions and fewer physical symptoms at three months' follow-up than students who wrote about *trivial* topics. His findings have been supported and expanded by Murray and his collaborators (Donnelly & Murray, 1991; Murray, Lamnin, & Carver, 1989; Murray & Segal, 1991).

Writing in any of its four structures does not decrease or eliminate the need for a professional. Rather, it provides a way to use the professional's time and energy more effectively, thereby decreasing time and costs of psychotherapy. Writing is complementary and supplementary to the therapist's personal contribution. Depending on its degree of structure and directives, writing is free from theoretical bias. For example, a central aim of cognitively oriented therapists is to uncover self-defeating thought patterns and self-statements. In contrast, therapists with psychodynamic or humanistic orientations could use writing to aid clients in reflecting on feelings associated with particular memories or psychological states (e.g., depression).

A review of the field of psychotherapy and the use of writing for paratherapeutic purposes readily shows that writing has not been used as a possible medium of therapeutic intervention (Freeman, Simon, Beutler, & Arkowitz, 1989; Garfield & Bergin, 1986; Graham, 1990). At best, it has been used for single-shot, ad hoc purposes or to log behavior. Therefore, to include writing in the practice of psychotherapy, a conceptualization of the therapeutic process is necessary to find a responsible rationale for its use. When writing is used in the context of a caring and compassionate therapeutic relationship, it can enhance and possibly shorten the process of psychotherapy. In some cases in our practice, it has precipitated a real breakthrough in dealing with such difficult problems as prolonged anxiety, extreme depression, and strong obsessions in individuals, conflicts in couples, and symptoms in families. Its advantages have yet to be fully explored, along with its limitations. In spite of evidence already gathered and published by this and other authors, more empirical evidence needs to be gathered to support its wider applicability. Because of its cost-cutting and timesaving potential, it deserves more attention from the psychotherapeutic community than it has received heretofore.

Through the systematic use of writing, this method can be adapted to current mental health delivery services. Schools could incorporate psychoeducational modules of written lessons. Outpatient and partial hospitalization programs can easily incorporate a writing approach, especially programmed writing. Future applications might also include interactive television and personal computer systems.

ISOMORPHISM BETWEEN THE PROFESSIONAL OFFICE AND OUTSIDE ENVIRONMENTS

Any intervention, whether therapeutic or paratherapeutic, is designed to help people improve their behavior at home and at their workplace. Consequently, we need to classify what can happen in the professional office and what should ideally happen at home and at work. Table 14.6 shows how these three media have isomorphic parallels between the therapist's office and behavior outside it, a relationship that behaviorists and learning theorists call generalization or transfer of training: How does behavior (insights, understanding, experiences, etc.) supposedly learned in the therapist's office generalize to settings outside that office? Is not the goal of all therapies to improve behavior outside the therapist's office? In this framework, the three media of treatment are used synergistically to improve behavior outside our offices. The classification ensuing from considering these media of intervention with the two settings where the interventions take place, and where change should supposedly occur, is summarized in Table 14.6.

No matter what theory determines what treatment, as long as treatment is based on the spoken word, isomorphic links between the two domains are going to be difficult if not impossible to obtain and to prove. Only when treatment is linked to evaluation through writing will we be able to link the two enterprises and achieve the match between evaluation and treatment that the past generation of therapists has been looking for (Howard et al., 1987; Seligman, 1990). We have been looking for the Holy Grail of match between theory and treatment without questioning critically whether our quest was appropriate or worth doing. This classification allows us to see that treatment needs to take place along a variety of media and that in combination, these media may allow us to intervene with more people in a more discriminating manner than has been the case heretofore.

THERAPEUTIC EMPHASIS

Most psychotherapies can be classified according to their therapeutic emphasis, using the ERAAwC model discussed in Chapter 1 (L'Abate, 1986). Therapies can be classified according to their emphasis on *E*motionality, as in the humanistic schools, *R*ationality, as in the psychodynamic schools, *A*ctivity, as in the behavioral schools, *Aw*areness, as in the Gestalt school, or *C*ontext, as in the family therapy movement. This model is supported by the work of Karasu (1986), who specified the relationship between specific techniques of different schools of psychotherapy in a similar way. He differentiated among Affective Experiencing (E), Cognitive Mastery (R), and Behavioral Regulation (A) in a way that is consistent with the ERAAwC model. For instance, *Affective Experiencing* consists of the following techniques: encounter, flooding, meditation, shared dialogue, body manipulation, group regression, massage, free association, isolation, role playing, and intravenous drugs. These techniques are respectively represented by the following schools: existential analysis, implosion therapy, Arica, Gestalt therapy, Rolfing, Erhard seminars, psychoanalysis, primal scream, psychodrama, and narcotherapy. *Cognitive Mastery* consists of techniques such as interpretation, clarification, attacking irrational ideas, providing information, thought stopping, search for meaning, correcting false beliefs, analysis of transference, paradoxical intention, analysis of body armor, and confronting decisions. The schools representing these techniques are psychoanalysis, supportive therapy, rational–emotive therapy, sex therapy, logotherapy, cognitive therapy, character analysis, and direct decision therapy. *Behavioral Regulation* consists of the following methods: conditioning, teaching and coaching, direct feedback, giving rewards, direct modeling, suggestion, punishment, and relaxation. These techniques are matched by the following schools: behavior therapy, assertiveness training, biofeedback, token economies, modeling therapy, hypnotherapy, aversiveness training, and systematic desensitization.

Karasu did not include marital or family therapies, which would encompass the contextual (C) dimension not considered by his otherwise apt classification. Royce and Muhlke (1991) found some evidence to support the validity of the first three components (ERA) in the selection of intervention strategies. Part of the same ERA(AwC) model was applied by Ulrici, L'Abate, and Wagner (1981) to a classification of psychoeducational skill training programs. In fact, the production of these programs can be used as a criterion of fruitfulness and hence usefulness for the various therapeutic schools. Only the humanistic and the behavioral schools have generated preventive, psychoeducational skill-training programs (L'Abate, 1990).

PRESCRIPTIVE VERSUS EXPLORATORY, REACTIVE, OR RELATIONSHIP THERAPIES

Ultimately, the function of a classification should facilitate the task of prescription, a task that thus far has taken place along subjective and difficult-to-replicate lines (Beutler, 1989; Howard et al., 1987; Perry, Frances, & Clarkin, 1985; Seligman, 1990). As long as talk remains the major medium of exchange between therapists and patients, this goal will remain unrealistic and unreachable. However, in using written homework assignments, especially programmed ones, we can achieve a level of prescription otherwise unreachable verbally (L'Abate, 1990, 1992c). As Barkham, Shapiro, and Firth-Cozens (1989) suggested, it may be possible to use prescriptive therapy at the beginning of therapy followed by more exploratory, relationship-oriented therapy later. The same approach could be recommended in working with character disorders. They may have to finish working on written programs to demonstrate their willingness and motivation to change. If change is demonstrated in writing, they may benefit then by a personal relationship based on talk.

SPECIFICITY VERSUS GENERALITY OR COMMONALITY

One of the major controversies in the field of psychotherapy (Frank, 1974; Karasu, 1986; Strupp, 1970, 1974) has been whether specific or nonspecific factors determine therapeutic outcome. For instance, is the success of a therapeutic approach due to the therapist's warmth, regard, and empathy, or is it due to the theoretical allegiance held by the therapist? Karasu, as previously reviewed, tried to solve the controversy by identifying the "three therapeutic change agents that all schools of therapy share as the basis of their different techniques" (p. 687): affective experiencing, cognitive mastery, and behavioral regulation.

On the basis of the previous classifications, it would seem that the issue could be dealt with in a different fashion. Specificity must be applied to the symptom or referring problem in ways that are already planned, prepared, tested, and rehearsed. Symptoms need to be dealt with by using objective, standardized, and, therefore, nomothetic methods based on structured, systematic programs to be completed by clients in writing. Generality (nonspecificity), on the other hand, deals with persons and personalities in an unplanned and unprepared manner. This approach refers to the style of the therapist or facilitator, which is subjectively spontaneous and individualized in an idiographic fashion. One approach deals with structuring skills, the other approach deals with relationships. Both sets of skills are important for therapeutic and paratherapeutic outcome (L'Abate, 1986, 1990). Style means being essentially available to our clients as human beings. Methods imply performance and production to deal with symptoms, as discussed later in this chapter.

ACTIVE VERSUS PASSIVE INTERVENTIONS

Another dimension that seems crucial in the process of helping people is the degree of activity for the therapist or facilitator. Rather than one aspect of the dimension, activity–passivity, being better than the other, instead both are necessary for positive outcome. At times, the intervener needs to be active; and at other times, he or she needs to be passive. Activity means the intervener must be directively prescriptive and conductively confrontational of issues and of problem solutions, an approach that requires structuring skills. Passivity in helping people does not mean apathy and lethargy, giving up, or abandoning people. It means being nondirectively reflective of their problems, and responsively supportive of their hurts, through the use of relationship skills of warmth, unconditional regard, empathy, and the ability to reframe positively what are perceived, by clients, to be negative issues. Therefore, activity can be equated with structuring skills whereas passivity can be equated with relationship skills or style.

The relevant aspect of any form of intervention is control; that is, to help establish or reestablish control in out-of-control systems, whether individual, dyadic, or multirelational. The major issue with control, however, in spite of a burgeoning literature on the subject (Gibbs 1982, 1989; Horwitz, 1990; Hunt, 1971; Langer, 1983), does not rely on academic treatises but on the reality of control. If we do not know how to achieve control because we do not know what it comprises, how can we help people learn to obtain it? To achieve this goal, we need to ask ourselves how are we controlled and how we control others in the "real" world. We go to work and we leave work, *when our employer tells us.* While we are at work, we perform chores requested of us by following established criteria in meeting appointments, deadlines, demands, and commitments. In other words, we obtain control by following a *routine* of appointments and *practicing* behavior needed for survival until we attain a criterion of mastery. ("If you want to stop the behavior, start it!") Without routine appointments with ourselves or loved ones to practice new skills, there would not be any control over ourselves and over our environment (L'Abate, 1984).

Consequently, if we want any therapeutic approach to succeed, we need to have our patients follow routine homework assignments *at prestated times,* practicing desirable behavior repeatedly to a level of mastery. The link between our office and external settings (home, work, leisure) cannot be achieved verbally because words are subject to unexpected distortions, inevitable deletions, and unwarranted generalizations. Consequently, if we want to help people change, we had better give them instructions *in writing* to be answered *in writing* at preestablished times and for specified durations. The viewpoint that if you want to stop

TABLE 14.7.   Guidelines to Teach and Learn Control of Self and Others

Guideline 1. *Regulation:*

If you want to stop IT (unpleasant thoughts, destructive thinking, tensions, painful feelings, etc.), start IT. Arrange it weekly, biweekly appointments at specific, preset times at least 24 hours ahead and for preset durations (1, 20, 30, 45, or 60 minutes at the most).

Guideline 2. *Approach:*

If you want to get rid of IT, approach IT instead of avoiding IT. Avoiding IT, as done in the past, will only continue to keep IT inside, still controlling you.

Guideline 3. *Write:*

During the time set to start IT, approach IT by writing about IT, instead of stewing, worrying, or obsessing and ultimately being controlled by IT. According to Pennebaker (1990, pp. 198–199), writing has the following advantages over thinking or talking: (a) It clears the mind, taking away cobwebs from it; (b) it resolves traumas from the past that stand in the way and interfere with the completion and accomplishment of important tasks in the present; (c) it helps in recalling, acquiring, considering, and remembering new information; (d) it fosters problem solving by clarifying and integrating information at hand by allowing you to focus and concentrate on it in a way that cannot be done by just thinking or talking about it; and (e) freewriting promotes forced writing; by allowing you to improve on a first draft about anything, you can then go back and add more details and specifics that may have been lacking.

---

certain, not all, undesirable behaviors, we have to start them (L'Abate, 1984) is in keeping with Powers' (1991) position: "A control system regulates input, not output" (p. 152).

Therapists vary as to their notions of control. On one hand, we have the humanists who limit control to the professional office and require very little else outside it. On the other hand, we have behaviorists who want to determine generalization from the professional office to outside it, home or office, through sequences of appropriate reinforcements and consequences (Bandura, 1989). Most therapists, likely, fall somewhere along this continuum. Thus far, however, few therapists seem to understand that control is achieved through (a) regulation of preset, prearranged appointments; (b) increment of cognitive controls through homework assignments in writing; and (c) feedback from the therapist about the homework. Thus, issues of control would be another dimension along which methods of intervention can be classified. Rules to teach control in self and others are in Table 14.7.

LINKING PRACTICE WITH THEORY

This chapter has taken a position in favor of explicitness and specificity in the differential treatment of disordered personality development and psychopathology. We have presented a multilevel, integrative theory of personality development according to a continuum of experiencing-expressing, to different levels of interpretation (Chapter 1), and to a continuum of likeness (Chapter 3). This theory stresses the crucial roles of the ability to love, as expressed in Presence, and the ability to negotiate Performance and Production, as expressed in Doing and Having. The ability to love is based on the attribution of importance to self and to intimate others and the ability to be intimate. These dimensions are crucial and relevant to an understanding and treatment of any deviation from hypothetical or presumptive norms. The ability to negotiate is made up by a structure and a process. The latter is based on the level of functionality–dysfunctionality (the ARC model), the integration of various components (the ERAAwC model), and the priorities necessary for motivation to negotiate.

To begin with, the aim of all psychological interventions is to *empower* and to *enable* people to function in more rewarding ways toward themselves and close others than they have done in the past (Dunst, Trivelle, & Deal, 1988; Figley, 1989). Whether it is done directly or indirectly, psychological interventions have that effect. If they are humanistically inclined, these interventions tend to improve the feeling of *empowerment* and self-importance in clients seeking support. If they are behaviorally inclined, these interventions tend to improve competencies and skills and *enable* people to deal successfully with life situations. Improved skills may or may not lead to increased feelings of empowerment, which, in turn, may or may not lead to greater ability to negotiate. Either way, therefore, psychological interventions, indirectly or directly, tend to improve the ability to love and the ability to negotiate in people who cannot do either well. The two concepts of *empowerment* and of *enablement* match the two basic concepts of this theory, the ability to love (importance and intimacy) and the ability to negotiate power issues (performance and production).

THE AIMS OF PSYCHOLOGICAL INTERVENTIONS

As hypothesized in Chapter 6, at the bottom of all self-defeating behaviors, whether they are intrapersonal or interpersonal in expression, there is unexpressed, unresolved hurt that is experienced partially or in full force. The human tendency is to escape the unpleasant sensation of hurt for the sake of psychological survival. Flight may take many different forms and can be made in many directions. Each pain-avoidant flight pattern results in the development of a behavioral repertoire designed to escape the burden of processing, experiencing, confronting, and expressing that core hurt. Flight can be either inward or outward or both. Instead of classifying self-defeating, hurt-denying behaviors dichotomously as either affective disorders or behavior/character disorders, it may be more accurate to postulate that all self-defeating behaviors are the consequence of the avoidance or denial of hurt.

Selflessness

Selfless people, who are able to nurture, but who are either not able to receive nurturing or are unable to choose mates who are capable of nurturing, may respond to pain through four major flight patterns—all of an inward, internalizing nature. These four patterns are (a) medicating or anesthetizing hurt, (b) somatizing hurt, (c) expiating hurt, and (d) self-isolating from hurt. The first behavioral expression of hurt-avoidance that typifies the selfless individual is self-medicating hurt through the use and combination of drugs (either prescription or nonprescription) or alcohol. These substances inhibit the sensation of emotional hurt or stress. However, the substance abuser may offer several rationalizations for the use of drugs or alcohol that do not appear related to, or cognizant of, personal pain.

Somatization is another behavioral expression, however conscious, of unexpressed hurt. It is estimated that 1 in 10 hospitalized individuals has no physical or physiological basis for the illnesses or physical complaints he or she expresses. Often, somatized hurt that can be medically legitimized is the singular course by which selfless persons can demand physical and/or emotional attention. Somatized emotional hurt not only offers selfless individuals license to nurture themselves, it offers them the permission they need to make demands on their (usually selfish) intimates.

Expiating hurt, as a behavioral flight pattern from hurt, may be described as self-inflicted martyrdom that results in overserving the spouse or family. This overserving, overresponsive behavior (typically a reactive response to an underresponsive spouse or several family members) is maintained because it offers the selfless person a sense of identity and self-worth, however distorted and destructive it may be. Overserving may help selfless individuals gain the sense that they are compensating for being a burden on the marital or family system (a cognitive distortion that is frequently reinforced by an exploiting, selfish spouse). The fourth modality of hurt avoidance, is evident in the "flight inside" pattern of isolating the (selfless) self behind the wall of depression. Much like the somatizer's physiological escape from (over-) responsibilities, individuals in this category take flight emotionally into the blackness of despair, in which *A*ctivity and *R*ationality dissolve, and all that remains is self-disintegration within an *E*motionality that is severed from any human connection that could offer life support. It is possible that the elevation of crisis to this degree typifies the "living space" (as opposed to healthy Being) of most individuals immediately prior to suicide, or suicide attempts.

When a crisis erupts with the selfless partner, the family or spouse may deny the crisis and continue accepting the hurt-avoidant flight pattern of the family member. They may ignore the crisis, as they have probably done in reacting to the minicrises leading up to the upheaval, or they may reject the family member's flight pattern and coerce him or her into attitudinal or behavioral modification. Unless a self-rewarding modification is induced, it is likely that the individual will avoid and repress further his or her core hurt, and not comply with family and therapy pressures at a self-presentational level.

Selfishness

Similar problems occur with families whose selfish member experiences distress of crisis proportions, when that member and his or her family are coerced into therapy. Behavior modification, when elicited or enforced without appropriate attention given to the affective disorder fueling it (E; the affective disorder of hurt avoidance) may lead to behavioral modification at the superficial, self-presentational level of interaction. Interpersonal distress will not be alleviated and its symptoms may be manipulated. Without direct emotional confrontation, the symptoms will continue to distort the person's cognitions and will create "smoke" until the "bonfire" of the core hurt is addressed.

The normative behavioral expressions of affective disorders in a selfish person, who is able to accept nurturance but unable to offer it, may be categorized in three modalities: (a) exploitation, (b) retaliation, and (c) preoccupation. Exploitation, as a flight pattern, is developed and maintained in relationships between selfish and selfless persons, in which one partner, often the man, exploits the spouse and/or children, who extend love, nurturance, and services to him. Equivalent and reciprocal nurturance and emotional presence are not offered by the selfish person. Reciprocity, if it takes place, is offered through information, services, possessions, or currency (the modalities of Doing and Having because Being is unavailable to family members and is therefore unavailable for sharing).

The mode of retaliation, a reactive behavioral response to unexpressed hurt, is evidenced in the selfish family member's tendency to express abuse toward other family members (or co-workers) physically, psychologically, sexually, or politically (abuse of power). Behaviors associated with preoccupation are evident in the selfish family member's driven involvement in work, leisure activities, academic pursuits, consumerism, and other self-promotional activities that could be identified as expressions of Doing and Having. Chemical and liquid dependencies on "high" inducing substances are also indicative of a selfish person's behavioral attempt to ameliorate emotional distress of unexpressed hurt. In response to the nonverbal message of distress of selfish family members, the family may submit to the member's exploitation, retaliation, and preoccupation; they may ignore it; or they may, after escalation of events precipitate a crisis, reject the flight pattern of their selfish family member.

Unless the family intervenes in the flight pattern of the selfish person, he or she will continue in his or her self-defeating flight pattern. Thus, he or she will continue to (a) exploit family members; (b) retaliate physically, psychologically, politically, sexually, in aggressive, other-inflicting behaviors; and (c) preoccupy him- or herself with self-promotional activities at the expense of the spousal and familial system.

Once again, as in the selfless family member's therapy experience, the goal of therapy is to "EAR" an individual's suffering, and to recognize its ripple effect on the family. "EARing" the family will entail (a) responding to the muffled pain and distorted *E*motionality of the family member, through confrontation, expression, and processing of unresolved hurt; (b) offering specific intervention to improve self(victorious)-control of the family member's *A*ctivity, especially in the crisis stage of therapy; and (c) reality-testing and correcting the cognitive distortions that have resulted in the self-defeating, selfish flight pattern from pain, thereby helping the family members achieve more adequate *R*ationality.

As with the selfless person and family who are induced to go into therapy, unless the intervention confronts the issue of emotionality, and specifically, unexpressed hurt, the selfish person, like the selfless person, might alter the symptomatology of hurt avoidance, but will not resolve the core hurt beneath it. As in the case of the selfless member's family, the selfish family member's kin are offered a variation of the individual's flight pattern, but flight remains the objective. In this reactive response to intrapersonal and interpersonal stress, there is additional collusion between the family and the individual as the family enforces a behavioral expression of unexpressed hurt and emotionality that facilitates status quo maintenance. However, the individual remains the victim of his or her unexpressed hurt.

The goal of any psychological intervention is to help family members learn not to collude (through exploiting, submitting to, or ignoring the behavioral disorder) with the identified patient. The therapist teaches members to hear the family member's muffled weeping and to allow his or her tears to be shed through EARing the individual's behavioral expressions of silenced emotional hurt. The recovery process can then begin for both the specific family member and for the entire family.

LINKING THEORY WITH PRACTICE

How are the practices of tertiary, secondary, and primary prevention linked with a developmental theory of interpersonal competence? Links between theory and practice are summarized in Table 14.8. These links are predicated on viewing therapy and prevention as consisting of two basic sets of relationship and structuring skills. From the viewpoint of a horizontal continuum of behavior that ranges from a receptively receiving, subjectively experiencing input side at one extreme to the other extreme of an expressing, behaviorally objective output side (Chapter 1, Figure 1.1), both relationship and structuring approaches can be integrated as two sides of the same coin, with psychodynamic, rational approaches representing the middle-point processing throughput from receiving to expressing (L'Abate, 1986).

Both relationship skills can be integrated with structuring skills because *both* sets of skills are necessary for successful outcome in therapy and prevention. Although relationship skills are necessary for starting and maintaining a therapeutic relationship, they are insufficient to produce change, especially in couples and families. Structuring skills may be insufficient to start and maintain a relationship, but they are necessary to produce changes in individuals as well as in couples and families. Relationship skills relate to the modality of Being: (a) being able to be present and to be available emotionally to the self and to another verbally and nonverbally without demands for performance, production, perfection, or problem solving; (b) asserting the inherent importance and worth of clients as autonomous, self-determining human beings through expressions of unconditional regard, warmth, and empathy; and (c) positive reframing of negative behaviors (Table 14.8).

The second set of skills—structuring—is basic to an engineering approach to symptoms and problems through repeatable methods of stepwise interventions found on a more expressively active, even intrusively directive mode of interventions based on prescriptions, task assignments, and homework assignments away from the therapist's office. This approach is favored by behaviorally oriented therapists (Meichenbaum, 1985; Rimm & Cunningham, 1985; Wilson, 1984) as well as marital and family therapists (Foley, 1984; Foster & Gurman, 1985). This approach favors Doing and Having, by asking clients to perform and produce (service) any time they process and complete homework assignments (information).

TABLE 14.8. Relationships between a Developmental Theory of Interpersonal Competence and Skills in Therapy and in Prevention

Being	Doing and Having
Presence	Performance (Power) Production
Relationship skills	Structuring Skills
Therapeutic style	Paratherapeutic method
Asserting clients' inherent worth and importance	Assessing and asserting the seriousness of referral problem and symptom
Dealing with clients as persons and not as objects	Dealing specifically with the symptom
Global, holistic, and subjective	Detailed, particularistic, and objective
Necessary to start and maintain relationship but insufficient to help produce changes in clients, especially couples and families	Insufficient to start and maintain relationship but necessary to help produce changes in clients, especially couples and families
Being available emotionally to self and to client(s)	Systematic and planned homework assignments in writing

The equation of relationship skills with Presence and of structuring skills with Performance and Production is supported by Huston and Rempel (1989), already quoted in Chapter 1. They distinguished between the two literatures by referring to them respectively as attitudinal–dispositional and behavioral. In relation to a developmental theory of interpersonal competence, the attitudinal–dispositional view would tend to support a postulate about the ability to love, whereas the behavioral view would tend to support a postulate about the ability to negotiate as the two most fundamental processes for individual, dyadic, and family living. This distinction reappears in therapy as two sets of skills: relationship and structuring skills. This distinction allows one to relate a developmental theory of interpersonal competence to the practice of therapy and programmed writing.

LIKENESS AND THERAPY

Furthermore, some aspects of psychological interventions can be linked to a continuum of likeness discussed in Chapter 3. For instance, Wills (1978) reviewed the role of similarity and attraction in the therapeutic relationship:

> Similarity of attitudes, interests and values is a basic determinant of innate personal attraction. A large number of studies have demonstrated that the attraction between persons is a direct function of the similarity between them, and this is usually termed the principle of similarity and attraction. . . . This process has wide generality, and in many contexts it can be predicted reliably that persons will like others who are similar to themselves and will tend to dislike persons who are dissimilar to themselves. (p. 982)

Wills (1978) goes on to cite a variety of studies showing a positive relationship between similarity in the therapist–client dyad and therapeutic outcome, when such a similarity includes social class, interests, and values, and orientations to interpersonal relations. In addition, Wills reviewed the level of authoritarianism and negativity in helpers, which would relate to a demand for sameness as defined by: ". . . a controlling, restrictive (and sometimes punitive) orientation toward clients, together with derogation of their personal attributes" (p. 982). This attitude translates itself in "programs almost exclusively oriented toward control of patients, emphasizing strict rules for patient behavior (and staff determination of those rules), highly structured activities for patients, and physical neatness of the ward" (Wills, 1978; p. 982). Many of these characteristics are reminiscent of parental behaviors prescribed for noncompliant children where rigidity, authoritarianism, and

TABLE 14.9.   Suggestions for a Hierarchy of Mental Health Personnel

Level of Training	Skills and Responsibilities

Doctorate or equivalent	Crisis intervention
	Treatment plans based on conclusions from evaluation (history, interview, objective tests, and diagnosis)
	Delegation of therapeutic responsibilities:
	  matching of treatment with helpers or
	  matching problem with solution;
	  assumption of some therapeutic responsibilities
	Supervision and support of master-level personnel
	Quality control, maintenance of ethical and professional standards
	Research leadership

Master or equivalent	Carrying out most therapeutic, paratherapeutic, and pretherapeutic responsibilities; prolonged face-to-face contact before, during, and after crisis Support and supervision of bachelor-level personnel
Bachelor or equivalent	Administration and scoring of standard tests Assignment, review, and feedback of written homework assignments Administration of primary and secondary preventive activities

inadequate negotiation are designed to produce blindly uncritical conformism. That practice often boomerangs to produce rebellion and rejection in the offspring.

IMPLICATIONS OF THIS CLASSIFICATION FOR A HIERARCHY OF MENTAL HEALTH PERSONNEL

This classification begs the question: "Who is going to perform all these services?" There are not sufficient doctorate-level personnel to perform all the various services that are necessary to help all the people at risk, in need, and in crisis. Consequently, we will need to start differentiating among different types and levels of personnel according to a hierarchical perspective, a ladder or lattice of human services, as summarized in Table 14.9. As this table shows, a classification of methods of intervention will allow a parallel differentiation among different types of personnel from professional to clerical. Whether this proposal will be implemented is a matter of policy that is outside the realm of this writing.

CONCLUSION

A complex classification of psychotherapies according to traditional and more recent categories or dimensions allows us to see what we need to learn to help people in trouble. In addition to the verbal modality, training programs in psychotherapy may need to develop additional courses in nonverbal and written media of intervention. Once we have learned a vast armamentarium of different intervention methods, we should be able to find out how to use the three major media of treatment—verbal, nonverbal, and written—synergistically, to improve our chances of success.

Long gone are the days when we could conclude the effectiveness of any form of treatment on a dichotomous black–white, true–false, applicable–nonapplicable basis. With so many forms of treatment available, we can no longer base our choices and selections of treatment(s) on an all-or-none basis. Instead, we need to choose one or more forms of treatment on the basis of *specificity of treatment* and *matching of a patient's needs with a specific treatment.* Nonetheless, we cannot choose or dismiss any legitimate and professionally available form of treatment only on grounds of fruitfulness or popularity. Other criteria must be considered, such as cost-effectiveness, specificity in client-treatment matching, and personal and interpersonal relevance.

We also will rely on other mental health professions and on a hierarchy of personnel for whatever their particular contribution may be. If one of our clients is extremely upset, he or she may need medical care, such as a prescribed tranquilizer or medication, and nonmedical approaches, such as a massage or a hot tub, provided therapist and client understand that a temporary crutch cannot be used for life (unless that is what the client wants—another form, albeit legitimate, of addiction). An appropriate and effective course of treatment for any dysfunctionality would involve multiple treatment modalities used synergistically with a variety of specialized personnel.

PART SIX

Conclusion

CHAPTER 15

The Adequacy of the Theory

There is nothing as practical as a good theory.
(LEWIN, 1935)

. . . . what counts as objective truth is not the result of rationally subjecting hypotheses to empirical test, but emerges from a network of social agreements.
(GERGEN, 1991, p. 93)

To claim superiority of position on the basis of factual accuracy is specious, for accounts of "the way the world is" don't grow from nature but from the application of a socially shared perspective.
(GERGEN, 1991, p. 94)

The purpose of this chapter is to ascertain how the theory presented in the previous chapters can be evaluated conceptually and methodologically. How does this theory stack up against the criteria listed in the introductory chapter? No author can render that judgment. It will be up to the reader to reach and render it. The criteria that concern us the most are validity and consistency, as well as whether the definition of personality used here can encompass psychopathology. Conceptually, this theory needs to be evaluated in terms of how well it compares with other psychological models that have been borrowed and used in developing it. This developmental theory of interpersonal competence has integrated many concepts borrowed from other psychological disciplines. For instance, the notion of what a theory is and requires (Chapter 1) seems to be in line with what a psychological theory needs to be in order to be testable. It cannot be said, however, that the definition of personality adopted here (Chapter 2) is in line with other definitions, if any (Pervin, 1990). The concept of development over the life cycle seems to be in line with most contemporary views of development, whereas well-known concepts of imitation have been redefined in different terms according to a continuum of likeness (Chapter 3). Developmental terms, such as attachment and dependence (Chapter 4), have been defined as extreme in approach–avoidance tendencies; and control functions, such as discharge–delay, have been made a function of time (Chapter 5).

The greatest debt of gratitude, however, is owed to social psychology, where social comparison theory (Festinger, 1954) is at the basis of a continuum of likeness (Chapter 3), and resource exchange theory (Foà & Foà, 1974) is at the basis of attribution of self-importance (Chapter 6) and the zest of this theory. Both processes are postulated as being basic to development (Chapters 3 and 6); attribution theory (Kelley, 1967) is also used in the attribution of importance to self and to others (Chapter 6). Previous attempts have been piecemeal with limited integration into a larger view (Kihlstrom, 1987). Resource exchange theory is basic to the whole of Part Three, on the competencies of Being, Doing, and Having. Ecological theory (Barker, 1968) was influential in developing the concept of setting, considered in Part Four.

Consequently, this chapter will show how the present theory relates to well-known and already established developmental and social psychological concepts, and how the theory can be expanded to encompass not only psychopathology (discussed in Chapter 6), but also sex, sexual behavior, and especially addictions.

The rest of this chapter will review supportive viewpoints, minor theories, and models that have been useful in constructing this theory. Thus, most of the epistemological evidence reviewed in this chapter is inferential in supporting the theory. Empirical evidence that is indirectly related or directly derived from this theory is still at its beginnings (L'Abate, 1990; L'Abate, 1991; Stevens & L'Abate, 1989). The various theories or models that form the background of this theory follow.

HISTORICAL ANTECEDENTS

No theory can be constructed without referring to past and present theories that have been influential in its development. Most of this influence may have been indirect rather than direct. However, no one can create anything without referring to past theories and viewpoints. Among those that have been most influential are psychoanalysis and object relations theory, linguistics and general semantics, and family psychology and therapy. The latter will be left out for reasons of space, but their undeniable influence is present in each word of this text.

Psychoanalysis

No specific reference is needed here to acknowledge Sigmund Freud's contribution. He and his followers started to interpret symptoms and behavior according to schemes not previously considered in the history of thinking. The major error made by this school was equating interpretation with change (interpretation of symptomatic behavior will *ipso facto* produce change in the behavior). Unfortunately, this was not the case, because all that interpretation did was to rely unduly on rationality, often bypassing the emotional, interpersonal, and contextual basis of the symptom. Sometimes, however, mostly by chance, interpretation would help in a hit-or-miss fashion. Although not isomorphic, interpretation and change are occasionally linked in some nonlinear and still unknown fashion (L'Abate, 1986). In spite of this incorrect equation, interpretation became the major therapeutic tool of change in psychoanalysis, and as such was here to stay.

The most relevant contribution of psychoanalysis to the present theory lies in the concept of defensive behavior, which thus far has been conceptualized in terms that, with the exception of the defense of repression, have been difficult, if not impossible, to verify. Once defenses are conceptualized as extensions and exaggerations of basic approach–avoidance and discharge–delay functions, we can relate them to visible and possibly quantifiable dimensions. More recently, there have been attempts to link psychoanalysis with social psychological concepts (Curtis, 1991).

Linguistics and General Semantics

Sapir (1921) and Whorf (Carroll, 1956) were part of the linguistic school of relativism that demonstrated the cultural determinism of language. As a famous linguist (Whatmough, 1956) concluded: "For language is a constant of human life, like breathing or the beating of the heart, independent of an alleged external reality, and independent of its own fluctuations and variations" (p. 148). Language is relative to the culture it represents, and, therefore, it illustrates how we think and how our thinking has been determined by the most immediate culture nearly all of us experience after birth, the culture of the family. Thus, our linguistic habits represent the learning and the modeling that goes on every minute of our lives in the closeness of our families. Nowhere is this conclusion more evident than in the families of schizophrenics. Language, like the attribution of importance and self-differentiation, is automatic to our learning to become persons. Consequently, we are not aware of how we act in expressing our importance any more than we know how we learned to talk.

If we conceive general semantics as applied linguistics, then we must acknowledge the contribution of Alfred Korzybski (1933) about the way language affects thinking and must recognize that many errors in our thinking are derived from how we talk (Chase, 1938). Language is an abstraction ("The map is not the territory")—a poor and limited representation of the complex physical and human reality. As Watzlawick (1978) amply acknowledged, Korzybski was one of the pioneers predating in many ways the neurolinguistic programming school. His analysis of linguistic errors formed the basis for the field of general semantics, which in many ways either predated or runs parallel to the communication school started by Ruesch and Bateson (1951). Although language is a poor representative of our reality, we have nothing to replace it, and consequently, we need to improve it. Watzlawick's conclusion (1978), influenced a great deal by Korzybski, seems apt here:

> Perhaps the most murderous element in human history is the delusion of a "real" reality, with all the consequences that logically follow from it . . . (p. 221) [I]t requires a very high degree of maturity and tolerance for others to live with relative truth, with questions for which there are no answers, with the knowledge that one knows nothing. . . . (p. 222)

The major contribution of the linguistic and general semantics schools to the present theory relies on the relativity of language and that most of the concepts we use to make sense of our reality are indeed attributions. From these schools, it was a skip and a jump to progress to neurolinguistic programming. This relativistic position is consistent and in some ways supports, the practice of multiple, positive reframings in psychotherapy. For instance, depression can be considered as a representative model of dysfunctionality where multiple, positive reframings are not only possible but in some ways mandatory. Rather than offering depressed people a single-minded interpretation, we want to present a variety of options from which they can choose the positive reframing that best fits their worldview (L'Abate, 1986).

Historically, neurolinguistic programming is a direct offshoot of linguistics and general semantics. Errors deriving from processes of generalization, deletion, and distortion were pointed out by Bandler and Grinder (1975) and Grinder and Bandler (1976) on the basis of their analysis of therapeutic dialogues. The inordinate claims of successes by the followers of this technique are not matched by empirical as well as by clinical evidence. Nonetheless, as with psychoanalysis, interpretation of linguistic habits and errors remains a significant contribution in its own right, even if the evidence for its therapeutic gains leaves much to be desired.

VALIDITY FOR THE EXTRATHEORETICAL ASSUMPTIONS OF THE THEORY

Extratheoretical refers to all the assumptions made in the text before Part Two, which introduced the assumptions relevant to this theory. For instance, Chapter 1 revealed two major assumptions about the importance of an experiencing–expressing continuum and descriptive and explanatory levels of interpretation. In Chapter 2, we made some assumptions about the nature of the self as a relational, interactive, and transactive construct that achieves meaning in prolonged, close, and committed (intimate) relationships. Chapter 3 postulated a continuum of likeness to describe the genotypical sublevel of development. There was an attempt at each step to muster logical and empirical evidence. By their very nature, however, some of these assumptions are assertions that we want to believe as valid regardless of their evidential base.

Impression Formation and Management

The issue of impression formation and management is relevant to our understanding of behavior in terms of levels of description and explanation considered in Chapter 1 (Schlenker, 1980; Snyder & Swann, 1976). Although socially we may put our best foot forward to make a good impression, we differ in how we appear to others external to our family. The discrepancy between these two levels of public and private description, that have been called presentational and phenotypical respectively, is important to an understanding of personality functioning–dysfunctioning. Some people stress external appearance at the expense of substance, some reverse this trend, and some people balance these two levels.

As soon as we accept the importance and validity of these two levels, however, we need to find how we can explain them, their consistencies, inconsistencies, and contradictions (Wakefield, 1989). At an internal, often unconscious level (traits), we may use intrapsychic concepts, such as self-esteem and self-perception to explain why members of a family present themselves publicly in one way and behave in another way in the privacy of their homes. Once we accept such a structural or situational explanation, we would have to introduce a historical view to explain the internal constructs we have used to "explain" discrepancies or consistencies between public and private behaviors (L'Abate, 1976).

Social Comparison

Basic to the development of styles in intimate relationships lies the differentiation of an individual according to a continuum of likeness, as discussed in Chapter 3. Expansion of the social comparison theory (Festinger, 1954; Kruglanski & Mayseless, 1990; Suls & Miller, 1977; Suls & Wills, 1990; Wood, 1989) to a continuum of likeness consisted of adding to the original dichotomy of similar–dissimilar, the dialectical ranges of same–opposite and symbiotic–autistic yielding a bell-shaped, dialectical continuum of likeness (L'Abate, Weinstein et al., 1989). This continuum is at the core of the three styles, AA, RR, and CC.

The presence of reactivity in intimate relationships is supported by the work of Gottman (1979), who showed that, given a certain amount of provocation in any couple, the degree of reactivity (immediate and thoughtless response, retaliation, or revenge), characterized clinical couples more than functional couples. The latter were able to defuse the provocation and go on with a minimum of uproar. Another source of evidence for the three styles in intimate relationships can be found in the work of Lewis (1989). Lewis and his collaborators found four different levels of competence in families. At the highest level of competence, spouses are close, committed, well individuated (differentiated), open, and spontaneous with a wide range of feelings and clear boundaries between themselves and their children. The lower level of competence is indicated by pained families whose spouses show definite conflicts in the area of closeness and intimacy and distance regulation. Next to this level is the male dominant–female submissive family, with little affect and virtually no negotiation. The lowest level of competence is shown by conflicted families, with chronic disagreements, little closeness, no intimacy, and low commitment. On the basis of the three styles in intimate relationships (Chapter 3), the highest level of competence, according to Lewis's topology, fits in the conductive–creative style; the next two levels would fit into the reactive–repetitive style; whereas the lowest level would fit into the abusive–reactive style.

VALIDITY FOR THE ASSUMPTIONS OF THE THEORY

The two assumptions of space and time leading to the two postulates of ability to love and to negotiate are supported by the work of Olson and his associates (Olson, Russell, & Sprenkle, 1989). This model is based on two basic dimensions that are considered basic to ultimate relationships, cohesion and adaptability. Cohesion is defined as the ". . . emotional bonding that family members have toward one another" (p. 9). Adaptability is defined as ". . . the ability of a marital or family system to change power structure, role relationships, and relationships rules in response to situational and developmental stress" (p. 12). Cohesion subsumes a dimension characterized by four steps from low to high cohesion: disengaged, separated, connected, and enmeshed. This dimension resembles the continuum of likeness, where symbiosis would represent enmeshment and autism would represent disengagement, while separated–connected would represent various levels of same–opposite and similar–different. Adaptability subsumes a dimension characterized by four steps from low to high adaptability: rigid, structured, flexible, and chaotic. This dimension would resemble the self-importance model of Chapter 6 to the extent that selfulness would result from structured-flexible problem solving ("I win, you win"); whereas rigid–chaotic would describe various gradations and types of selfish ("I win, you lose"), self-less ("You win, I lose"), and non-self positions ("We both lose").

Olson and his co-workers arrived at this model, not only empirically, through results of various factor analyses, but also on the basis of comparing strikingly similar epistemological evidence. They reviewed a variety of theorists who, although using different concepts, showed a convergence for a two-factor view of behavior in personality development and intimate relationships (p. 9). Beavers and Voeller (1983) used centripetal–centrifugal for cohesion and adaptability. While Benjamin (1977) worked with affiliation and interdependence, Epstein, Bishop, and Levin (1978) utilized affective involvement and behavior control–problem solving. For Gottman (1979), validation and contracting were synonymous with cohesion and adaptability. Kantor and Lehr (1975) researched affect and power dimensions, whereas L'Abate (1986) used intimacy and power. Leary (1957) and Constantine (1986) chose affection–hostility and dominance–submission. Leff and Vaughn (1985) analyzed distance and problem solving. Parsons and Bales (1955) used expressive and instrumental roles, and Reiss (1981) studied coordination and closure. L'Abate and Colondier (1987) also reviewed additional epistemological evidence to support the two dimensions of intimacy and power, including the work of McAdams (1988), whose analysis of Thematic Apperception Test (TAT) stories yielded two major factors, intimacy and power, providing striking support at the intrapsychic level for the same two factors at interpersonal and intimate levels.

The fundamental issue with these two factors, however, does not rest with their validity, for which there is sufficient theoretical and empirical support. What is relevant here is the question, How do these concepts develop? Like most models, Olson et al.'s model may describe well what goes on in intimate relationships. As noted in Chapter 1, however, description does not mean or denote explanation. If we link both factors to the two assumptions and postulates of the theory, space—the ability to love, and time—the ability to negotiate, we can begin to tentatively explain how these two factors develop over time.

Space and Social Settings

Space is where we live before conception from the cradle to cremation or equivalent (Altman, 1975; L'Abate, 1964, 1976, 1983a, 1985a; Linder, 1970). Living in space means having to modulate, modify, and moderate our approach–avoidance tendencies into workable, functional choices of whom, what, when, how, and why we approach and whom, what, when, how, and why we avoid at the same time. Any act of approach toward somebody or something is a choice and possibly an act of avoidance of someone or something else. These acts transform themselves over time, going toward a functional, selective, careful balance of these tendencies in most cases, and toward a dysfunctional amplification of one at the expense of the other. From these tendencies, we develop attachments, dependencies, denial of dependencies, and (when we mature into adulthood), interdependencies. Here is where nonverbal behavior becomes relevant to intimacy and closeness in prolonged and committed relationships (Noller, 1984, 1985). The ultimate act of intimacy—crying and sharing grief together—is nonverbal, expressed in the request, "Be here now with me when I am hurting." This request demands the emotional presence of a loved one in times of grief and makes no demands for performance, production, problem solving, or perfection. This presence is usually communicated nonverbally as well as verbally, but it is best expressed when the person is able and willing to share the hurts of a loved one as well as the joys (L'Abate, 1986).

Space is not only how we share it with loved ones in our homes, emotionally and practically, but also how we choose to travel to work, leisure, and transitory (malls, beauty salons, barbershops, bars) settings (Barker, 1968; Schoggen, 1989). In most cases, we may have no choice. However, we do have choices in how we prioritize these various settings for our well-being and the well-being of loved ones. Is the work setting more important than home? Is shopping at the mall better than spending time at a bar? Some of our approach–avoidance tendencies may be modulated and modified by the impression we want to make on others.

Time

The evidence for the importance of time has been reviewed in Chapter 5. Admittedly, the jump from time to the ability to negotiate may be a long and tortuous one. On the other hand, negotiation is based on the ability to express feelings in an appropriate, nonjudgmental fashion, concentrating on solving task demands and respecting another's feelings and opinions. The win–win position present in selful position ("We" rather than "I" or "You") requires modulating and modifying discharge–delay functions until we reach an appropriate atmosphere where mutual problem solving may take place. In many intimate, selful relationships, this process may proceed tacitly, nonverbally, and automatically. In less than selful positions—reactive ones—the process may be coupled with uproars and interferences that prolong it even though they may not preclude it. In abusive-apathetic relationships negotiation may never take place.

Attribution Theory

Heider (1958) is the acknowledged (Kelley, 1967) social psychologist who stressed the process of attribution—that most, if not all, causes of human events are hypothetical guesses at best or downright inventions stemming from our perceptions. As Kelley (1967) stated: "Attribution refers to the process of inferring or perceiving the dispositional properties of entities in the environment" (p. 193). This position was elaborated further by Jones et al. (1971), who among others, refer to the importance of labeling as a major form of attribution often leading to faulty and pathogenic generalizations and stereotypes. Attribution theory also leads toward the same conclusions stated earlier by Korsybski, without acknowledging, his contribution, however.

The attribution of attributions—that a great deal of our reality is of our own making—is not too different from early views of general semantics about the relativity of our perceptions (Weary, Stanley, & Harvey, 1989). Nonetheless, the importance of subjective perceptions is especially relevant to how and what we do and say about ourselves and others. Attributions speak about the importance of the phenomenological reality of individual perceptions, especially in close relationships where distortions, deletions, and generalizations are more apt to be exaggerated, amplified, or denied and suppressed (Mahoney, 1991). The importance of attributions is especially relevant to how family members see themselves and each other and how they exchange these attributions. The most important attribution, fundamental to how families are formed and maintained, is the attribution of love.

Commitment and Close Relationships

The proof of the pudding in personality development consists of how we behave in close, committed, and usually lasting relationships such as marriage and parenthood. The real test is not how we come off in short-lived, superficial, or contrived laboratory situations or relationships (Kiesler, 1971; Schwartz & Merten, 1980; Smedes, 1988). Thus, the study of commitment to long-range relationships becomes crucial for our understanding of why some relationships last and some break up. What kind of person will marry what other kind of person? Who will give up and who will not, no matter what happens? Can we reduce commitment to individual personality traits and characteristics, or is this process only a function of two people's interaction independent from other personality characteristics? Chapter 6 represents an initial effort to discern what may be going on in close and prolonged relationships with different types of personality makeup. Direct testing of this model of self-importance can be carried out through the Problems in Relationships Scale (L'Abate, 1992c) and the Intimacy Scale developed by Cusinato and L'Abate (1994), among others.

Self-Definition and Self-Importance

The most important source of epistemological support for the model of self-importance and self-definition was developed completely independently of the present formulation. McClintock and Keil (1983) presented a model that in many ways is similar to the one presented here

(Chapter 6). On the horizontal axis, their model included a dimension maximizing a person's own outcome characterized by masochism at the left side and individualism at the right. The vertical axis dealt with outcome toward others and was made up by altruism at the top and by aggression at the bottom. These orthogonal dimensions were intersected by two other dimensions, sadomasochism in the lower left quadrant defined as masochism–aggression and cooperation in the upper right quadrant, defined as individualism–altruism; martyrdom appeared in the upper left quadrant, defined as masochism–altruism; and in the lower right quadrant, competition was positioned, defined as aggression–individualism.

If this model were rotated by 45 degrees it would be somewhat equivalent to the model in Chapter 6. Individualism would identify selfulness, whereas masochism would identify no-self. Aggression would identify with selfishness, altruism with selflessness. Cooperation would be found in the quadrant defined by the selful position, and competition would be found in the quadrant characterized by selfulness–selfishness. Martyrdom would be found in the quadrant characterized by no-self and selflessness. Sadomasochism would be found in the quadrant characterized by non-self-selfishness, as seen in many extreme character disorders, such as criminality. As Curtis and other contributors argued (1991), there is such a thing as a self-defeating personality, whose internal genotype, as well as intimate and interpersonal styles should be close to the selflessness position.

Game Theory

The outcome of win–win, lose–win, win–lose, and lose–lose in intimate relationships (L'Abate, 1976, 1985a) can be related to game theory propounded by Luce and Raiffa (1957) and Pruitt (1983). Ultimately, the outcome of close and prolonged relationships can be positive and multiplicatively improving ($+ + = \times$), as in conductive–creative relationships, remain the same ($+ - = 0$), as in reactive-repetitive relationships, or end up in negatively divisive outcomes ($- - = -/-$), as in murder, suicide, mental illness, or criminality in abusive-apathetic relationships (L'Abate, 1976). This human arithmetic is very close to people who suffer from emotional and relational scars. They are keenly aware of how much they have lost and how defeated they were by abusive–apathetic relationships in their families of origin that may have been repeated in their families of procreation.

Self-Disclosure and Intimacy

Self-disclosure of vulnerability, fallibility, and neediness which make up intimacy, can take place when two people share equality of (attributed) importance and reciprocity of positively rewarding, loving relationships, as in win–win selfulness (Clark & Reis, 1988; L'Abate, 1986; Thoits, 1986). The work of Pennebaker (1990) supports the original notion that intimacy consists of the sharing of hurts, discussed in Chapter 6. It is present in conductive–creative relationships characterized by commitment, reciprocity, and equality. In reactive–repetitive relationships, intimacy can be sporadic and short-lived. In abusive–apathetic relationships, if there is intimacy at all, it is shown contradictorily, as in the case of the wife batterer who cannot live with or without his wife and would rather kill her than allow her to leave him. Here, symbiosis and autism are intertwined.

Development and Resource Exchange Theory

To delineate links between resource exchange theory and this theory, the significance of the social context as a contributor to personality development will be discussed as it is verified independently in various areas of study. Different schools of thought have generated empirical findings in an attempt to define variables that account for developmental competence versus incompetence.

These distinct areas within psychology (developmental, clinical, personality) recognize the importance of the psychosocial environment in determining competence and the nature of personality development. In discussing a theoretical derivation of pathological personalities, Millon (1986) reaffirmed the view that "pathology always reflects a person–environment interaction" (p. 645). Kegan (1982) discussed problem and process in human development with the focus on the evolving self. He described the constitutions of the self and elaborated on "the two yearnings in human experience," (p. 107). Each subsumed the other. Both are observed according to appropriately specific situations. Except for object-relations theorists, most of the other theorists seem to go to great lengths to avoid dealing with the family as the matrix of personality development and psychopathology.

SEX AND SEXUALITY

This theoretical framework has been applied toward a tentative classification of sex and sexuality (L'Abate & Hewitt, 1988b), which can also serve as another way of illustrating how this theory of interpersonal competence in intimate relationships is related to a theory of resource exchange (Foà & Foà, 1974), or more specifically, how resource exchange theory can be expanded to cover sex and sexuality in intimate relationships (Table 15.1). Sex and sexuality as acts of love are related to being available or emotionally present to the partner. Sex and sexuality as a

TABLE 15.1.   Toward a Classification of Sex and Sexuality According to a Theory of Personality Development and Resource Exchange Theory*

Modalities	Resources	Methods	Outcomes
Being	Importance	Attribution of importance to self and loved ones	Presence
	Intimacy	Seeing the good, caring, forgiveness, sharing of hurts (intimacy)	
Doing	Information	Books, articles	
	Services	Early experiences	
		One-night stands	Performance
		Recreational sex	
Having	Goods, possessions	Paraphernalia Pornography	
	Money	Surrogates, prostitutes	
		Mistresses, gigolos	
		Marital arrangements where sex is exchanged for financial security	Production

* From L'Abate and Hewitt (1988a,b).

physical act are related to performance. When money enters in the exchange, sex and sexuality performed becomes production. Sexual decisions that need to be negotiated relate either to performance or to production. As stated repeatedly, love and status are not negotiable. When they are negotiated, they become commodities that lose their personal, intimate quality and become linked to sex as performance and production, but not to presence. When presence is defective, there will be an exaggeration and overreliance on sex and sexuality as either performance or production, as in the paraphylias.

IMPLICATIONS OF THE THEORY FOR A CLASSIFICATION OF ADDICTIONS

In addition to the implications of this theory for an understanding of functionalities and dysfunctionalities in personality development as considered in Chapter 6, this theory has direct implications for an understanding of addictions and addictive behaviors. To find support for this theory, however, other existing theories of addictions need to be considered critically in their implications for our understanding. What theory, among so many, can we use that would be relevant to an understanding of addictions (Blane & Leonard, 1987)? For instance, Levin (1987) used Kohut's (1971) self-theory, a recent offshoot of psychoanalytic theory, to understand the narcissistic personality of some addicts (Frosch, 1985;

McFadden, 1988). However, there are some addicts who may fail to show such a characteristic. In fact, there are addicts who are more concerned about the welfare of others than about their own welfare, as in religious fanaticism, in excessive spending, or in addictive, codependent love relationships. How can we explain altruistic, compulsive embezzling and giving to others, for instance? Furthermore, characteristics of narcissism have usually been defined impressionistically and clinically. However, we should have more objective evidence that narcissism can be validly measured and selectively applied instead of being used wholesale to explain most addictive behaviors. Thus, psychoanalytic theory, no matter how encompassing and inclusive it may be, is not only difficult to evaluate and verify but is rather expensive and, as a whole, practically inapplicable to the treatment of addictions. This conclusion, however, does not preclude its application to specific cases where the patient may have the financial, emotional, and intellectual resources to benefit from this type of treatment.

What theory shall we use to make such a choice? Psychoanalytic theory, *at its very best,* may apply to 5% of the overall population of addictions. Systems thinking and psychoanalysis may be extremely encompassing, but at the same time, they are too general and vague to allow verifiability on better grounds than the verbal and the rhetorical. Furthermore, both psychoanalytic approaches and systems thinking have failed to produce psychoeducational programs for primary and secondary prevention of addictions (L'Abate, 1990). According to the criterion of fruitfulness discussed in Chapter 1, in producing programs for primary and secondary prevention, only the humanistic and the behavioral schools have produced enough programs to fulfill this criterion.

Marlatt (Marlatt & Gordon, 1985), among others, used social learning and behavioral theory to make sense of addictions from the viewpoint of classical conditioning (Cappell & Greeley, 1987; Siegel, Krank, & Hinson, 1988), where reinforcement and gratification are part of the reward system that keeps the addiction going (Abrams & Niaura, 1987; McCrady, Dean, Dubreuil, & Swanson, 1985; Pomerleau & Pomerleau, 1988; Shaffer & Schneider, 1985; Shipley, 1987; Zinberg & Shaffer, 1985). Anxieties (internal tensions and drives) are used as explanatory concepts to understand addictions and their reinforcement value as drive-reduction, whatever the drive may be, be it inadequate self-concept, poor self-esteem, self-efficacy, or other intrapsychically inferred concepts.

Undoubtedly, there are more theories of addictions than there are addictions. But can the present theory serve as an umbrella in helping us make sense of most, if not all, addictions? Can this theory allow us to see addictions as being in continuity and in contiguity with functional or "normal" behavior? We do subscribe, unabashedly, to a view of addictions that implies a *defect* notion. Addicts are defective in certain personal or personality characteristics that make addictions one of the most difficult conditions to treat. In fact, many addicts do not want treatment. No one can help anyone recover unless that person wants recovery. No one can be helped against her or his will. We are aware of the multiple causes that precipitate and accompany addictions.

There may well be genetic and physiological determinants and predispositions, and if they are not the determinants, they may be the consequences of abuse. Many of these are either determinants or consequences that we cannot control (Fingarette, 1988). Consequently, we want to put our energies in using workable, practical, theoretical and treatment models based on psychological approaches. In addictions, Being is confused with either Doing (information and services) and/or Having (money and possessions): "If you loved me you would do . . . ," or "If you loved me you would buy . . . ," as in conditional rather than unconditional love. Either one or both abilities, the ability to love and the ability to negotiate, are defective in addictions. Addicted individuals either love themselves and gratify themselves at the expense of loved ones, or love others more than themselves, giving more importance to others than to themselves, thus depleting themselves of self-worth and of importance, as in the case of codependent individuals.

Surely, addicts are able to fool some people some of the time. However, they are not able to fool them or themselves all the times. Eventually, the addict's external facade, a house of cards, a superficial and external facade of euphoric hail-fellow-well-met gives way to what he or she really is: a frightened little boy or girl who plays adult games beyond his chronological or emotional age. How does this process start and expand as individuals move from the cradle to the coffin? The answer is: *developmentally and progressively.*

Status, Self-Definition, and Self-Importance

The most important deficit that we attribute to most addictions is a defective, negative, and/or incomplete sense of self-importance, the no-self position. This sense of self-importance or status is basic to the genesis, development, and establishment of a positive sense of personal identity. The main features of addictions found repeatedly in the relevant literature are having "low self-esteem," "deep feelings of inadequacy," or "feelings of worthlessness." These feelings result from profound experiences of abuse, neglect, and rejection by parents and by peers (Jacobs, 1987). Instead, as discussed in Chapter 6, we prefer to use the concept of *importance,* which is a personal and interpersonal attribution, rather than terms such as *self-esteem, feelings of inadequacy,* or *worthlessness,* which are all inferred and hypothetical terms with little if any relational value.

In most addictions, individuals make up for their inability to feel and be important and intimate by stressing Doing and Having something illegitimate instead, such as the addiction itself. They may love themselves, but their inability to love others as well makes it impossible to obtain equality, reciprocity, and intimacy in close and prolonged relationships. Furthermore, selfishness is really not based on the ability to love the self. Addicts may gratify themselves, but self-gratification is not love, especially when it occurs at the expense of others. It is still indulgence. By the same token, the selfless individual cannot really love others in the full sense of the term. By minimizing the sense of self-importance, giving is another form of internal manipulation, to feel important on the basis of purchased external acceptance and approval rather than from an internal acceptance and attribution of importance. Addictions give many individuals an ephemeral feeling of importance and power that they would not obtain otherwise. Yet, they cannot share hurts with intimate others and cannot negotiate in a way that everybody wins.

Gender Differences in Proneness to Addiction

The model of status, self-definition, and self-importance presented in Chapter 6 is especially useful in understanding the many gender differences that exist among addictions. For instance, women tend to become addicted to heroin faster than men (Anglin, Hser, & McGlothlin, 1987). Furthermore, two major types of alcoholism are strongly related to gender differences (Cloninger, 1987). Type 1 alcoholism is associated with guilt and fear about dependence on alcohol. The alcoholics may abstain for periods of time, but lose control once they start drinking. The personalities of this type of alcoholic are more likely to be emotionally dependent, passive or anxious, perfectionistic and introverted, all characteristics of the selfless individual. Women usually tend to develop loss-of-control alcoholism more than men, who tend to follow the Type 2 pattern, characterized by an inability to abstain altogether. This pattern is associated with impulsivity, risk taking, and a tendency for antisocial behavior, such as fighting in bars and driving under the influence, characteristics of selfish individuals.

Cloninger (1987) further reduced alcoholism to three psychological dimensions: (a) novelty seeking, such as taking action and enjoying risks, (b) harm avoidance, such as cautiousness and apprehension, and (c) reward dependence, such as emotional dependence, eagerness to help others, and hypersensitivity to social cues. Type 1 alcoholics, mostly women, tend to avoid harm and novelty seeking while remaining emotionally dependent, whereas Type 2 alcoholics, mostly men, exhibit the opposite characteristics. These differences could be interpreted as supporting the

model of self-importance and self-definition that tends to perceive dysfunctional men as being socialized for selfishness, and dysfunctional
women for selflessness. This conclusion is also supported by evidence on
how boys are socialized in comparison with girls ". . . from very early
ages, boys in groups communicate through domination and aggression,
while girls communicate in ways that facilitate exchange . . . girls have
difficulty influencing boys" (DeAngelis, 1989, p. 12).

Reactivity and Repetition

The child who is the product of either abusive and/or apathetic relationships, will grow up with the same repertoire of abusive–apathetic responses learned since childhood. Adults raised in this environment
typically react repetitively and habitually from a contradictory context of
abuse or apathy based either on immediacy and fast discharge, or delay
and withdrawal from dealing with whatever is troubling the individual.
Only rarely do reactive individuals tend to proact or to act in a positive
way that will assert and establish the importance of both parties in the
relationship. Some individuals raised under reactive conditions may be
able, because of their life experiences, to grow up and out from reactive
family relationships, achieving thus a modicum of selfulness. Others may
sink further down into the No-Self position. Hence, polarization between
selfish–selfless extremes allow us to understand one characteristic of
obsessive-compulsive and addictive behavior: repetitiveness, resulting
from a reactive identification and style.

The self-importance model elaborated in Chapter 6 helps us understand addictions, *in part,* as defects in self-definition, which result from
faulty, inadequate, inconsistently harsh or punitive, or incompetently inadequate parental and familial socialization practices, rather than as the
outcome of physical or genetic causes. These practices are all founded
on the same process: the ultimate discounting of self or others in their
importance. Instead of looking just for physical causes, which I do not
discount, it would be more effective and rewarding to look at the socialization practices that each addict has experienced. We may not be able to
change the genetic makeup of an addict, but we can hope to help addicts
change themselves, *if* our theoretical models are close to their reality.

Defensiveness and Denial

The major defensive reaction of most addicts is *denial,* which is the developmental outcome of learned avoidance of personal responsibility and of
reality testing (Dorpat, 1985). In the past, denial was attributed to
"unconscious forces." Functional individuals tend to approach reality and
to confront and deal effectively with issues and problems. Dysfunctional

individuals and addicts learn to avoid reality through denial and other defensive reactions. The present model would understand denial more as a learned inadequacy in awareness rather than as an outcome due to mysterious unconscious forces or external reinforcements. Denial can be verbal as well as nonverbal. It can be limited to a specific addiction, or it can be generalized to most, if not all, spheres of life. Denial is the individual's attempt to negate the notion that the addiction is controlling his or her life, coupled with the inability to admit helplessness in gaining control. Denial is directed against the admission of vulnerability, fallibility, and neediness (L'Abate, 1986). These are the human qualities needed to develop intimate relationships that sometimes are strongly rejected by even nonaddicted adults, especially men in our society. Denial may pertain to lack of admission concerning the harmfulness of addiction to self and to others, or it could pertain to the minimization of the possible dangers that the person would incur with a continuation of the addiction. Ultimately, denial is avoidance of tensions, pains, and conflicts that the individual feels unable to cope with.

The overuse of denial may produce concomitant defensive reactions, such as deception and outright lying, all distortions of reality that help maintain the addiction. Thus, denial is symbiotic with the addiction. The exaggerated approach of pleasure at any cost represents a parallel avoidance of unpleasant and painful closeness and balanced functionality. These defensive reactions, however, are not acquired in a vacuum. They are learned from the way the family of origin defends and protects itself from assumed or expected attacks from the inside and the outside. Why should anyone want to achieve pleasure, release from tensions, or relief from either internal or external conflict through illegitimate or destructive means? What are the conditions of family life that did not allow the individual to learn to enjoy life through socially acceptable means? What are the characteristics of their families that did not promote the achievement of joy, pride, pleasure, and enjoyment through everyday interchange and exchange of tangible and intangible goods? Most addictions develop from unhappy to very unhappy family environments, where there was no joy in living and in *Being* with each other. Most of the families' energies were consumed in either *Doing* (working) or *Having* (possessing a modicum of goods) just to survive.

TOWARD A CLASSIFICATION OF ADDICTIONS

This theory has the potential to classify addictions as exaggerations in resources exchanged (Table 15.2). For instance, sexual offenses and abuses, interpersonal and love relationships, and violence may be seen as distortions in the sense of importance, where the process of victimization is

TABLE 15.2.   A Theory of Developmental Competence and the Classification of Addictions

Abilities	Modalities	Resources	Skills	Addictions
Ability to love	Being	Importance	Presence	Abuse Physical Verbal Sexual
		Intimacy		Promiscuity Love relationships
Ability to negotiate	Doing	Information	Performance	Religious fanaticism Television Reading (?)
		Services		Excessive work Excessive exercise
	Having	Money	Production	Excessive spending Gambling
		Goods		Food Substance abuse Alcoholism

based on discounting physically, sexually, verbally, and violently the importance of the other person, all distortions in the modality of Being. By the same token, in the modality of Doing, religious fanaticism would be based on an exaggerated use of faulty information, whereas workaholism and excessive exercise would be seen as exaggerations in services. In the modality of Having, excessive spending and gambling would be based on the overuse of money, and all the remaining addictions, such as smoking, alcoholism, eating disorders, and substance abuse, would be exaggerations in the (mis)use of goods and possessions.

This theory allows us to view addictions, personality disturbances, and psychopathologies, as being continuous and contiguous with each other and with functionalities and competencies. Selfulness becomes one of the criteria we can use to evaluate whether an addict is improved to the point that no further help is necessary. Reciprocal victories in intimate relationships, based on the affirmation of equality of importance but of differences in functions, become the ultimate criterion of success. If an individual has been able to achieve and maintain a level of self-importance that will allow for legitimate rather than for illegitimate pleasures, our job will be completed. Most legitimate pleasures in Being, even more important than Doing and Having, need to be achieved within the context of close, prolonged, warm, and effective relationships with family and with friends.

This theory also suggests that the sense of self-importance must be dealt with from the very outset of therapy, if we are to make any therapeutic headway. Furthermore, this theory suggests the importance of gender differences that, heretofore, might have been explained mostly on the basis of constitutional or cultural factors. As important as these factors may be, they are greatly overshadowed by factors of socialization in traditional gender roles, which are paramount in the etiology and maintenance of addictions. Family socialization factors link possible constitutional factors with cultural factors.

CONCLUSION

This developmental theory of personality development as interpersonal competence needs to be evaluated *epistemologically*, in terms of its logical consistency with other developmental and social psychological constructs, *experimentally*, in terms of its empirical validity to personality development, and *experientially* as well as *applicatively*, in terms of how it can be applied to an understanding and control of personality disorders, psychopathologies, paraphilias, and addictions. The theory was expanded to include a classification of sex and sexuality as well as addictions. Instruments that have been derived from the theory are paper-and-pencil and self-report tests (Chapter 13), structured enrichment programs, and programmed workbooks (L'Abate, 1990; L'Abate & Weinstein, 1987; L'Abate & Young, 1987). The reader who is interested in evaluating this theory is referred to those instruments and methods of intervention or is encouraged to create new ones, as long as they are derived directly from the theory.

References

Abrams, D. B., & Niaura, R. S. (1987). Social learning theory. In H. T. Blane & K. F. Leonard (Eds.), *Psychological theories of drinking and alcoholism* (pp. 131–178). New York: Guilford.

Abramson, P. R. (1981). *Personality.* New York: Holt, Rinehart and Winston.

Abt, L. E., & Stuart, I. R. (Eds.). (1982). *The newer therapies: A sourcebook.* New York: Van Nostrand Reinhold.

Adams, B. N. (1979). Mate selection in the United States: A theoretical summarization. In W. R. Burr, R. Hill, F. I. Nye, & I. R. Reiss (Eds.), *Contemporary theories about the family* (Vol. 1, pp. 259–267). New York: Free Press.

Ainsworth, M. D. S., Blehar, M., Waters, E., & Wall, S. (1978). *Patterns of attachment.* Hillsdale, NJ: Earlbaum.

Al-Issa, I. (1980). *The psychopathology of women.* Englewood Cliffs, NJ: Prentice-Hall.

Allport, G. W. (1968). *The person in psychology.* Boston, MA: Beacon Press.

Altman, L. (1975). *The dream of psychoanalysis.* New York: International Universities Press.

Andrews, D. A., Bonta, J., & Hoge, R. D. (1990). Classification for effective rehabilitation: Rediscovering psychology. *Criminal Justice and Behavior, 17,* 19–52.

Anglin, M. D., Hser, Y. I., & McGlothlin, W. H. (1987). Sex differences in addict careers: Becoming addicted. *American Journal of Drug and Alcohol Abuse, 13,* 59–71.

Anthony, E. J., & Cohler, B. J. (Eds.). (1987). *The invulnerable child.* New York: Guilford.

Arieti, S. (Ed.). (1966). *American handbook of psychiatry* (Vol. 3). New York: Basic Books.

Arieti, S., & Bemporad, J. R. (1980). The psychological organization of depression. *American Journal of Psychiatry, 137,* 1360–1365.

Aron, A., & Aron, E. N. (1986). *Love and the expansion of self: Understanding attraction and satisfaction.* New York: McGraw-Hill.

Ausloos, G. (1986). The march of time: Rigid or chaotic transactions, two different ways of living time. *Family Process, 25,* 549–557.

Bader, E., & Pearson, P. T. (1988). *In quest of the mythical mate: A developmental approach to diagnosis and treatment in couples therapy.* New York: Brunner/Mazel.

Baker, M. A. (Ed.). (1987). *Sex differences in human performance.* New York: Wiley.

Balswick, J., & Balswick, J. (1987). A theological basis for family relationships. *Journal of Psychology and Christianity, 6,* 37–49.

Bammel, G., & Burrus-Bammel, L. L. (1982). *Leisure and human behavior.* Dubuque, IA: Brown.

Bandler, R., & Grinder, J. (1975). *The structure of magic, I: A book about language and therapy.* Palo Alto, CA: Science & Behavior Books.

Bandura, A. (1977). Self-efficacy: Toward a unifying theory of behavioral change. *Psychological Review, 84,* 191–215.

Bandura, A. (1989). Human agency in social cognitive theory. *American Psychologist, 44,* 1175–1184.

Barker, R. G. (1968). *Ecological psychology: Concepts and methods for studying the environment of human behavior.* Stanford, CA: Stanford University Press.

Barkham, M., Shapiro, D. A., & Firth-Cozens, J. (1989). Personal questionnaire changes in prescriptive vs. exploratory psychotherapy. *British Journal of Clinical Psychology, 28,* 97–107.

Barnett, J. E. (1981). The natural history of a marriage. *Pilgrimage, 9,* 5–19.

Barrett, R. C., Biener, L., & Baruch, G. K. (Eds.). (1987). *Gender and stress.* New York: Free Press.

Baron, J. (1985). *Rationality and intelligence.* Cambridge, UK: Cambridge University Press.

Bastien, S., & Jacobs, A. (1974). Dear Sheila: An experimental study of the effectiveness of written communication as a form of psychotherapy. *Journal of Consulting and Clinical Psychology, 42,* 151.

Baumrind, D. (1975). The contributions of the family to the development of competence in children. *Schizophrenia Bulletin, 14,* 12–37.

Beavers, W. R., & Voeller, M. N. (1983). Parent adolescent communication and the Circumplex Model. *Child Development, 56,* 438–447.

Beck, A. T. (1976). *Cognitive therapy and the emotional disorders.* New York: New American Library.

Beck, A. T. (1988). *Love is never enough.* New York: Harper & Row.

Becker, E. (1973). *The denial of death.* New York: Free Press.

Bednar, R. L., Wells, M. G., & Peterson, S. R. (1989). *Self-esteem: Paradoxes and innovations in clinical theory and practice.* Washington, DC: American Psychological Association.

Belle, D. (1987). Gender differences and the social moderators of stress. In R. C. Barrett, L. Biener, & G. K. Baruch (Eds.), *Gender and stress* (pp. 257–276). New York: Free Press.

Bengtson, V. L., Olander, E. B., Haddad, A. A. (1976). The "generation gap" and aging family members: Toward a conceptual model. In J. F. Gubrium

(Ed.), *Time, roles, and self in old age* (pp. 237–263). New York: Human Sciences Press.

Benjamin, L. S. (1977). Structural analysis of a family in therapy. *Journal of Consulting and Clinical Psychology, 45,* 391–406.

Bennett, C. G. (1984). Know thyself. *Professional Psychology, 15,* 271–283.

Berger, P. L., & Luckman, T. (1966). *The social construction of reality.* New York: Doubleday.

Berglas, S. (1987). Self-handicapping model. In H. T. Blane & K. E. Leonard (Eds.), *Psychological theories of drinking and alcoholism* (pp. 305–345). New York: Guilford.

Berkowitz, L. (1978). Whatever happened to the frustration-aggression hypothesis? *American Behavioral Scientist, 21,* 691–708.

Bernal, G., & Baker, J. (1980). Multilevel couple therapy: Applying a meta-communication framework of couples' interaction. *Family Process, 19,* 367–376.

Bernard, H. S. (1981). Identity formation during late adolescence: A review of some empirical findings. *Adolescence, 16,* 349–358.

Beutler, L. E. (1989). Differential treatment selection: The role of diagnosis in psychotherapy. *Psychotherapy, 26,* 271–281.

Biener, L. (1987). Gender differences in the use of substances for coping. In R. C. Barnett, L. Biener, & G. K. Baruch (Eds.), *Gender and stress* (pp. 330–349). New York: Free Press.

Biringen, Z., & Robinson, J. (1991). Emotional availability in mother-child interactions: A reconceptualization of research. *American Journal of Orthopsychiatry, 61,* 258–271.

Blanck, R., & Blanck, G. (1968). *Marriage and personal development.* New York: Columbia University Press.

Blane, H. T., & Leonard, K. F. (Eds.). (1987). *Psychological theories of drinking and alcoholism.* New York: Guilford.

Blau, P. M. (1964). *Exchange and power in social life.* New York: Wiley.

Block, R. A. (1978). Remembered duration: Effects of event and sequence complexity. *Memory and Cognition, 6,* 320–326.

Block, R. A. (1982). Temporal judgments and contextual change. *Journal of Experimental Psychology: Learning, Memory, and Cognition, 8,* 530–544.

Block, R. A. (Ed.). (1990). *Cognitive models of psychological time.* Hillsdale, NJ: Earlbaum.

Bohen, H. H., & Viveros-Long, A. (1981). *Balancing jobs and family life: Do flexible work schedules help?* Philadelphia, PA: Temple University Press.

Borofsky, G. L. (1974). Issues in the diagnosis and classification of personality functioning. In A. L. Rabin (Ed.), *Clinical psychology: Issues of the seventies* (pp. 24–48). Lansing, MI: Michigan State University Press.

Boszormenyi-Nagy, I., & Krasner, B. R. (1986). *Between give and take: A clinical guide to contextual therapy.* New York: Brunner/Mazel.

Bowen, M. (1978). *Family therapy in clinical practice.* New York: Aronson.

Bowers, K. S. (1973). Situationalism in psychology: An analysis and critique. *Psychological Review, 80,* 307–336.

Bowlby, J. (1969). *Attachment and loss: Attachment* (Vol. 1, 2nd ed.). New York: Basic Books.

Bowlby, J. (1970). Disruption of affectional bonds and its effects on behavior. *Journal of Contemporary Psychotherapy, 2,* 75–86.

Bowlby, J. (1973). *Attachment and loss: Separation, anxiety and anger* (Vol. 2). New York: Basic Books.

Bowlby, J. (1980). *Attachment and loss: Sadness and depression* (Vol. 3). New York: Basic Books.

Bowlby, J. (1981). Psychoanalysis as a natural science. *International Review of Psychoanalysis, 8,* 243–256.

Bowlby, J. (1988). *A secure base: Parent-child attachment and healthy human development.* New York: Basic Books.

Brand, A. G. (1989). *The psychology of writing: The affective experience.* New York: Guilford.

Branden, N. (1969). *The psychology of self esteem: A new concept of man's psychological nature.* Los Angeles, CA: Nash Publishing.

Brehm, J. W. (1966). *A theory of psychological resistance.* New York: Academic Press.

Brehm, J. W., & Jones, R. A. (1970). The effect of dissonance on surprise consequences. *Journal of Experimental Social Psychology, 6,* 420–431.

Bretherton, I., & Waters, E. (Eds.). (1985). Growing points of attachment theory and research. *Monographs of the Society for Research in Child Development, 50* (No. 209).

Brickman, P., Rabinowitz, V. C., Karuza, J., Coates, D., Cohen, E., & Kidder, L. (1982). Models of helping and coping. *American Psychologist, 37,* 368–384.

Brody, N. (1980). Social motivation. *Annual Review of Psychology, 31,* 143–168.

Bronfenbrenner, U. (1958). The study of identification through interpersonal perception. In R. Tagium & L. Petrullo (Eds.), *Person perception and interpersonal behavior* (pp. 110–130). Palo Alto, CA: Stanford University Press.

Bronfenbrenner, U. (1960). Freudian theories of identification and three derivatives. *Child Development, 31,* 15–40.

Bronfenbrenner, U. (1986). Ecology of the family as a context for human development: Research prospectives. *Developmental Psychology, 22,* 723–742.

Broun, B. G. (1986). *Treatment of multiple personality.* Washington, DC: American Psychiatric Association.

Broun, B. G. (1988). The BASK model of dissociation: Part I. *Dissociation, 1,* 4–23.

Broverman, I. K., Vogel, S. R., Broverman, D. M., Clarkson, F. E., & Rosencrantz, P. S. (1972). Sex role sterotypes: A current reappraisal. *Journal of Social Issues, 28,* 59–78.

Burks, J., & Rubenstein, M. (1979). *Temperament styles in adult interaction: Applications in psychotherapy.* New York: Brunner/Mazel.

Caldwell-Brown, C., & Gottfried, A. W. (Eds.). (1985). *Play interactions: The role of toys and parental involvement in children's development.* Skillman, NJ: Johnson & Johnson.

Cancro, R. (Ed.). (1971). *Intelligence: Genetic and environmental influences.* New York: Grune & Stratton.

Cantor, N., & Kihlstrom, J. F. (1987). *Personality and social intelligence.* Englewood Cliffs, NJ: Prentice-Hall.

Caplan, F., & Caplan, T. (1973). *The power of play.* New York: Doubleday.

Cappell, H., & Greeley, J. (1987). Alcohol and tension reduction: An update on research and theory. In H. T. Blane & K. E. Leonard (Eds.), *Psychological theories of drinking and alcoholism* (pp. 15–54). New York: Guilford.

Carkhuff, R. (1980). *The art of helping.* Amherst, MA: Human Resource Development Press.

Carroll, J. B. (1956). *Language, thought, and reality: Selected readings of Benjamin Lee Whorf.* New York: Wiley.

Carson, R. C. (1989). Personality. *Annual Review of Psychology, 40,* 227–248.

Cartwright, D. S. (1979). *Theories and models of personality.* Dubuque, IA: Brown.

Chase, S. (1938). *The tyranny of words.* New York: Harcourt Brace & Co.

Chess, S., & Thomas, A. (1986). *Temperament in clinical practice.* New York: Guilford.

Chodorow, N. (1978). Mothering, object relations, and the female oedipal configuration. *Feminist Studies, 4,* 137–158.

Clark, M. S., & Mills, J. (1979). Interpersonal attraction in exchange and communal relationships. *Journal of Personality and Social Psychology, 17,* 12–24.

Clark, M. S., & Mills, J. (1986). Communications that should lead to perceived exploitation in communal and exchange relationships. *Journal of Social and Clinical Psychology, 4,* 225–234.

Clark, M. S., Mills, J., & Powell, M. (1986). Keeping track of needs in communal and exchange relationships. *Journal of Personality and Social Psychology, 51,* 333–338.

Clark, M. S., & Reis, H. T. (1988). Interpersonal processes in close relationships. *Annual Review of Psychology, 39,* 609–672.

Clark, M. S., & Wassell, B. (1985). Perceptions of exploitation in communal and exchange relationships. *Journal of Social and Personal Relationships, 2,* 403–418.

Clausen, J. A. (Ed.). (1968). *Socialization and society.* Boston, MA: Little, Brown & Co.

Cleary, P. D. (1987). Gender differences in stress-related disorders. In R. C. Barnett, L. Biener, & G. K. Baruch (Eds.), *Gender and stress* (pp. 39–72). New York: Free Press.

Cloninger, C. R. (1987). Neurogenetic adaptive mechanisms in alcoholism. *Science, 236,* 410–416.

Cohen, D. (1987). *The development of play.* New York: New York University Press.

Cole, J. P. (1971). *The problematic self in Kierkegaard and Freud.* New Haven, CT: Yale University Press.

Combrink-Graham, L. (1985). A developmental model for family systems. *Family Process, 24,* 139–150.

Constantine, L. (1986). *Family paradigms.* New York: Guilford.

Coopersmith, S. (1967). *The antecedents of self-esteem.* San Francisco, CA: Freeman.

Corlett, J. A. (1988). Perloff, utilitarianist, and existentialist: Problems with self interest and personal responsibility. *The American Psychologist, 43,* 481–482.

Corsini, R. J. (Ed.). (1984). *Current psychotherapies.* Itasca, IL: Peacock.

Cramer, S. H. (Ed.). (1984). *Perspectives on work and the family.* Rockville, MD: Aspen.

Crandall, R. (1984). Work and leisure in the life space. In M. D. Lee & R. N. Kanungo (Eds.), *Management of work and personal life: Problems and opportunities* (pp. 86–111). New York: Praeger.

Cronenwett, L. (1982). Father participation in child care: A critical review. *Research in Nursing and Health, 5,* 63–72.

Crosby, F. (1984). Job satisfaction and domestic life. In M. D. Lee & R. N. Kanungo (Eds.), *Management of work and personal life: Problems and opportunities* (pp. 41–60). New York: Praeger.

Crosby, J. F. (1985). *Illusion and disillusion: The self in love and marriage.* Belmont, CA: Wadsworth.

Csikszentmihalyi, M., & Rochberg-Halton, E. (1981). *The meaning of things: Domestic symbols and the self.* New York: Cambridge University Press.

Cummings, N. A. (1987). The future of psychotherapy: One psychologist's perspective. *American Journal of Psychotherapy, 41,* 349–360.

Curtis, R. C. (Ed.). (1991). *The relational self: Theoretical convergences in psychoanalysis and social psychology.* New York: Guilford.

Cusinato, M., & L'Abate, L. (1994). A spiral model of intimacy. In S. D. Johnson (Ed.), *Intimacy.* New York: Brunner/Mazel.

Davis, M., & Hadiks, D. (1990). Nonverbal behavior and client state changes during psychotherapy. *Journal of Clinical Psychology, 46,* 340–351.

de Vries, B., Birren, J. E., & Deutchman, D. E. (1990). Adult development through guided autobiography: The family context. *Family Relations, 39,* 3–7.

DeAngelis, T. (1989). Men's interaction style can be tough on women. *Psychology Monitor, 20,* 12.

Deci, E. L., & Ryan, R. M. (1985a). The support of autonomy and the control of behavior. *Journal of Personality and Social Psychology, 53,* 1024–1037.

Deci, E. L., & Ryan, R. M. (1985b). *Intrinsic motivation and self-determination in human behavior.* New York: Plenum.

Del Monte, R. (1976). *Locus of control and conceptual systems in personality differentiation.* M. A. thesis, Georgia State University, Atlanta, GA.

Denny, M. R. (Ed.). (1991). *Fear, avoidance, and phobias.* Hillsdale, NJ: Earlbaum.

Dewey, J., & Bentley, A. F. (1949). *Knowing and the known.* Boston, MA: Beacon Press.

Dix, T. (1991). The affective organization of parenting: Adaptive and maladaptive processes. *Psychological Bulletin, 110,* 3–25.

Dockrell, W. B. (Ed.). (1970). *On intelligence: The Toronto Symposium 1969.* London, UK: Methuen.

Donnelly, D. A., & Murray, E. J. (1991). Cognitive and emotional changes in written essays and therapy interviews. *Journal of Social and Clinical Psychology, 10,* 334–350.

Dorpat, T. L. (1985). *Denial and defense in the therapeutic situation.* New York: Aronson.

Duck, S. (Ed.). (1983). *Friends for life: The psychology of close relationships.* New York: St. Martin's Press.

Duhl, F. J., Kantor, D., & Duhl, B. S. (1973). Learning, space, and action in family therapy: A primer of sculpture. In D. A. Block (Ed.), *Techniques of family psychotherapy: A primer* (pp. 47–63). New York: Grune & Stratton.

Dumas, E. (1989). Let's not forget the content in behavioral assessment. *Behavioral Assessment, 11,* 231–247.

Dunne, E. E., & L'Abate, L. (1978). The family taboo in psychology textbooks. *Teaching of Psychology, 5,* 115–117.

Dunst, C., Trivette, C., & Deal, A. (1988). *Enabling and empowering families: Principles and guidelines for practice.* Cambridge, MA: Brookline Books.

Duval, S., & Wicklund, R. A. (1972). *A theory of objective self-awareness.* New York: Academic Press.

Ekehammar, B. (1974). Interactionism in personality from a historical perspective. *Psychological Bulletin, 81,* 1026–1048.

Ellis, M. (1985). Foreword. In M. G. Wade (Ed.), *Constraints on leisure* (pp. vii–viii). Springfield IL: Thomas.

Endler, N. S. (1983). Interactionism: A personality model, but not a theory. In M. M. Page (Ed.), *Nebraska symposium on motivation, 1982: Personality—current theory and research* (pp. 155–200). Lincoln, NE: University of Nebraska.

Endler, N. S., & Magnusson, D. (Eds.). (1976a). *Interactional psychology and personality.* Washington, DC: Hemisphere.

Endler, N. S., & Magnusson, D. (1976b). Toward an interactional psychology of personality. *Psychological Bulletin, 83,* 956–974.

Epstein, N. B., Bishop, D. S., & Levin, S. (1978). The McMaster model of family functioning. *Journal of Marriage and Family Counseling, 4,* 19–31.

Erikson, E. (1954). The dream specimen of psychoanalysis. *Journal of the American Psychoanalytic Association, 2,* 5–56.

Ewen, R. B. (1984). *An introduction to theories of personality.* Orlando, FL: Academic Press.

Eysenck, H. J. (Ed.). (1973). *The measurement of intelligence.* Baltimore, MD: Williams & Wilkins.

Fehr, B., & Perlman, D. (1985). The family as a social network and support system. In L. L'Abate (Ed.), *Handbook of family psychology and therapy* (pp. 323–356). Pacific Grove, CA: Brooks/Cole.

Fenton, W. S., Robinowitz, C. B., & Leaf, P. J. (1987). Male and female psychiatrists and their patients. *American Journal of Psychiatry, 144,* 358–361.

Festinger, L. (1954). A theory of social comparison processes. *Human Relations, 7,* 117–140.

Figley, C. R. (1989). *Helping traumatized families.* San Francisco, CA: Jossey-Bass.

Fingarette, H. (1988). *Heavy drinking: The myth of alcoholism as a disease.* Berkeley, CA: University of California Press.

Fisher, S. (1970). *Body experience in fantasy and behavior.* New York: Appleton-Century-Crofts.

Flavell, J. H. (1985). *Cognitive development* (2nd ed.). Englewood Cliffs, NJ: Prentice-Hall.

Flavell, J. H., & Wohlwill, J. F. (1969). Formal and functional aspects of cognitive development. In D. Elkind & J. H. Flavell (Eds.), *Studies in cognitive development: Essays in honor of Jean Piaget* (pp. 67–120). New York: Oxford University Press.

Foá, U., & Foá, E. (1974). *Societal structures of the mind.* Springfield, IL: Thomas.

Foley, V. D. (1984). *An introduction to family therapy.* New York: Grune & Stratton.

Ford, M. E. (1985). The concept of competence: Themes and variations. In H. A. Marlowe, Jr. & R. B. Weinberg (Eds.), *Competence development: Theory and practice in special populations* (pp. 3–49). Springfield, IL: Thomas.

Forehand, R. L., Walley, P. B., & Furery, W. M. (1984). Prevention in the home: Parent and family. In M. C. Roberts & L. Peterson (Eds.), *Prevention of problems in childhood: Psychological research and applications* (pp. 342–368). New York: Wiley.

Foster, S. W., & Gurman, A. S. (1985). Family therapies. In S. J. Lynn & J. P Garske (Eds.), *Contemporary psychotherapies: Models and methods* (pp. 377–418). Columbus, OH: Merrill.

Fox, N. A., Kimmerly, N. L., & Schafer, W. D. (1991). Attachment to mother/attachment to father: A meta-analysis. *Child Development, 62,* 210–225.

Frank, J. D. (1974). Psychotherapy: The restoration of morale. *American Journal of Psychiatry, 13,* 271–274.

Franken, D. A., & van Raaij, W. F. (1982). Satisfaction with leisure time activities. *Journal of Leisure Research, 24,* 337–351.

Fraser, J. T. (Ed.). (1989). *Time and mind: Interdisciplinary issues.* Madison, CT: International Universities Press.

Freeman, A., Simon, K. M., Beutler, L. E., & Arkowitz, H. (1989). *Comprehensive handbook of cognitive therapy.* New York: Plenum.

Frey, J., III. (1980). *Personality correlates of emotional masking.* Doctoral dissertation, Georgia State University, Atlanta, GA.

Fridgen, J. P. (1984). Leisure, work, and a changing society: An environmental perspective. In M. D. Lee & R. N. Kanungo (Eds.), *Management of work and personal life: Problems and opportunities* (pp. 260–257). New York: Praeger.

Friedman, M. M. (1986). *Family nursing: Theory and assessment.* Norwalk, CT: Appleton-Century-Crofts.

Friedman, W. J. (Ed.). (1982). *The developmental psychology of time.* New York: Academic Press.

Frosch, W. A. (1985). An analytic overview of addictions. In H. B. Milkman & H. J. Shaffer (Eds.), *The addictions: Multidisciplinary perspectives and treatments* (pp. 29–37). Lexington, MA: Heath.

Funt, M. (1988). *Grounds for marriage: Couples who make marriage work.* New York: Dodd, Mead and Co.

Gardner, H. (1983). *Frames of mind: The theory of multiple intelligences.* New York: Basic Books.

Garfield, S. L., & Bergin, A. E. (Eds.). (1986). *Handbook of psychotherapy and behavior change.* New York: Wiley.

Gatchel, R. J., & Mears, F. G. (1982). *Personality: Theory, assessment, and research.* New York: St. Martin's Press.

Geerken, M., & Gove, W. R. (Eds.). (1983). *At home and at work: The family's allocation of labor.* Newbury Park, CA: Sage.

Gentry, J. W., & Doering, M. (1979). Sex role orientation and leisure. *Journal of Leisure Research, 11,* 102–111.

Gergen, K. J. (1971). *The concept of self.* New York: Holt, Rinehart and Winston.

Gergen, K. J. (1991). *The saturated self: Dilemmas of identity in contemporary life.* New York: Basic Books.

Gerstel, N., & Gross, H. E. (Eds.). (1987). *Families and work.* Philadelphia, PA: Temple University Press.

Giacomo, P., & Weissmark, M. (1987). Toward a generative theory of the therapeutic field. *Family Process, 26,* 437–459.

Gibbs, J. P. (Ed.). (1982). *Social control: Views from the social sciences.* Beverly Hills, CA: Sage.

Gibbs, J. P. (1989). *Control: Sociology's central notion.* Urbana, IL: University of Illinois Press.

Gilligan, C. (1982). New maps of developments: New visions of maturity. *American Journal of Orthopsychiatry, 52,* 199–212.

Gjerde, P. F. (1986). Arousal and the disruption of language production processes in schizophrenia. *Behavioral and Brain Sciences, 9,* 524.

Glickauf-Hughes, C., & Wells, M. (1991). Current conceptualization on masochism: Genesis and object relations. *American Journal of Psychotherapy, 45,* 53–68.

Goffman, I. (1956). *The presentation of the self in everyday life.* New York: Doubleday.

Goldsmith, E. B. (Ed.). (1989). *Work and family: Theory, research, and applications.* Newbury Park, CA: Sage.

Goodrich, M. E. (1984). *Concurrent validation of the Georgia State University Marital Evaluation Questionnaire.* Unpublished doctoral dissertation, Georgia State University, Atlanta, GA.

Gordon, T. (1970). *Parent effectiveness training.* New York: Macmillan.

Gottman, J. M. (1979). *Marital interaction.* New York: Basic Books.

Graham, H. (1990). *Time, energy and the psychology of healing.* London, UK: Kingsley.

Greenberg, E., & Steinberg, L. (1986). *When teenagers work: The psychological and social costs of adolescent employment.* New York: Basic Books.

Gregson, R. A. M. (1975). *Psychometrics of similarity.* New York: Academic Press.

Grinder, J., & Bandler, R. (1976). *The structure of magic, II: A book about communication and change.* Palo Alto, CA: Science & Behavior Books.

Grotevant, H. D., & Cooper, C. R. (1986). Individuation in family relationships: A perspective on individual differences in the development of identity and role-taking skill in adolescence. *Human Development, 29,* 82–100.

Guidano, V. R. (1987). *Complexity of the self: A developmental approach to psychopathology and therapy.* New York: Guilford.

Gur, R. C., & Sackheim, H. A. (1979). Self-deception: A concept in search of a phenomenon. *Journal of Personality and Social Psychology, 37,* 147–169.

Gutmann, D. (1976). Individual adaptation in the middle years: Developmental issues in the masculine mid-life crisis. *Journal of Geriatric Psychiatry, 9,* 41–59.

Hackman, J. R., Hoffman, L. W., Moos, R. H., Osipow, S. H., & Tornatzky, L. G. (1986). *Psychology and work: Productivity, change, and employment.* Washington, DC: American Psychological Association.

Haley, J. (1973). *Uncommon therapy.* New York: Norton.

Hall, C. S., & Lindsey, G. (1978). *Theories of personality.* New York: Wiley.

Hall, R. H. (1986). *Dimensions of work.* Newbury Park, CA: Sage.

Hamachek, D. E. (1978). *Encounters with the self.* New York: Holt, Rinehart and Winston.

Harner, L. (1982). Talking about the past and the future. In W. J. Friedman (Ed.), *The developmental psychology of time* (pp. 141–169). New York: Academic Press.

Harper, R. A. (1975). *The new psychotherapies.* Englewood Cliffs, NJ: Prentice-Hall.

Hart, J. T., & Tomlinson, T. M. (1970). *New directions in client-centered therapy.* Boston, MA: Houghton Mifflin Co.

Harter, S. (1983). The determinants and mediational role of global self-worth in children. In N. Eisenberg, (Ed.), *Contemporary topics in developmental psychology* (pp. 129–242). New York: Wiley.

Harter, S. (1986). Cognitive developmental process in the integration of concepts about emotions and the self. *Social Cognition, 4,* 119–151.

Hartocollis, P. (1983). *Time and timelessness: The varieties of temporal experience, a psychoanalytic inquiry.* New York: International Universities Press.

Harvey, A. B. (1984). The context of discretionary activities. In M. D. Lee & R. N. Kanungo (Eds.), *Management of work and personal life: Problems and opportunities* (pp. 112–132). New York: Praeger.

Harvey, O. J. (1966). System structure, flexibility and creativity. In O. J. Harvey (Ed.), *Experience, structure and adaptability* (pp. 39–65). New York: Springer.

Hayes, S. C., & Melancon, S. M. (1989). Comprehensive distancing, paradox, and the treatment of emotional avoidance. In L. M. Ascher (Ed.), *Therapeutic paradox* (pp. 184–218). New York: Guilford.

Heider, F. (1958). *The psychology of interpersonal relations.* New York: Wiley.

Helson, R., & Mitchell, V. (1978). Personality. *Annual Review of Psychology, 29,* 555–585.

Hergenhahn, B. R. (1984). *An introduction to theories of personality.* Englewood Cliffs, NJ: Prentice-Hall.

Herron, R. E., & Sutton-Smith, B. (1982). *Child's play.* Malabar, FL: Krieger.

Higgins, E. T. (1990). Personality, social psychology, and person-situation relations: Standards and knowledge activation as a common language. In L. A. Pervin (Ed.), *Handbook of personality theory and research* (pp. 301–338). New York: Guilford.

Higgins, R. L., Snyder, C. R., & Berglas, S. (1990). *Self-handicapping: The paradox that isn't.* New York: Plenum.

Hill, C. E., & Stephany, A. (1990). Relation of nonverbal behavior to client reactions. *Journal of Counseling Psychology, 37,* 22–26.

Hirschman, E. C. (1984). Leisure motives and sex roles. *Journal of Leisure Research, 16,* 209–223.

Hoffman, L. W. (1972). Early childhood experiences and women's achievement motives. *Journal of Social Issues, 28,* 129–155.

Hoffman, M. L. (1977). Personality and social development. *Annual Review of Psychology, 28–29,* 5–32.

Hoffman, M. L. (1979). Development of moral thought, feeling, and behavior. *American Psychologist, 10,* 958–966.

Holland, J. (1973). *Making occupational choices: A theory of careers.* Englewood Cliffs, NJ: Prentice-Hall.

Holland, N. N. (1985). *The I.* New Haven, CT: Yale University Press.

Holman, T. B., & Epperson, A. (1984). Family and leisure: A review of literature with research recommendations. *Journal of Leisure Research, 16,* 277–292.

Homans, G. C. (1950). *The human group.* New York: Harcourt Brace.

Horn, J. L. (1968). Organization of abilities and the development of intelligence. *Psychological Review, 75,* 242–259.

Horwitz, A. V. (1990). *The logic of social control.* New York: Plenum.

House, J. S. (1981). *Work stress and social support: Readings.* Boston, MA: Addison-Wesley.

Howard, G. S., & Myers, P. R. (1990). Predicting human behavior: Comparing idiographic, nomothetic, and agentic methodologies. *Journal of Counseling Psychology, 37,* 227–233.

Howard, G. S., Nance, D. W., & Myers, P. (1987). *Adaptive counseling and therapy: A systematic approach to selecting effective treatments.* San Francisco, CA: Jossey-Bass.

Hunt, J. M. (Ed.). (1972). *Human intelligence.* New Brunswick, NJ: Transaction Books.

Hunt, W. A. (Ed.). (1971). *Human behavior and its control.* Cambridge, MA: Schenkman.

Huston, T. L., & Rempel, J. K. (1989). Interpersonal attitudes, dispositions, and behavior in family and other close relationships. *Journal of Family Psychology, 3,* 177–198.

Hutton, J. B. (1984). Teacher ratings of problem behaviors: Which student behaviors "concern" and "disturb" teachers? *Psychology in the Schools, 21,* 482–484.

Hytten, F. I., & Leitch, I. (1971). *The physiology of human pregnancy.* London: Blackwell Scientific Publications.

Iso-Ahola, S. E., & Buttimer, K. J. (1981). The emergence of work and leisure ethic from early adolescence to early adulthood. *Journal of Leisure Research, 13,* 282–288.

Jacobs, D. F. (1987). A general theory of addictions: Application to treatment and rehabilitation planning for pathological gamblers. In T. Galski (Ed.), *The handbook of pathological gambling* (pp. 169–194). Springfield, IL: Thomas.

James, W. (1890). *Principles of psychology.* New York: Holt.

Jensen, L. C., & Kingston, M. (1986). *Parenting.* New York: Holt, Rinehart and Winston.

Jessor, R., & Feshbach, S. (1967). *Cognition, personality and clinical psychology.* San Francisco, CA: Jossey-Bass.

Johnson, T. B., Levis, M., & L'Abate, L. (1986). Treatment of depression in a couple with systematic homework assignments. *Journal of Psychotherapy and the Family, 2,* 117–128.

Jones, E. E., Kanouse, D. E., Kelley, H. H., Nisbett, R. E., Valins, S., & Weiner, B. (1971). *Attribution: Perceiving the causes of behavior.* Morristown, NJ: General Learning Press.

Jones, J. M. (1988). Cultural differences in temporal perspectives: Instrumental and expressive behaviors in time. In J. E. McGrath (Ed.), *The social psychology of time: New perspectives* (pp. 25–38). Newbury Park, CA: Sage.

Jung, C. G. (1954). *The development of personality.* Princeton, NJ: Princeton University Press.

Jung, C. G. (1983). *The essential Jung.* Princeton, NJ: Princeton University Press.

Jurkovic, G. J., & Ulrici, D. K. (1980). Developing conceptions of marital issues: A cognitive-developmental analysis. Paper read at the Meeting of the American Association of Psychiatric Services for Children, New Orleans, November, 1980.

Juster, F. T., & Stafford, F. P. (Eds.). (1985). *Time, goods, and well-being.* Ann Arbor, MI: Institute for Social Research.

Kagan, J. (1958). The concept of identification. *Psychological Review, 65,* 296–305.

Kantor, D., & Lehr, W. (1975). *Inside the family.* San Francisco, CA: Jossey-Bass.

Kanungo, R. N., & Misra, S. (1984). An uneasy look at work, non-work, and leisure. In M. D. Lee & R. N. Kanungo (Eds.), *Management of work and personal life: Problems and opportunities* (pp. 143–165). New York: Praeger.

Kaplan, H. B. (1975). *Self-attitudes and deviant behavior.* Pacific Palisades, CA: Goodyear Publishing.

Karasek, R., & Theorell, T. (1990). *Healthy work: Stress, productivity, and the reconstruction of working life.* New York: Basic Books.

Karasu, T. B. (1986). The specificity vs. nonspecificity dilemma: Toward identifying therapeutic change agents. *American Journal of Psychiatry, 143,* 687–695.

Kaye, K., & Furstenberg, F. F., Jr. (Eds.). (1985). Family development and the child: Special issue. *Child Development, 56* (Whole No. 2), 279–501.

Keeney, B. P., & Sprenkle, D. H. (1982). Ecosystemic epistemology: Critical implications for the aesthetics and pragmatics of family therapy. *Family Process, 21,* 1–10.

Kegan, R. (1982). *The evolving self: Problem and process in human development.* Cambridge, MA: Harvard University Press.

Kelley, H. H. (1967). Attribution theory in social psychology. In D. Levine (Ed.), *Nebraska symposium on motivation* (pp. 192–238). Lincoln, NE: University of Nebraska Press.

Kelly, J. R., & McGrath, J. E. (1988). *On time and method.* Newbury Park, CA.: Sage.

Kessler, R. C. (1985). Social factors in psychopathology: Stress, social support, and coping processes. *Annual Review of Psychology, 36,* 531–572.

Kiesler, C. A. (1971). *The psychology of commitment: Experiments linking behavior to belief.* New York: Academic Press.

Kihlstrom, J. F. (1987). Introduction to the special issue: Integrating personality and social psychology. *Journal of Personality and Social Psychology, 53,* 989–992.

Kihlstrom, J. F. (1990). The psychological unconscious. In L. A. Pervin (Ed.), *Handbook of personality theory and research* (pp. 445–464). New York: Guilford.

Kingston, P. W., & Nock, S. L. (1985). Consequences of the family work day. *Journal of Marriage and the Family, 47,* 619–629.

Kitchens, J. A. (1991). *Understanding and treating codependence.* Englewood Cliffs, NJ: Prentice-Hall.

Klaus, M. H., & Kennell, J. H. (1982). *Parent-infant bonding.* St. Louis, MO: Mosby.

Kleinmuntz, B. (1967). *Personality measurement: An introduction.* Homewood, IL: Dorsey Press.

Klinger, E. (1977). *Meaning and void: Inner experience and the incentives in people's lives.* Minneapolis, MN: University of Minnesota Press.

Kohlberg, L. (1968). Stage and sequence: The cognitive development approach to socialization. In D. A. Goslin (Ed.), *Handbook of socialization theory and research* (pp. 387–480). Chicago: Rand-McNally.

Kohut, H. (1971). *The analysis of self.* New York: International Press.

Kokin, M., & Walker, I. (1989). *Women who are married to alcoholics: Help and hope for nonalcoholic partners.* New York: Morrow.

Korzybski, A. (1933). *Science and sanity: An introduction to non-aristotelian systems and general semantics.* Lakeville, CT: International Non-Aristotelian Library.

Kruglanski, A. K., & Mayseless, O. (1990). Classic and current social comparison research: Expanding the perspective. *Psychological Bulletin, 108,* 195–208.

L'Abate, L. (1964). *Principles of clinical psychology.* New York: Grune & Stratton.

L'Abate, L. (1971). Receptive-expressive functions in kindergarten children and adolescents. *Psychology in the Schools, 8,* 253–259.

L'Abate, L. (1973). The laboratory method in clinical child psychology: Three applications. *Journal of Clinical Child Psychology, 2,* 8–10.

L'Abate, L. (1975). Pathogenic role rigidity in fathers: Some observations. *Journal of Marriage and Family Counseling, 1,* 69–79.

L'Abate, L. (1976). *Understanding and helping the individual in the family.* New York: Grune & Stratton.

L'Abate, L. (1979). Aggression and construction in children's monitored play therapy. *Journal of Counseling and Psychotherapy, 2,* 137–158.

L'Abate, L. (1980). Inexpressive males or overexpressive females: A reply to Balswick. *Family Relations, 29,* 229–230.

L'Abate, L. (1983a). *Family psychology: Theory, therapy, and training.* Washington, DC: University Press of America.

L'Abate, L. (1983b). Styles in intimate relationships: The A-R-C model. *The Personnel and Guidance Journal, 61,* 277–283.

L'Abate, L. (1984). Beyond paradox: Issues of control. *American Journal of Family Therapy, 12,* 12–20.

L'Abate, L. (1985a). Descriptive and explanatory levels in family therapy: Distance, defeats, and dependence. In L. L'Abate (Ed.), *Handbook of family psychology and therapy* (pp. 1218–1245). Pacific Grove, CA: Brooks/Cole.

L'Abate, L. (Ed.). (1985b). *Handbook of family psychology and therapy* (Vols. I & II). Pacific Grove, CA: Brooks/Cole.

L'Abate, L. (1986). *Systematic family therapy.* New York: Brunner/Mazel.

L'Abate, L. (1987a). The denial of depression. In L. L'Abate (Ed.), *Family psychology II: Theory, therapy, enrichment and training* (pp. 153–165). Lanham, MD: University Press of America.

L'Abate, L. (1987b). Therapeutic writing through homework assignments. In L. L'Abate (Ed.), *Family psychology II: Theory, therapy, enrichment, and training* (pp. 123–136). Washington, DC: University Press of America.

L'Abate, L. (1990). *Building family competence: Primary and secondary prevention strategies.* Newbury Park, CA: Sage.

L'Abate, L. (1991). The use of writing in psychotherapy. *American Journal of Psychotherapy, 45,* 87–98.

L'Abate, L. (1992a). Family psychology and family therapy: Comparisons and contrasts. *American Journal of Family Therapy, 19,* 3–12.

L'Abate, L. (1992b). *Programmed writing: A self-administered approach for interventions with individuals, couples and families.* Pacific Grove, CA: Brooks/Cole.

L'Abate, L. (1994). What is developmental family psychology? In L. L'Abate (Ed.), *Handbook of developmental family psychology and psychopathology.* New York: Wiley.

L'Abate, L. (Submitted for publication). *Hurt: A fundamental but neglected emotion.*

L'Abate, L. (In preparation). *The laboratory method in clinical psychology.*

L'Abate, L., & Bagarozzi, D. A. (1993). *Sourcebook for marriage and family evaluation.* New York: Brunner/Mazel.

L'Abate, L., Boyce, J., Fraizer, L., & Russ, D. A. (1992). Programmed writing: Research in progress. *Comprehensive Mental Health Care, 2,* 45–62.

L'Abate, L., & Colondier, G. (1987). The emperor has no clothes! Long live the emperor! A critique of family systems thinking and a reductionistic proposal. *American Journal of Family Therapy, 15,* 16–23.

L'Abate, L., & Frey, J., III. (1981). The E-R-A model: The role of feelings in family therapy reconsidered; Implications for a classification of theories of family therapy. *Journal of Marital and Family Therapy, 7,* 143–150.

L'Abate, L., Ganahl, G., & Hansen, J. C. (1986). *Methods of family therapy.* Englewood Cliffs, NJ: Prentice-Hall.

L'Abate, L., & Harrison, M. G. (1992). Treating codependency. In L. L'Abate, J. E. Farrar, & D. A. Serritella, (Eds.), *Handbook of differential treatments for addictions* (pp. 286–307). Boston, MA: Allyn & Bacon.

L'Abate, L., & Hewitt, D. (1988a). Power and presence: When complementarity becomes polarity. In J. F. Crosby (Ed.), *When one wants out and the other doesn't: Doing therapy with polarized couples* (pp. 136–152). New York: Brunner/Mazel.

L'Abate, L., & Hewitt, D. (1988b). Toward a classification of sex and sexual behavior. *Journal of Sex and Marital Therapy, 14,* 29–39.

L'Abate, L., & Kunkel, D. (research in progress). Problems in relationships: Assessment and applications. Department of Psychology, Georgia State University, Atlanta, GA.

L'Abate, L., & L'Abate, B. L. (1979). The paradoxes of intimacy. *Family Therapy, 6,* 175–184.

L'Abate, L., & L'Abate, B. L. (1981). Marriage: The dream and the reality. *Family Relations, 30,* 121–136.

L'Abate, L., & McHenry, S. (1983). *Handbook of marital interventions.* New York: Grune & Stratton.

L'Abate, L., & Milan, M. (Eds.). (1985). *Handbook of social skills training and research.* New York: Wiley.

L'Abate, L., & Platzman, K. (1991). The practice of programmed writing (PW) in therapy and prevention with families. *American Journal of Family Therapy, 19,* 1–10.

L'Abate, L., & Swindell, D. H. (1970). Religiosity, dogmatism, and repression-sensitization. *Journal for the Scientific Study of Religion, 9,* 249–251.

L'Abate, L., & Talmadge, W. (1987). Love, intimacy, and sex. In G. R. Weeks & L. Hof (Eds.), *Integrating sex and marital therapy: A clinical guide* (pp. 23–34). New York: Brunner/Mazel.

L'Abate, L., & Wagner, V. (1985). Theory-derived, family-oriented test-batteries. In L. L'Abate (Ed.), *Handbook of family psychology and therapy* (pp. 106–132). Pacific Grove, CA: Brooks/Cole.

L'Abate, L., & Wagner, V. (1988). Testing a theory of developmental competence in the family. *American Journal of Family Psychology. 16,* 23–35.

L'Abate, L., & Weinstein, S. (1987). *Structured enrichment programs for couples and families.* New York: Brunner/Mazel.

L'Abate, L., Weinstein, S. E., Fraizer, L., & Russ, D. (1989). *The continuum of likeness in intimate relationships: Theory and research.* Unpublished manuscript. Department of Psychology, Georgia State University, Atlanta, GA.

L'Abate, L., & Wildman. (1973). Unpublished manuscript. Georgia State University, Atlanta, GA.

L'Abate, L., & Young, L. (1987). *Casebook of structured enrichment programs for couples and families.* New York: Brunner/Mazel.

LaBier, D. (1986). *Modern madness: The emotional fallout of success.* Reading, MA: Addison-Wesley.

Landy, F. J. (1989). *Psychology of work behavior.* Pacific Grove, CA: Brooks/Cole.

Lange, A., & van der Hart, O. (1983). *Directive family therapy.* New York: Brunner/Mazel.

Langer, E. J. (1983). *The psychology of control.* Beverly Hills, CA: Sage.

Lauer, R. H. (1981). *Temporal man: The meaning and uses of social time.* New York: Praeger.

Lazarus, R. S., & Folkman, S. (1984). *Stress, appraisal, and coping.* New York: Springer.

Lazarus, R. S., Kanner, A. D., & Folkman, S. (1980). Emotions: A cognitive-phenomenological analysis. In R. Plutchik & H. Kellerman (Eds.), *Theories of emotion* (pp. 189–217). New York: Academic Press.

Leary, T. (1957). *Interpersonal diagnosis of personality.* New York: Ronald Press.

Lee, M. D. (1984). Life space design. In M. D. Lee & R. N. Kanungo (Eds.), *Management of work and personal life: Problems and opportunities* (pp. 206–227). New York: Praeger.

Lee, M. D., & Kanungo, R. N. (1984a). Effective management of work and personal life: Implications and speculations. In M. D. Lee & R. N. Kanungo (Eds.), *Management of work and personal life: Problems and opportunities* (pp. 258–273). New York: Praeger.

Lee, M. D., & Kanungo, R. N. (Eds.) (1984b). *Management of work and personal life: Problems and opportunities.* New York: Praeger.

Lee, M. D., & Kanungo, R. N. (1984c). Work and personal-life coordination in a changing society. In M. D. Lee & R. N. Kanungo (Eds.), *Management of work and personal life: Problems and opportunities* (pp. 1–9). New York: Praeger.

Lee, P. C., & Stewart, R. S. (Eds.). (1976). *Sex differences: Cultural and developmental dimensions.* New York: Urizen Books.

Leff, J., & Vaughn, C. (1985). *Expressed emotion in families.* New York: Guilford.

Lenneberg, E. H. (1967). *Biological foundations of language.* New York: Wiley.

Lesse, S. (1987). Psychotherapy in a changing post-industrial society. *American Journal of Psychotherapy, 41,* 336–348.

Levant, R. F. (1986). *Psychoeducational approaches to family therapy and counseling.* New York: Springer.

Levin, J. D. (1987). *Treatment of alcoholism and other addictions: A self-psychology approach.* New York: Aronson.

LeVine, R. A. (1973). *Culture, behavior, and personality.* Chicago, IL: Aldine.

Levinson, D. J. (1986). A conception of adult personality. *American Psychologist, 41,* 3–13.

Levy, J. (1978). *Play behavior.* New York: Wiley.

Levy, L. H. (1970). *Conceptions of personality: Theories and research.* New York: Random House.

Lewin, K. (1935). *A dynamic theory of personality: Selected papers.* New York: MGraw-Hill.

Lewis, H. (1971). *Shame and guilt in neurosis.* New York: International Universities Press.

Lewis, J. M. (1989). *The birth of the family: An empirical inquiry.* New York: Brunner/Mazel.

Lewis, J. M., Beavers, W. R., Gossett, J. T. , & Phillips, V. A. (1976). *No single thread: Psychological health in family systems.* New York: Brunner/Mazel.

Lewis, R. A., & Spanier, G. B. (1979). Theorizing about the quality and stability of marriage. In W. R. Burr, R. Hill, F. I. Nye, & I. R. Reiss (Eds.), *Contemporary theories about the family* (Vol. 1, pp. 268–294). New York: Free Press.

Lidz, T. (1983). *The person: His and her development throughout the life cycle.* New York: Basic Books.

Lieberman, J. N. (1977). *Playfulness: Its relationship to imagination and creativity.* New York: Academic Press.

Linder, S. B. (1970). *The hurried leisure class.* New York: Columbia University Press.

Lindgren, H. C. (1991). *The Psychology of money.* Malabar, FL: Krieger.

Lips, H. M., & Colwill, N. L. (1978). *The psychology of sex differences.* Englewood Cliffs, NJ: Prentice-Hall.

Locke, E. A. (1988). The virtue of selfishness. *The American Psychologist, 43,* 481.

Luce, R. D., & Raiffa, H. (1957). *Games and decisions.* New York: Wiley.

Lynch, M. D., Norem-Hebeisen, A. A., & Gergen, K. (1981). *Self-concept: Advances in theory and research.* Cambridge, MA: Ballinger.

Lynn, D. B. (1969). *Parental and sex role identification: A theoretical formulation.* Berkeley, CA: McCutchan Publishing.

Lynn, S. J., & Garske, J. P. (Eds.). (1985). *Contemporary psychotherapies: Models and methods.* Columbus, OH: Merrill.

Maccoby, E. E. (1968). What coping requires. *Ontario Journal of Educational Research, 10,* 163–170.

Maccoby, E. E. (1980). *Social development: Psychological growth and the parent-child relationship.* New York: Harcourt Brace Jovanovich.

Maddi, S. (1985). Existential psychotherapy. In S. J. Lynn & J. P. Garske (Eds.), *Contemporary psychotherapies: Models and methods* (pp. 191–219). Columbus, OH: Merrill.

Maddi, S. L. (1980). *Personality theories: A comparative analysis.* Homewood, IL: Dorsey Press.

Magnusson, D., & Allen, V. P. (Eds.). (1984). *Human development: An interactional perspective.* New York: Academic Press.

Magnusson, D., & Endler, N. S. (Eds.). (1977). *Personality at the crossroads: Current issues in interactional psychology.* Hillsdale, NJ: Earlbaum.

Mahler, M. (1968). *On human symbiosis and the vicissitudes of individuation.* New York: International Universities Press.

Mahoney, M. J. (1991). *Human change processes: The scientific foundations of psychotherapy.* New York: Basic Books.

Mahrer, A. R. (1978). *Experiencing: Humanistic theory of psychology and psychiatry.* New York: Brunner/Mazel.

Marks, S. R. (1977). Multiple roles and role strain: Some notes on human energy, time and commitment. *American Sociological Review, 42,* 921–936.

Marks, S. R. (1986). *Three corners: Exploring marriage and the self.* Lexington, MA: Lexington Books.

Marlatt, G. A., & Gordon, J. R. (Eds). (1985). *Relapse prevention.* New York: Guilford.

Marlowe, H. A., Jr., & Weinberg, R. B. (Eds.). (1985). *Competence development: Theory and practice in special populations.* Springfield, IL: Thomas.

Massermanm, J. H. (Ed.). (1970). *The dynamics of work and marriage.* New York: Grune & Stratton.

Massey, R. F. (1981). *Personality theories: Comparisons and syntheses.* New York: Van Nostrand.

Matteson, M. T., & Ivancevich, J. M. (1987). *Controlling work stress: Effective human resource and management strategies.* San Francisco, CA: Jossey-Bass.

Maxmen, J. S. (1986). *Essential psychopathology.* New York: Norton.

May, R. (1953). *Man's search for himself.* New York: Dell.

May, R. (1980). *Psychology and the human dilemma.* New York: Norton.

May, R., & Yalom, I. (1984). Existential psychotherapy. In R. J. Corsini (Ed.), *Current psychotherapies* (pp. 354–391). Itaska, IL: Peacock.

McAdams, D. P. (1988). *Power, intimacy, and the life story: Personological inquiries into identity.* New York: Guilford.

McClintock, C. G., & Keil, L. J. (1983). Social values: Their definition, their development, and their impact upon human decision making in settings of outcome interdependence. In H. H. Blumberg, A. P. Hare, V. Kent, & M. Davies (Eds.), *Small groups and social interaction* (Vol. 2, pp. 123–143). New York: Wiley.

McCrady, B. S., Dean, L., Dubreuil, E., & Swanson, S. (1985). The problem drinkers' project: A programmatic application of social-learning-based treatment. In G. A. Marlatt & J. R. Gordon (Eds.), *Relapse prevention* (pp. 417–471). New York: Guilford.

McFadden, J. (1988). Guilt is soluble in alcohol: An ego analytic view. In S. Peele (Ed.), *Visions of addictions: Major contemporary perspectives on addictions and alcoholism* (pp. 183–200). Lexington, MA: Lexington Books.

McGee, R. S. (1987). *The search for significance.* Houston, TX: Rapha.

McGrath, E., Keita, G. P., Strickland, B. R., & Russo, N. F. (Eds.). (1990). *Women and depression: Risk factors and treatment issues.* Washington, DC: American Psychological Association.

McGrath, J. E. (Ed.). (1988). *The social psychology of time: New perspectives.* Newbury Park, CA: Sage.

McGrath, J. E., & Kelly, J. R. (1986). *Time and human interaction: The social psychology of time.* New York: Guilford.

McNeil, D. (1968). Production and perception: The view from language. *Ontario Journal of Educational Research, 10,* 181–185.

McNeil, E. B. (1969). *Human socialization.* Belmont, CA: Brooks/Cole.

McReynolds, P. (Ed.). (1968). *Advances in psychological assessment* (Vol. 1). Palo Alto, CA: Science & Behavior Books.

McReynolds, P. (Ed.). (1971). *Advances in personality assessment* (Vol. 2). Palo Alto, CA: Science & Behavior Books.

Meader, B. D., & Rogers, C. R. (1984). Person-centered psychotherapy. In R. J. Corsini (Ed.), *Current psychotherapies* (pp. 142–195). Itaska, IL: Peacock.

Megargee, E. L. (Ed.). (1966). *Research in clinical assessment.* New York: Harper & Row.

Meichenbaum, D. (1985). Cognitive-behavioral therapies. In S. J. Lynn & J. P. Garske (Eds.), *Contemporary psychotherapies* (pp. 261–286). Columbus, OH: Merrill.

Melges, F. T. (1982). *Time and inner future: A temporal approach to psychiatric disorders.* New York: Wiley.

Melito, R. (1985). Adaptation in family systems: A developmental perspective. *Family Process, 24,* 89–100.

Mercer, R. T. (1986). *First-time motherhood.* New York: Springer.

Miller, I. J. (1989). The therapeutic empathic communication (TEC) process. *American Journal of Psychotherapy, 48,* 531–545.

Millon, T. (1986). A theoretical derivation of pathological personalities. In T. Millon & G. L. Klerman (Eds.), *Contemporary directions in psychopathology: Towards the DSM IV* (pp. 639–669). New York: Guilford.

Minuchin, S. (1974). *Families and family therapy.* Cambridge, MA: Harvard University Press.

Mischel, W. (1968). *Personality and assessment.* New York: Wiley.

Mischel, W. (1979). On the interface of cognition and personality: Beyond the person x situation debate. *American Psychologist, 34,* 740–754.

Mischel, W. (1981). *Introduction to personality.* New York: Holt, Rinehart and Winston.

Mischel, W. (1983). Alternatives in the pursuit of the predictability and consistency of persons: Stable data that yield unstable interpretations. *Journal of Personality, 51,* 578–604.

Mischel, W., & Peake, P. K. (1983). Analyzing the construction of consistency in personality. In M. M. Page (Ed.), *Nebraska symposium on motivation, 1982: Personality—current theory & research* (pp. 233–262). Lincoln, NE: University of Nebraska Press.

Monte, C. F. (1980). *Beneath the mask: An introduction to theories of personality.* New York: Holt, Rinehart and Winston.

Moos, R. H. (1973). Conceptualizations of human environments. *American Psychologist, 28,* 652–665.

Moos, R. H. (1974). *Evaluating treatment environments: A social ecological approach.* New York: Wiley-Interscience.

Moos, R. H. (1976). *The human context: Environmental determinants of behavior.* New York: Wiley.

Morris, P. W., Horne, A. M., Jessell, J. C., Passmore, J. L., Walker, J. M., & Sayger, T. V. (1988). Behavioral and cognitive characteristics of fathers of aggressive and well-behaved boys. *Journal of Cognitive Psychotherapy: An International Quarterly, 2,* 251–265.

Murray, E. J., Lamnin, A. D., & Carver, C. S. (1989). Emotional expression in written essays and psychotherapy. *Journal of Social and Clinical Psychology, 8,* 414–429.

Murray, E. J., & Segal, D. L. (1991). Emotional processing in vocal and written expression of feelings about traumatic experiences. Unpublished manuscript. University of Miami, Coral Gables, FL.

Murstein, B. L. (1976). *Who will marry whom? Theories and research in marital choice.* New York: Springer.

Nahemow, L., & Lawdon, M. P. (1983). Similarity and propinquity: Making friends with "different" people. In H. H. Blumberg, A. P. Hare, V. Kent, & M. Davies (Eds.), *Small groups and social interaction* (pp. 279–292). New York: Wiley.

Near, J. P. (1984). Predictive and explanatory models of work and non-work. In M. D. Lee & R. N. Kanungo (Eds.), *Management of work and personal life: Problems and opportunities* (pp. 67–85). New York: Praeger.

Newman, P. R., & Newman, B. M. (1988). Parenthood and adult development. *Marriage and Family Review, 12,* 313–337.

Nichol, II. (1977). A developmental hierarchy of dyadic relationships. *Canadian Psychiatric Association Journal, 22,* 3–9.

Nieva, V. F. (1984). Work and family roles. In M. D. Lee & R. N. Kanungo (Eds.), *Management of work and personal life: Problems and opportunities* (pp. 15–40). New York: Praeger.

Niles, F. S. (1979). The adolescent girls' perception of parents and peers. *Adolescence, 14,* 591–597.

Nisbett, R. E., & Wilson, T. (1977). Telling more than we can know: Verbal reports on mental processes. *Psychological Review, 84,* 231–259.

Nock, S. L., & Kingston, P. W. (1984). The family work day. *Journal of Marriage and the Family, 46,* 333–343.

Noller, P. (1984). *Nonverbal communication and marital interaction.* New York: Pergamon.

Noller, P. (1985). Negative communication in marriage. *Journal of Social and Personal Relationships, 2,* 289–301.

Norcross, J. C. (Ed.). (1986). *Handbook of eclectic psychotherapy.* New York: Brunner/Mazel.

Nystrand, M. (1977). Language as discovery and exploration: Heuristic and explicative uses of language. In M. Nystrand (Ed.), *Language as a way of knowing: A book of readings* (pp. 95–124). Toronto: The Ontario Institute for Studies in Education.

Olsen, D. R., & Pagliuso, S. M. (1968). From perceiving to performing: An aspect of cognitive growth. *Ontario Journal of Educational Research, 10,* 155–231.

Olson, D. H., Russell, C. S., & Sprenkle, D. H. (Eds.). (1989). *Circumplex model: Systematic assessment and treatment of families.* New York: Haworth Press.

Omer, H. (1989). Specifics and nonspecifics in psychotherapy. *American Journal of Psychotherapy, 43,* 181–192.

Orthner, D. K. (1975). Leisure activity patterns and marital satisfaction over the marital career. *Journal of Marriage and the Family, 37,* 91–102.

Orthner, D. K., & Mancini, J. A. (1989, May). *Benefits of leisure for family bonding.* Paper prepared for the Benefits of Leisure Conference, Snowbird, UT.

Otto, L. B. (1979). Antecedents and consequences of marital timing. In W. R. Burr, R. Hill, F. I. Nye, & I. L. Reiss (Eds.), *Contemporary theories about the family* (pp. 101–126). New York: Free Press.

Outler, A. C. (1987). Problems of selfhood in a Christian perspective. In P. Young-Eisendrath & J. A. Hall (Eds.), *The book of the self* (pp. 407–420). New York: New York University Press.

Owen-Smith, P. (1985). *Family process and self-concept in early childhood.* Doctoral dissertation, Georgia State University, Atlanta, GA.

Page, M. M. (Ed.). (1983). *Nebraska symposium on motivation 1982: Personality—current theory and research.* Lincoln, NE: University of Nebraska Press.

Parkes, C. M., & Stevenson-Hinde, J. (Eds.). (1982). *The place of attachment in human behavior.* New York: Basic Books.

Parsons, T., & Bales, R. F. (1955). *Family socialization and interaction processes.* Glencoe, IL: Free Press.

Pasamanick, B., Roberts, D. W., Lemkau, P. W., & Krueger, D. B. (1959). A survey of mental disease in an urban population: Prevalence by race and income. In B. Pasamanick (Ed.), *Epidemiology of mental disorder* (pp. 183–201). Washington, DC: American Association for the Advancement of Science.

Peele, S., & Brodsky, A. (1975). *Love and addiction.* New York: New American Library.

Peery, J. C. (1979). Popular, amiable, isolated, rejected: A reconception of sociometric status in preschool children. *Child Development, 50,* 1231–1234.

Pennebaker, J. W. (1990). *Opening up: The healing power of confiding in others.* New York: Morrow.

Perloff, R. (1987). Self interest and personal responsibility redux. *American Psychologist, 42,* 3–11.

Perry, S., Frances, A., & Clarkin, J. (1985). *A DSM-III casebook of differential therapeutics: A clinical guide to treatment selection.* New York: Brunner/Mazel.

Pervin, L. A. (1980). *Personality: Theory, assessment, and research.* New York: Wiley.

Pervin, L. A. (1985). Personality: Current controversies, issues, and direction. *Annual Review of Psychology, 36,* 83–114.

Pervin, L. A. (Ed.). (1990). *Handbook of personality theory and research.* New York: Guilford.

Peterson, C. (1992). *Personality.* Fort Worth, TX: Harcourt Brace Jovanovich.

Phillips, E. L., & Wiener, D. N. (1966). *Short-term psychotherapy and structured behavior change.* New York: McGraw-Hill.

Phillips, L. (1968). *Human adaptation and its failures.* New York: Academic Press.

Piaget, J. (1970). Piaget's theory. In P. H. Mussen (Ed.), *Carmichael's manual of child psychology* (pp. 703–732). New York: Wiley.

Piers, M. W. (Ed.). (1972). *Play and development: A symposium.* New York: Norton.

Pittman, T. S., Cooper, E. E., & Smith, T. W. (1977). Attribution of causality and the overjustification effect. *Personality and Social Psychology Bulletin, 3,* 280–283.

Plas, J. M., & Hoover-Dempsey, K. V. (1988). *Working up a storm: Anger, anxiety, joy, and tears on the job—and how to handle them.* New York: Norton.

Pleck, J. H. (1981). *The myth of masculinity.* Boston: MIT Press.

Pleck, J. H. (1985). *Working wives/working husbands.* Beverly Hills, CA: Sage.

Pomerleau, O. F., & Pomerleau, C. S. (1988). A biobehavioral view of substance abuse and addictions. In S. Peele (Ed.), *Visions of addictions: Major contemporary perspectives on addictions and alcoholism* (pp. 117–139). Lexington, MA: Lexington Books.

Powers, W. T. (1991). Commentary on Bandura's "Human Agency." *American Psychologist, 46,* 151–153.

Prentice, D. A. (1987). Psychological correspondence of possessions, attitudes, and values. *Journal of Personality and Social Psychology, 53,* 993–1003.

Prochanska, J. O. (1984). *Systems of psychotherapy: A transtheoretical analysis.* Chicago, IL: Dorsey Press.

Pruitt, D. G. (1983). Experimental gaming and the goal expectation hypothesis. In H. H. Blumberg, A. P. Hare, V. Kent, & M. Davies (Eds.), *Small groups and social interaction* (Vol. 2, pp. 107–121). New York: Wiley.

Quick, J. C., Hess, R. E., Hermalin, J., & Quick, J. D. (Eds.). (1990). *Career stress in changing times.* New York: Haworth Press.

Rand, A. (1964). *The virtue of selfishness.* New York: Signet.

Rapoport, R., & Rapoport, R. N. (1975). *Leisure and the family life cycle.* Boston, MA: Routledge & Kegan Paul.

Raskin, N. J. (1985). Client-centered therapy. In S. J. Lynn & J. P. Garske (Eds.), *Contemporary psychotherapies: Models and methods* (pp. 155–190). Columbus, OH: Merrill.

Raush, H. L., Barry, W. A., Hertel, R. K., & Swain, M. A. (1974). *Communication, conflict, and marriage.* San Francisco, CA: Jossey-Bass.

Reichenbach, H. (1969). *The rise of scientific philosophy.* Berkeley, CA: University of California Press.

Reiss, D. (1981). *The family's construction of reality.* Cambridge, MA: Harvard University Press.

Repetti, R. L. (1987). Linkages between work and family roles. In S. Oskamp (Ed.), *Family processes and problems: Social psychological aspects* (pp. 98–127). Newbury Park, CA: Sage.

Richman, N., Stevenson, J., & Graham, P. (1985). Sex differences in outcome of pre-school behavior problems. In A. R. Nicol (Ed.), *Longitudinal studies in child psychology and psychiatry: Practical lessons from research experience* (pp. 75–89). New York: Wiley.

Rimm, D. C., & Cunningham, H. M. (1985). Behavior therapies. In S. J. Lynn & J. P. Garske (Eds.), *Contemporary psychotherapies: Models and methods* (pp. 221–259). Columbus, OH: Merrill.

Robins, L. (1986). Epidemiology of antisocial personality. In G. Klerman, M. M. Weissman, P. S. Applebaum, and L. Roth (Eds.), *Social epidemiologic and legal psychiatry* (Vol. 5, pp. 231–244). New York: Basic Books.

Robinson, J. P. (1984). Work, free time, and the quality of life. In M. D. Lee & R. N. Kanungo (Eds.), *Management of work and personal life: Problems and opportunities* (pp. 133–142). New York: Praeger.

Rogers, C. R. (1957). The necessary and sufficient conditions of therapeutic personality change. *Journal of Consulting Psychology, 21,* 95–103.

Rogers, C. R. (1961). *On becoming a person.* Boston, MA: Houghton-Mifflin.

Rollins, B. C., & Thomas, D. L. (1979). Parental support, power, and control techniques in the socialization of children. In W. R. Burr, R. Hill, F. I. Nye, & I. L. Reiss (Eds.), *Contemporary theories about the family* (Vol. 1, pp. 317–364). New York: Free Press.

Rosenberg, M. (1979). *Conceiving the self.* New York: Basic Books.

Rossi, A. S., & Rossi, P. H. (1990). *Of human bonding.* New York: Aldine de Gruyter.

Rothbart, M. K. (1971). Birth order and mother-child interaction in an achievement situation. *Journal of Personality and Social Psychology, 17,* 113–120.

Rothbart, M. K., & Rothbart, M. (1976). Birth order, sex of child, and maternal help-giving. *Sex Roles, 2,* 39–46.

Rothman, F., & Wetz, J. R. (1989). *Child psychotherapy and the quest for control.* Newbury Park, CA: Sage.

Royce, W. S., & Muehlke, C. V. (1991). Therapists' causal attributions of clients' problems and selection of intervention strategies. *Psychological Reports, 68,* 379–386.

Rubin, R. (1984). *Maternal identity and the maternal experience.* New York: Springer.

Ruesch, J., & Bateson, G. (1951). *Communication: The social matrix of psychiatry.* New York: Norton.

Rutter, M. (1974). *The qualities of mothering: Maternal deprivation.* New York: Aronson.

Rutter, M. (1981). *Scientific foundations of developmental psychiatry.* Baltimore, MD: University Park Press.

Rychlack, J. F. (1968). *A philosophy of science for personality theory.* Boston, MA: Houghton Mifflin.

Sabatelli, R. M., & Mazor, A. (1985). Differentiation, individuation, and identity formation: The integration of family system and individual developmental perspectives. *Adolescence, 20,* 619–633.

Sackheim, H. A., & Gur, R. C. (1978). Self-deception, self-confrontation and consciousness. In G. E. Schwartz & D. Shapiro (Eds.), *Consciousness and self-regulation: Advances in Research* (Vol. 2, pp. 305–347). New York: Plenum.

Saltzman, N., & Norcross, J. C. (Eds.). (1990). *Therapy wars: Contention and convergence in differing clinical approaches.* San Francisco, CA: Jossey-Bass.

Sapir, E. (1921). *Language: An introduction to the study of speech.* New York: Harcourt Brace & Company.

Satir, V. (1972). *Peoplemaking.* Palo Alto, CA: Science & Behavior Books.

Scanzoni, J. (1972). *Sexual bargaining: Power politics in the American marriage.* Englewood Cliffs, NJ: Prentice-Hall.

Scanzoni, J., & Polonko, K. (1980). A conceptual approach to explicit marital negotiation. *Journal of Marriage and the Family, 42,* 31–44.

Scarr, S. (1985). Constructing psychology: Making facts and fables for our times. *American Psychologist, 40,* 499–512.

Scharfstein, B. A. (1989). *The dilemma of context.* New York: New York University Press.

Scheff, T. J., Retzinger, S. M., & Ryan, M. T. (1989). Crime, violence, and self-esteem: Review and proposals. In A. M. Mecca, N. J. Smelser, & J. Vasconcellos (Eds.), *The social importance of self-esteem* (pp. 165–199). Berkeley, CA: University of California Press.

Scheier, M. F., & Carver, C. S. (1977). Self-focused attention and the experience of emotion: Attraction, repulsion, elation, and depression. *Journal of Personality and Social Psychology, 35,* 625–636.

Schlenker, B. R. (1980). *Impression management: The self-concept, social identity, and interpersonal relations.* Monterey, CA: Brooks/Cole.

Schneider, K. J. (1990). *The paradoxical self: Toward an understanding of our contradictory nature.* New York: Plenum.

Schoggen, P. (1989). *Behavior settings: A revision and extension of Roger G. Barker's ecological psychology.* Stanford, CA: Stanford University Press.

Schuler, R. S. (1984). Organizational and occupational stress and coping: A model and overview. In M. D. Lee & R. N. Kanungo (Eds.), *Management of work and personal life: Problems and opportunities* (pp. 172–205). New York: Praeger.

Schultz, D. (1981). *Theories of personality.* Belmont, CA: Brooks/Cole.

Schvaneveldt, J. D., & Ihinger, M. (1979). Sibling relationships in the family. In W. R. Burr, R. Hill, F. I. Nye, & I. L. Reiss (Eds.), *Contemporary theories about the family* (Vol. 1, pp. 453–467). New York: Free Press.

Schwartz, G., & Merten, D. (1980). *Love and commitment.* Beverly Hills, CA: Sage.

Schwartzman, H. B. (1978). *Transformations: The anthropology of children's play.* New York: Plenum.

Seligman, L. (1990). *Selecting effective treatments.* San Francisco, CA: Jossey-Bass.

Seltzer, L. F. (1986). *Paradoxical strategies in psychotherapy: A comprehensive overview and guidebook.* New York: Wiley-Interscience.

Sevy, B. A. (1988). The concurrent validity of the Correctional Officers' Interest Blank. *Public Personal Management, 17,* 135–144.

Shaffer, H. J., & Schneider, R. J. (1985). Trends in behavioral psychology and the addictions. In H. B. Milkman & H. J. Shaffer (Eds.), *The addictions: Multidisciplinary perspectives and treatments* (pp. 39–55). Lexington, MA: Heath.

Shaver, P., & Hendrick, C. (Eds.). (1987). *Sex and gender.* Newbury, CA: Sage.

Shelton, J. L., & Levy, R. L. (1981). *Behavioral assignments and treatment compliance.* Champaign, IL: Research Press.

Shipley, T. E., Jr. (1987). Opponent process theory. In H. T. Blane & K. E. Leonard (Eds.), *Psychological theories of drinking and alcoholism* (pp. 346–387). New York: Guilford.

Siegel, S., Krank, M. D., & Hinson, R. E. (1988). Anticipation of pharmacological and nonpharmacological events: Classical conditioning and addictive behavior. In S. Peele (Ed.), *Visions of addictions: Major contemporary perspectives on addiction and alcoholism* (pp. 85–116). Lexington, MA: Lexington Books.

Simons, R. L., Whitbeck, L. B., Conger, R. D., & W. Chyi-In. (1991). Intergenerational transmission of harsh parenting. *Developmental Psychology, 27,* 159–171.

Singer, J. L. (1984). *The human personality.* New York: Harcourt Brace Jovanovich.

Singer, J. L. (1987). Developments in the study of private experiences. *Annual Review of Psychology, 38,* 533–574.

Singer, J. L., & Bonanno, G. A. (1990). Personality and private experience: The individual variations in consciousness and in attention to subjective phenomena. In L. A. Pervin (Ed.), *Handbook of personality theory and research* (pp. 419–444). New York: Guilford.

Sloan, S. Z., & L'Abate, L. (1985). Intimacy. In L. L'Abate (Ed.), *Handbook of family psychology and therapy* (pp. 305–329). Pacific Grove, CA: Brooks/Cole.

Slovenko, R., & Knight, J. A. (Eds.). (1967). *Motivation in play, games, and sports.* Springfield, IL: Thomas.

Smedes, L. B. (1988). *Caring and commitment: Learning to live the love we promise.* San Francisco, CA: Harper & Row.

Snyder, M. (1974). The self-monitoring of expressive behavior. *Journal of Personality and Social Psychology, 30,* 526–537.

Snyder, M., & Swann, W. B., Jr. (1976). When actions reflect attitudes: The politics of impression management. *Journal of Personality and Social Psychology, 34,* 1034–1042.

Snyder, M., & Tanke, E. D. (1976). Behavior and attitudes: Some people are more consistent than others. *Journal of Personality, 44,* 501–517.

Sobel, S. B., & Russo, N. F. (Eds.). (1981). Special issue: Sex roles, equality, and mental health. *Professional Psychology, 11,* 1–18.

Somers, M. N. (1987). Parenting in the 1980s: Programming perspectives and issues. *Volta Review, 89,* 68–77.

Spiegel, J. (1971). *Transactions: The interplay between individual, family, and society.* New York: Science House.

Staats, A. W. (1971). *Child learning, intelligence, and personality: Principles of a behavioral interaction approach.* New York: Harper & Row.

Stafford, L., & Canary, D. (1991). Maintenance strategies and romantic relationships, gender, and relational characteristics. *Journal of Social and Personal Relationships, 8,* 217–242.

Staines, G. L., & Pleck, J. H. (1983). *The impact of work schedules on the family.* Ann Arbor, MI: University of Michigan Press.

Staines, G. L., & Pleck, J. H. (1984). Nonstandard work schedules and family life. *Journal of Applied Psychology, 69,* 515–523.

Stamps, S. M., & Stamps, M. B. (1985). Race, class, and leisure activities of urban residents. *Journal of Leisure Activities, 17,* 40–55.

Stauffer, J. R. (1987). Marital intimacy: Road blocks and therapeutic interventions. *Family Therapy, 14,* 179–185.

Steffenhagen, R. A., & Burns, J. D. (1987). *The social dynamics of self esteem: Theory to therapy.* New York: Praeger.

Stein, A. H., & Bailey, M. M. (1973). The socialization of achievement orientation in females. *Psychological Bulletin, 80,* 345–366.

Stein, S. L., & Weston, L. C. (1982). College women's attitudes toward women and identity achievement. *Adolescence, 17,* 895–899.

Steinmetz, S. (1979). Disciplinary techniques and their relationship to aggressiveness, dependency, and conscience. In W. R. Burr, R. Hill, F. I. Nye, & I. L. Reiss (Eds.), *Contemporary theories about the family* (Vol. 1, pp. 405–438). New York: Free Press.

Sternberg, R. J. (1986). *Intelligence applied: Understanding and increasing your intellectual skills.* New York: Harcourt Brace Jovanovich.

Stevens, F. E., & L'Abate, L. (1989). Validity and reliability of a theory-derived measure of intimacy. *American Journal of Family Therapy, 17,* 359–368.

Stewart, L., & Livson, N. (1966). Smoking and rebelliousness: A longitudinal study from childhood to maturity. *Journal of Consulting Psychology, 30,* 225–229.

Strupp, H. H. (1970). Specific vs. nonspecific factors in psychotherapy and the problem of control. *Archives of General Psychiatry, 23,* 393–401.

Strupp, H. H. (1974). Some observations on the fallacy of value-free psychotherapy and the empty organism: Comments on a case study. *Journal of Abnormal Psychology, 83,* 199–201.

Suls, J. M., & Miller, R. L. (1977). *Social comparison processes: Theoretical and empirical perspectives.* Washington, DC: Hemisphere.

Suls, J. M., & Wills, T. A. (1990). *Social comparison: Contemporary theory and research.* Hillsdale, NJ: Earlbaum.

Sundstrom, E. (1986). *Work places: The psychology of the physical environment in offices and factories.* Cambridge, UK: Cambridge University Press.

Sutton-Smith, B. (1986). *Toys as culture.* New York: Garder Press.

Swanson-Kauffman, K. M. (Ed.). (1987). *Women's work, families, and health: The balancing act.* New York: Hemisphere.

Tageson, C. W. (1982). *Humanistic psychology: A synthesis.* Homewood, IL: Dorsey Press.

Tamashiro, R. T. (1978). Developmental stages in the conceptualization of marriage. *The Family Coordinator, 27,* 237–244.

Tapp, J. L., & Kohlberg, L. (1971). Developing senses of law and legal justice. *Journal of Social Issues, 27,* 65–93.

Taylor, I. A. (1960). Similarities in the structure of extreme social attitudes. *Psychological Monographs: General and Applied, 74* (Whole No. 489).

Taylor, J. L. (1986). *In search of self: Life, death and Walter Percy.* Cambridge, MA: Cowley.

Thoits, P. A. (1986). Social support as coping assistance. *Journal of Counseling and Clinical Psychology, 54,* 416–423.

Thompson, L. (1990). Negotiation behavior and outcomes: Empirical evidence and theoretical issues. *Psychological Bulletin, 108,* 515–532.

Trickett, P. K., Aber, J. L., Carlson, V., & Cicchetti, D. (1991). Relationship of socioeconomic status to the etiology and developmental sequelae of physical child abuse. *Developmental Psychology, 27,* 148–158.

Ulrich, D. N., & Dunne, H. P., Jr. (1986). *To love and work: A systemic interlocking of family, workplace, and career.* New York: Brunner/Mazel.

Ulrici, D. K. (1984). *An objective assessment of developmental stages of marital understanding.* Unpublished doctoral dissertation, Georgia State University, Atlanta, GA.

Ulrici, D., L'Abate, L., & Wagner, V. (1981). The ERA model: A heuristic framework for classification of skill training programs for couples and families. *Family Relations, 30,* 307–315.

Vaillant, G. E. (1986). Comments on Robin Room's "Dependence and society": Deconstruction deconstructed. *British Journal of Addiction, 81,* 58.

Van Dusen, R. A., & Sheldon, E. B. (1976). The changing status of American women: A life cycle perspective. *American Psychologist, 31,* 106–116.

Vernon, P. E. (1964). *Personality assessment: A critical survey.* New York: Wiley.

Vernon, P. E. (1969). *Intelligence and cultural environment.* New York: Barnes & Noble.

Veroff, J., & Feld, S. (1970). *Marriage and work in America: A study of motives and roles.* New York: Van Nostrand Reinhold.

Waanders, D. D. (1987). Ethical reflections on the differentiation of self in marriage. *Journal of Pastoral Care, 41,* 100–110.

Wade, M. G. (1985). Preface. In M. G. Wade (Ed.), *Constraints on leisure* (pp. ix–x). Springfield, IL: Thomas.

Wakefield, J. C. (1989). Levels of explanation in personality theory. In D. M. Buss & N. Cantor (Eds.), *Emerging issues in personality psychology* (pp. 333–346). New York: Springer-Verlag.

Walker, K., & Woods, M. (1976). *Time use: A measure of household production of family goods and services*. Washington, DC: American Home Economics Association.

Watzlawick, P. (1978). *How real is real?: Communication, disinformation, confusion*. New York: Random House.

Weary, G., Stanley, M. A., & Harvey, J. H. (1989). *Attribution*. New York: Springer-Verlag.

Weeks, G. R., & L'Abate, L. (1982). *Paradoxical psychotherapy: Theory and practice with individuals, couples, and families*. New York: Bruner/Mazel.

Weiner, B. (1991). Metaphors in motivation and attribution. *American Psychologist, 46*, 921–930.

Weiner, M. (1978). Money myths in marriage. *Clinical Social Work Journal, 6*, 53–56.

Weintraub, M. D. (1981). *Verbal behavior: Adaptations in psychopathology*. New York: Springer.

Wethington, E., McLeod, J. D., & Kessler, R. C. (1987). The importance of life events for explaining sex differences in psychological stress. In R. C. Barnett, L. Biener, & G. K. Baruch (Eds.), *Gender and stress* (pp. 144–158). New York: Free Press.

Whatmough, J. (1956). *Language: A modern synthesis*. London, UK: Secker & Warburg.

White, J. M. (1991). *Dynamics of family development*. New York: Guilford.

White, R. W. (1959). Motivation reconsidered: The concept of competence. *Psychological Review, 66*, 297–333.

Wildman, R. W., II, & L'Abate, L. (1979). The AVOM: A model-derived, age-limited, and modality-related test of intellectual functioning. *Psychology in the Schools, 16*, 408–413.

Wills, T. A. (1978). Perceptions of clients by professional helpers. *Psychological Bulletin, 85*, 968–1000.

Wilson, G. T. (1984). Behavior therapy. In R. J. Corsini (Ed.), *Current psychotherapies* (pp. 239–278). Itaska, IL: Peacock.

Wine, J. D., & Smye, M. D. (Eds.). (1980). *Social competence*. New York: Guilford.

Winnicott, D. W. (1965). *The maturational processes and the facilitating environment: Studies in the theory of emotional development*. New York: International Universities Press.

Witkin, H. A. (1965). Psychological differentiation and forms of pathology. *Journal of Abnormal Psychology, 70*, 317–336.

Wolf, A. W., Schubert, D. S., Patterson, M. B., Grande, T. P., Brocco, K. J., & Peddleton, L. (1988). Associations among major psychiatric diagnoses. *Journal of Consulting and Clinical Psychology, 56,* 292–294.

Wood, J. V. (1989). Theory and research concerning social comparisons of personal attributes. *Psychological Bulletin, 106,* 231–248.

Woody, R. H. (Ed.). (1980). *Encyclopedia of clinical assessment* (Vols. I & II). San Francisco, CA: Jossey-Bass.

Woody, R. H., & Woody, J. D. (Eds.). (1972). *Clinical assessment in counseling and psychotherapy.* New York: Appleton-Century-Crofts.

Wylie, R. (1961). *The self-concept: A critical survey of pertinent research literature.* Lincoln, NE: University of Nebraska Press.

Wylie, R. (1974). *The self concept* (Rev. Ed., Vol. 1). A review of methodological considerations of measuring instruments. Lincoln, NE: University of Nebraska Press.

Wylie, R. (1978). *The Self Concept Revised Edition: Vol. 2.* Lincoln, NE: University of Nebraska Press.

Yablonsky, L. (1991). *The emotional meaning of money.* New York: Gardner.

Yeates, K. O., Schultz, L. H., & Selman, R. L. (1990). Bridging the gaps in child-clinical assessment: Toward the application of social-cognitive developmental theory. *Clinical Psychology Review, 10,* 567–588.

Zajonc, R. B. (1965). Social facilitation. *Science, 149,* 269–274.

Zeig, J. K., & Munion, W. M. (Eds.). (1990). *What is psychotherapy?: Contemporary perspectives.* San Francisco, CA: Jossey-Bass.

Zinberg, N. E., & Shaffer, H. J. (1985). The social psychology of intoxicant use: The interaction of personality and social setting. In H. B. Milkman & H. J. Shaffer (Eds.), *The addictions: Multidisciplinary perspectives and treatments* (pp. 57–74). Lexington, MA: D. C. Books.

Author Index

Subject Index